Pullingthe**trigger**®

There is recovery and a place beyond. We promise.

Adam Shaw, a mental illness survivor and mental health advocate, and Lauren Callaghan, an industry-leading clinical psychologist, are the founders of the global mental health publishing enterprise, **Pulling**the**trigger**®. With their TV appearances and global education programmes, Adam, Lauren and their amazing team are helping more people around the world understand, recover from, and talk about their mental health issues.

The **Pulling**the**trigger**® range – user-friendly self-help books with an innovative approach to supporting people recovering from mental health issues.

The**inspirational**series™ – remarkable, real-life stories of men and women who have overcome mental illness to lead fulfilling lives.

Why have we called our books Pullingthe**trigger**®?

Many things can 'trigger' mental health issues. So what do you do if something makes you feel bad? You stay away from it, right?

I bet you've been avoiding your triggers all your life. But now we know that avoiding them only makes things worse. So here's the game changer: you need to learn how to pull those triggers instead of running away from them – and our **Pulling**the**trigger**® series shows you how. Your recovery is within reach, we promise.

This is more than recovery, it's a way of life.

Adam Shaw & Lauren Callaghan.

First published in Great Britain 2017 by Trigger Press

Trigger Press is a trading style of Shaw Callaghan Ltd & Shaw Callaghan 23 USA, INC.

The Foundation Centre
Navigation House, 48 Millgate, Newark
Nottinghamshire NG24 4TS UK

www.trigger-press.com

British Library Cataloguing in Publication Data

A CIP catalogue record for this book is available upon request
from the British Library

ISBN: 978-1-911246-53-4

This book is also available in the following e-Book formats:

MOBI: 978-1-911246-56-5
EPUB: 978-1-911246-54-1
PDF: 978-1-911246-55-8

Cover design and typeset by Fusion Graphic Design Ltd

Project Management by Out of House Publishing

Printed and bound in Great Britain by Bell & Bain, Glasgow

Paper from responsible sources

The**inspirational**series™
Overcoming adversity and thriving

Walk a Mile
Tales of a Wondering Loon
By Chris Young

We are proud to introduce The**inspirational**series™. Part of the **Pulling**the**trigger**® family of innovative self-help mental health books, The**inspirational**series™ tells the stories of the people who have battled and beaten mental health issues. For more information visit: www.pulling-the-trigger.com

THE AUTHOR

Chris Young is an ex-social worker from Northamptonshire, UK. In 2008 he was diagnosed with borderline personality disorder.

In 2011 Chris began his endeavour *Walk a Mile In my Shoes*. He walks around the edge of the UK – the edge of society being where many people with mental health problems feel they are – without spending any money and relying on the kindness of strangers. He invites other people to join him on these walks in order to discuss mental health and tackle stigma one step at a time.

Chris has a wonderful way of looking at the world despite his BPD. He goes about life assuming that everyone, no matter who they are or what background they're from, is fantastic. That way, he can open up a healthy and productive conversation about mental health with everyone he meets.

Thank you for purchasing this book.
You are making an incredible difference.

All of The**inspirational**series™ products have substantial
enterprising and philanthropic value and generate proceeds that
contribute towards our global mental health charity,
The Shaw Mind Foundation

MISSION STATEMENT

*'We aim to bring to an end the suffering and despair caused
by mental health issues. Our goal is to make help and support
available for every single person in society, from all walks of life.
We will never stop offering hope. These are our promises.'*

Pulling the Trigger and The Shaw Mind Foundation

Supporting children, adults and families
for better mental health. **#lets**do**stuff**

The Shaw Mind Foundation (www.shawmindfoundation.org) offers
unconditional support for all who are affected by mental health
issues. We are a global foundation that is not for profit. Our core
ethos is to help those with mental health issues and their families at
the point of need. We also continue to run and invest in mental health
treatment approaches in local communities around the globe, which
support those from the most vulnerable and socially deprived areas
of society. Please join us and help us make an incredible difference
to those who are suffering with mental health issues. **#lets**do**stuff**.

The**inspirational**series™
Overcoming adversity and thriving

Walk a Mile
Tales of a Wondering Loon
By Chris Young

We are proud to introduce The**inspirational**series™. Part of the **Pulling**the**trigger**® family of innovative self-help mental health books, The**inspirational**series™ tells the stories of the people who have battled and beaten mental health issues. For more information visit: www.pulling-the-trigger.com

THE AUTHOR

Chris Young is an ex-social worker from Northamptonshire, UK. In 2008 he was diagnosed with borderline personality disorder.

In 2011 Chris began his endeavour *Walk a Mile In my Shoes*. He walks around the edge of the UK – the edge of society being where many people with mental health problems feel they are – without spending any money and relying on the kindness of strangers. He invites other people to join him on these walks in order to discuss mental health and tackle stigma one step at a time.

Chris has a wonderful way of looking at the world despite his BPD. He goes about life assuming that everyone, no matter who they are or what background they're from, is fantastic. That way, he can open up a healthy and productive conversation about mental health with everyone he meets.

Thank you for purchasing this book.
You are making an incredible difference.

All of The**inspirational**series™ products have substantial enterprising and philanthropic value and generate proceeds that contribute towards our global mental health charity,
The Shaw Mind Foundation

MISSION STATEMENT

'We aim to bring to an end the suffering and despair caused by mental health issues. Our goal is to make help and support available for every single person in society, from all walks of life. We will never stop offering hope. These are our promises.'

Pulling the Trigger and The Shaw Mind Foundation

Supporting children, adults and families
for better mental health. **#lets**do**stuff**

The Shaw Mind Foundation (www.shawmindfoundation.org) offers unconditional support for all who are affected by mental health issues. We are a global foundation that is not for profit. Our core ethos is to help those with mental health issues and their families at the point of need. We also continue to run and invest in mental health treatment approaches in local communities around the globe, which support those from the most vulnerable and socially deprived areas of society. Please join us and help us make an incredible difference to those who are suffering with mental health issues. **#lets**do**stuff**.

This book is dedicated to my lovely wife, Ella.

And to Ben and Kate – whenever they need me.

Trigger Warning: The book contains references to attempted suicide, dissociation, and very graphic self-harm.

Disclaimer: Some names and identifying details have been changed to protect the privacy of individuals.

CHAPTER 1

LIVING ON
THE BORDERLINE

I was diagnosed with borderline personality disorder in January 2008. At this time, I was a middle manager in a local authority. This is the story of my gradual transition from gamekeeper to poacher.

Had I been waiting for some manner of surgery or medical intervention, then my treatment – in line with department of health directives – would have started within 18 weeks. However, since I have a mental health problem, the time between referral and treatment is not dictated by any such directives. Psychiatric waiting lists are locally managed with no clear guidelines to ensure consistency or equity of care.

'So what do you think I've got?' I was terribly earnest. This diagnosis had been a long time in the making.

'I don't like labelling people,' Dr Brown, my psychiatrist, was just as intense.

'But if you were to give me a label?'

'Well then, Mr Young, I'd have to say you display many of the traits of borderline personality disorder.'

Had I been one of my less knowledgeable colleagues or a member of the general public I might have thought, 'Oh, that's all right then – I've nearly got a personality disorder,' or, 'borderline personality disorder, what the hell's that?'

That, however, was not the case.

The latest version of the *Diagnostic and Statistical Manual of Mental Disorders* (DSM-IV), which is used by the American Psychiatric Association, describes BPD as a cluster of symptoms. If a patient displays five or more of these then they can receive the diagnosis:

1. Frantic efforts to avoid real or imagined abandonment. [Not including suicidal or self-mutilating behaviour covered in Criterion 5.]

2. A pattern of unstable and intense interpersonal relationships characterised by alternating between extremes of idealization and devaluation.

3. Identity disturbance: markedly and persistently unstable self-image or sense of self.

4. Impulsivity in at least two areas that are potentially self-damaging (e.g. promiscuous sex, eating disorders, binge eating, substance abuse, reckless driving). [Again, not including suicidal or self-mutilating behaviour covered in Criterion 5.]

5. Recurrent suicidal behaviour, gestures, threats, or self-mutilating behaviour such as cutting, interfering with the healing of scars (excoriation) or picking at oneself.

6. Affective instability due to a marked reactivity of mood (e.g. intense episodic dysphoria, irritability, or anxiety usually lasting a few hours and only rarely more than a few days).

7. Chronic feelings of emptiness, worthlessness.

8. Inappropriate anger or difficulty controlling anger (e.g. frequent displays of temper, constant anger, recurrent physical fights).

9. Transient, stress-related paranoid ideation, delusions or severe dissociative symptoms.

Personally, I display around eight of these traits.

In the UK we use a different diagnostic tool: *The World Health Organisation's International Statistical Classification of Diseases and Related Health Problems, 10th Revision* (ICD-10). In this they talk of a comparable condition: Emotionally unstable personality disorder – borderline type.

'So what?' I hear you cry. Does it really matter that there are different tools and definitions for the same condition?

It does when all of the health professionals I've worked with use the American rather than the UK model. For a condition where confusion and misunderstanding is already rife among the public, health professionals, and those who may have attracted the diagnosis, it is essential that there is just one clear definition of BPD that we are all working to.

I recently met an old colleague and friend of mine who I hadn't seen for a few months. We soon got chatting and she told me about another friend who had contracted cancer and was dealing with all the treatments attached to that. We both made all the appropriate concerned noises, but, being British, nothing too over the top. We were, after all, in a public place!

Jane had heard that I'd recently left social work due to my mental health. Again, all the right quiet noises were made. She'd worked with me at the time when I was first told that I had depression.

'Turned out it wasn't depression after all,' I smiled brightly at her, 'I've been diagnosed with borderline personality disorder.'

Jane's hands flew up to her cheeks as her face contorted into an expression that had only previously been seen in Munch's The Scream. She took a step back and squealed.

She may have said, 'Oh my god.'

'It's not a death sentence,' I said, in an attempt to dilute the situation.

'Sure,' she said, taking some steps to compose herself. 'We'll speak later.' And off she went.

The interesting thing about Jane is that she is a mental health officer – the Scottish equivalent of the approved social worker in England. So, what would cause a normally composed mental health professional to react in such a way to that seemingly harmless label, 'borderline personality disorder'?

Over the years BPD has attracted a number of preconceived notions that are now held by many people working in health and social care:

- People with BPD are dishonest and manipulative
- People with BPD are dangerous – after all, Josef Fritzl has been diagnosed with a personality disorder
- BPD is untreatable and the sufferer will have it for life
- BPD is the 'dustbin diagnosis' for people who don't easily fit under the umbrella of one of the other, more well known mental health conditions
- There are some GPs who don't recognise BPD as an authentic condition.

It is hardly surprising, then, that when I received this diagnosis I thought, 'Oh my bloody god. I'm doomed.'

I did what anyone else in my position would have done. I read everything I could get my hands on regarding my condition.

In the meantime, I had to leave the job I'd been doing for 15 years because of my mental health. I'd wanted to be a social worker since the age of 12 and had reached the dizzy heights of middle management. My symptoms were now making this role untenable. At home, my behaviour was becoming more and more erratic and antisocial, causing the downward spiral of distress to my family, feeding into my feelings of alienation as a result.

So I made the decision to move out. I felt I could no longer expose my children and my wife to my unpredictable symptoms.

Suddenly, I was homeless. Suddenly, I was going through the humiliation of applying for Incapacity Benefit, Disability Living Allowance, and Housing Benefit to supplement my social work pension of £218 per month. The whole process felt degrading; at times I felt pilloried, in the stocks, for a paltry extra £35 per week.

Unexpectedly, my reading had revealed a whole raft of treatments that were available for my condition.

In the States, Marcia Linehan had developed a treatment for BPD called dialectical behavioural therapy (DBT), a kind of spin-off of cognitive behavioural therapy that has been used with significant success since 1993. In it, she recognises that BPD is a complex condition that requires a variety of approaches to deal with it. In the UK, Fonagy and Bateman have developed mentalisation, a type of psychotherapeutic intervention that focuses on enhancing the patient's capacity to think about and regulate their mental states. Again, they are experiencing similar levels of success in the treatment of BPD to Linehan.

There is also individual and group psychotherapy. There are therapeutic communities where individuals are removed from mainstream society and placed in what is deemed to be a more validating environment to enable them to focus on their needs.

Although there is no specific BPD drug, pharmacology has a great deal to offer the BPD sufferer. There is a raft of drugs that can be taken in therapeutic doses to stabilise mood and emotions, which enable the person with BPD to make the most of their talking treatments.

The shocking thing for me was that neither I, nor my health and social work colleagues, had any notion of what was around to support BPD sufferers.

A huge problem for the professionals working in this area is motivation. When one believes that a condition is untreatable and merely manageable, then one is a damn sight less likely to pull out all the stops in an attempt to help treat it. So suspicion, fear and resignation reign where, at the very least, there should be hope.

In January 2017, the National Institute for Health and Care Excellence (NICE) published guidelines on the treatment and management of borderline personality disorder. In it, they outline all of the above diagnostic tools, treatments, therapies, and medications that are being used with varying levels of success to help combat this condition. They talk of the need for more research so that patients, taxpayers, and health trusts can get more bangs for their buck.

Therein lies a major problem. Health trusts want to put their money into the most effective treatments. Research is an expensive luxury that they are reluctant to plough the taxpayer's pound into without there being a promise of clear results.

On top of this the NICE guidelines are exactly that – *guidelines*. In a world where professionals are more inclined to follow protocols that are mandatory as opposed to discretionary, they are much less likely to read through the 476 pages of the guidelines when there is no obligation to.

All of which left me, as gamekeeper turned poacher, on a discretionary waiting list waiting for a discretionary therapy while taking discretionary medication with a diagnosis that isn't recognised by all the relevant bodies.

That said, I feel I have been desperately lucky. After a year on a waiting list, I received group psychotherapy alongside a small therapeutic dose of Quetiapine, which took the edges off my self-harming and suicidal thoughts.

People who attract the label of borderline personality disorder need to be in a position where they receive a clear diagnosis along with a prognosis. From this, they should be able to make an informed choice as to what treatments would best suit them.

In a world where 1 in 4 of us will be profoundly touched by some manner of mental illness at some time in our lives, it really is time that psychiatric services were given the same recognition as the other health and social care services.

Because of the complex range of issues in the BPD sufferer's life, they can place a high demand on health and social care services if they continue unmanaged.

Here's some more info on BPD from NICE guidelines:

People with borderline personality disorder may engage in a variety of destructive and impulsive behaviours including self-harm, eating problems and excessive use of alcohol and illicit substances. Self-harming behaviour in borderline personality disorder is associated with a variety of different meanings for the individual, including relief from acute distress and feelings, such as emptiness and anger, and to reconnect with feelings after a period of dissociation. As a result of the frequency with which they self-harm, people with borderline personality disorder are at increased risk of suicide (Cheng et al., 1997), with 60 to 70% attempting suicide at some point in their life (Oldham, 2006). The rate of completed suicide in people with borderline personality disorder has been estimated to be approximately 10% (Oldham, 2006). A well-documented association exists between borderline personality disorder and depression (Skodol et al., 1999; Zanarini et al., 1998), and the combination of the two conditions has been shown to increase the number and seriousness of suicide attempts (Soloff et al., 2000).

NICE, January 2009

Research is required now to explore the efficacy of the variety of therapies used in the treatment and management of BPD. Without effective support, BPD sufferers will place a higher demand on services, completely outweighing any perceived financial savings made from placing them on lengthy waiting lists.

Finally, comprehensive multidisciplinary training is required to ensure that health and social care professionals are aware of the spectrum of treatments and therapies available to BPD sufferers. This will ensure that service users receive the input they require and the professionals will achieve more of the job satisfaction they crave as a result.

The status quo is not an option. Without radical change now, BPD sufferers will continue to demand a disproportionate amount of services without receiving the input they require.

Borderline personality disorder, for me, is a condition that affects relationships. It can have negative effects on the sufferer and those around them. It can also have positive effects, in that I can be very insightful regarding the needs, hopes and aspirations of others.

I am hugely affected by emotion. Whether it be positive (like love and joy), or negative (like hate and anger), I can twist myself into some terrible shapes in an attempt to experience these feelings at the same time as running away from them. As such, starting friendships and relationships can be a fairly straightforward task for me. Maintaining them is another thing altogether.

Ever since I was 12 years old, my life has been marked by guilt, lies and intrigue. As I grew up, different people would get to know different elements of my truth and my world. That is why I chose to write much of my story from the perspective of my relationships with different people.

And so, without further ado, here it is.

CHAPTER 2

GAMEKEEPER
TURNED POACHER

If I'd had my wits about me, I would have had some recollection as to how I had appeared on Ward 6 at the Royal Edinburgh Hospital that day in late December 1993. It sounds kind of innocuous, doesn't it? The Royal Edinburgh Hospital. The Royal Ed. Edinburgh's Bin of Loons. Had I been firing on all cylinders, I would have been struck with the smell that exuded from the carpet in the communal area. It was a heady mix of tea, coffee, biscuits – probably digestives – some undisclosed medicines, bodily fluids and, of course, piss.

The following memories later gradually trickled back to me over a period of weeks, months and in some cases, years.

The male nurse who admitted me to the ward, who was dressed in non-threatening civilian clothing, was a tall bespectacled fellow, whose role it was to ask me exactly the same questions as the admitting psychiatrist, whose role it was, interestingly, to ask me exactly the same questions as the GP.

The psychiatrist did add one thing. If I, at any time, attempted to leave the ward, I would be sectioned. Even in my somewhat unhinged state I was overcome with the righteous indignation of the patient who had been admitted voluntarily. Why say that? Was it just in case I was under some bizarre delusion as to who was in charge here? I was all too aware who was in charge. It sure as hell wasn't me.

Bizarrely, I thought of my time working as a nursing assistant on a long-stay ward in a psychiatric hospital. We were taught control and restraint, part of which was actually being controlled and restrained. It had taken six male nurses to get me down. And that was without me kicking and / or punching. I was acting on the mindset that if anyone was going to section me, I definitely wasn't going to come quietly. What a knob. Only I could be competitive about being held under the Mental Health (Scotland) Act.

That morning, before I'd found myself on Ward 6, I'd been at a Social Work Team meeting at the Western General Hospital. It was held in the hospital's chaplaincy. The meeting started at 9.30, most people drifted in by 10.00 and the ambient 'god music' started, somewhat comedically, at 10.30. This was my first qualified social work job. 'A community care social worker in a busy hospital team' I think the advert had said. I had qualified in late June that year and had started work in July. Seamless.

It was what I'd always wanted to do. I had always wanted to be there for others. Probably because when I was younger, no one had been there for me. Just for the record, especially for all those potential social-workery types, this may not have been the best motivation in the world.

I sat in the meeting smiling and joking. Perhaps I was a little detached. Perhaps I was a little flippant, even sarcastic at times. No one noticed what was going on behind the scenes. Because I'd been a student at the Western, I hadn't received any induction when I'd started work there. I'd been a good student, so I was expected to hit the ground running. So I had.

I loved working on the care of the elderly ward. They hadn't had a dedicated social worker for some time, so they were pretty delighted with me too. They had a backlog of work and they merrily chucked whatever they had at me – and I lapped it up.

Until that day in the team meeting where my boss explained that my post was also to involve covering the medical wards. It was my role to take any referrals from those two acute wards – as well as the care of the elderly – and do any work that was involved with them. Trust me, it was a lot of work.

Following the guidelines from the tutors on my course and from any social work textbook you care to read, I challenged him. I explained that this amount of work would put me under a lot of stress and that it was unlikely that I'd be able to do my job. There, I'd admitted it. There was no shame in showing weakness. I was a new worker for goodness' sake. Cue understanding from my manager? Cue support from my colleagues?

Nope, not one single supportive breath came from anyone. I could almost hear the relieved, internal thoughts of the others. *Thank fuck it's not me.*

No, these would be my wards. I would be responsible for these people. But now that I had adopted this tidy clutch of wards, there were days when I was receiving 13 – count them, 13 – referrals. It was a huge number and it really piled the pressure onto my shoulders. Add to this my similarity to a box of frogs, things weren't looking too promising.

Sure, I did the stress thing. I did the detached, walking into things thing, and the not listening to people thing. But on that fateful day, in the team meeting, with the god music playing, I felt wonderfully relaxed.

The 20 godzillion referrals didn't matter. The million phone calls a minute could fuck right off. I didn't feel giddy. My mind wasn't racing. Nor was my pulse. I was hori-fucking-zontal.

In case you hadn't noticed, this wasn't a good thing.

In my mind, I was failing at the job I'd always wanted to do. I'd also indiscriminately shagged a variety of women both at Edinburgh University and, er, not at the university. I also felt my marriage was a sham. At the time, in my mind at least, there was little else in the world. So, the question wasn't *if* I was going to kill myself, it was *how*

I was going to kill myself. It was during the meeting I had worked out that little riddle.

During one of my many and varied conversations with one of the medical consultants, they told me that an overdose of paracetamol really hurts. That was ticked off as not really the thing to do.

One of my colleagues had a mug of coffee. She had a habit of not going back to the social work office after the meeting and often got someone to take her mug for her.

I was that volunteer. After the meeting, the mug and I took a little trip down to the men's toilet along the corridor.

Here was my cunning plan: break the mug, take one of the sharp remnants and carve out a vertical hole in my left wrist.

As I sat on the toilet (I was using it as my own seat in my own little private office), a feeling of absolute relaxation and serenity washed over me. I have never felt so calm. My mind was a gentle wind blowing across the wheat field near the house where I grew up. The sky was a vivid blue. The sparrows in the nearby hedgerow were having an altercation. Perfect.

A quiet yet persistent voice came into my mind. 'Chris, if you kill yourself, you'll be dead.'

'This is Chris Young, stating the fucking obvious, News at Ten.'

Suddenly it was like being held hostage. The Chris that had allowed me to bathe in that wonderful imagery was suddenly red with anger.

Just fucking do it!

What have you got to live for?

Chris, if you kill yourself, you'll be dead.

I was paralysed with fear. I could hardly move. All the muscles in my body were solid with tension. I was instantly covered in a cold sweat. My pulse was racing, my breathing rapid. I had to get out. I got to my office. If I phoned my GP, I'd be okay.

'Hello, doctors' surgery?'

'Yes, er, hi, I'd like to see a doctor … er, today please.'

'Is it a medical emergency?'

'Er, I, er … no.'

'You can see someone in two days, shall I book you in?'

'No, no.' Quietly, defeated.

My office was hidden away in the depths of the hospital, far from the wards and the main social work office. I had to be with someone. I phoned Mabel.

'Mabel? Hi.'

She was an experienced social worker who worked mainly with terminally ill folk from the oncology wards. I told her everything. Suddenly she was with me, her hand on my shoulder while she phoned my GP. 'I'm going to be unashamedly brutal with you, Chris.' She was direct as ever. 'Think of Ben and what he'd do with no dad.'

My two-year-old son. She was right.

Just fucking do it!

'Yes, it is a medical emergency,' Mabel told the receptionist. 'I'm bringing him in now and he will be seen by a GP when he gets there.'

Mabel manhandled me across the car park. I was so tense I could hardly walk. I was crying so much I was unable to talk. She drove me to the GP and then to the Royal Ed. She sat in with me during all the interviews with the GP and the psychiatrists. She said goodbye to me at the door of Ward 6 as she handed me on to my nursing friend.

'Smart / casual', he wrote next to 'appearance' on his form. 'Eyes – grey.'

My eyes are blue. Bright blue. How could they be grey? I remembered my dad's eyes when he died. They'd gone from vibrant blue to grey.

They gave me a single room. I was on suicide watch every 15 minutes to start off. Really, they shouldn't have bothered. Absolved of any and all responsibility, I slept for 18 hours. Safe.

My first visitor was Poppy, my wife. She appeared to be in a bit of a state of shock. Her husband, the man she'd known for six years, was languishing in hospital with his head in bits. She had spoken to my manager who, apparently, had got straight into the blame game.

'If you didn't spend all your time training ... If you had taken his name when you got married ... If ... '

Shit, was there anything else he could pin on her? Yes, Poppy did spend a lot of time running, cycling, and swimming. That was the deal before we got married, so why should it change afterwards?

So often, in situations such as these, people want a scapegoat – someone to blame.

What do you bring someone who has disconnected from the rest of the world? Grapes? Flowers? Poppy brought me two brightly coloured wooden angelfish. I kept those fish on my desk at work for years. They served as a kind of memory. A warning. She also brought herself. And her brother and sister-in-law. They made all the right noises. They were friendly and supportive. But it was Christmas 1993. Poppy's husband was in a psychiatric hospital. She had a two-year-old boy. This was not the way it was supposed to be.

In the meantime, I busied myself getting to know the ward staff. I was of the same opinion as most of the other patients on the ward – 'I'm not like any of these nutters.' I was demonstrating to myself that I was normal and that, by definition, the rest of the folk on the ward were anything but.

An older man befriended me. He was about 60, grey round the sides and bald on top. He was built like a boxer. He was notable partly because he called me Charles.

'It's Chris.'

'Sorry.' Pause. 'Anyway Charles, are you going to get something to eat?'

The boxer found himself in Ward 6 most Christmases. The simple reason being that his wife had died on Christmas day. Ho-ho-fucking-ho. Each year he was overwhelmed with the pain and grief of it all. Every Christmas felt like the one where she'd died of cancer. He was a lovely, warm and gentle man. We never kept in touch.

Christmas Day 1993 – I was having Christmas dinner with a fireman and a local council administrator. The fireman was terribly intense. 'If I can't look after myself, how am I supposed to look after the public?' The administrator and I nodded sagely.

We sat in silence for a while, looking at our fellow ward-mates, each displaying different types and levels of illness, from sitting in an almost catatonic state to yelling at someone who wasn't there.

The fireman looked around and then leant towards the middle of the table. Conspiratorially, he beckoned us to join him. 'Have you ever read *One Flew over the Cuckoo's Nest*? This is just like that.'

I had. It was.

After a few days sleeping and chatting to boxing man, fireman and admin-man, the powers that be decided it might be time for me to venture forth back into the community. This was the first time I'd met the head honcho psychiatrist.

This reminded me of all the case conferences and ward rounds I'd attended in my professional life. Two really stood out in my memory:

The multidisciplinary team in another hospital ward consisted of about ten professionals including psychiatrists, nurses, occupational therapists, physiotherapists, speech therapists, and good old social workers. We had one meeting in a room that felt roughly the size of a broom cupboard. A patient was brought in using one of the hospital wheelchairs. He was sound asleep. According to his notes he had dementia, probably Alzheimer's.

'How are they treating you here?' bellowed the consultant psychiatrist. His spotty bow tie and bad suit combo made him look not unlike a second-rate TV host.

Not surprisingly, the patient's eyes sprang open. He looked shocked at the fright of being awoken so suddenly and with ten folk huddled together, staring at him. He might have said, 'Huuh?'

'Is the food to your taste?' continued the bastard son of Ted Rogers and Bruce Forsyth.

'Huuh?' the patient said again, before being ushered out. The purpose of this little charade was?

The second case was even more fascinating. I had been working with a twenty-something year-old man for a few months. He had been diagnosed as having schizophrenia. I had no pretensions of being a medical man, but in all the time I'd worked with him, I hadn't spotted any behaviours from him that might suggest that he was seeing, hearing or believing things that weren't there.

But what did I know? I was crackers myself.

This particular case conference had a similar number of medical, nursing, and social work staff hanging around. While we were waiting for my client to be beckoned in, one of the more junior doctors dropped an interesting bombshell. 'I wasn't very busy last night so I took the opportunity to read X's case notes. Did you know that no one, apart from his mother, has ever seen him display psychotic symptoms?'

We had all encountered his mother. She didn't have a great relationship with her son. He wanted to have nothing to do with her. He was adamant that she had nothing to do with any decisions made about his care. The label of schizophrenia had been given to him by the consultant psychiatrist's predecessor.

'I'm sure Dr (Thingy) would never have made his diagnosis based on what the patient's mother said.'

We all mumbled something that suggested we weren't terribly convinced. Munchausen's by proxy was mentioned.

My client ambled in, nodding at me and a few of the others. A few questions were fired at him, which he answered confidently and concisely. He was finally asked to leave.

'Well, he looks like a schizophrenic.'

The consultant's words were met with silence. My particular silence meant, 'What the fuck does a schizophrenic look like?' There are times when I just wish I hadn't kept my gob shut. This was one of those times.

I knew this side of medicine was as much an art as it was a science. And so I had no idea what to expect from my own brand of mental health professionals when my own case came up for review.

The psychiatrist asked me loads of questions regarding my mood and what supports I had at home. He suggested follow-up input, including community psychiatry and psychotherapy. It all sounded a great deal more satisfactory than those two surreal meetings I'd witnessed before. I left hospital feeling altogether more optimistic.

Free! I was free, I tell you!

Over time, my community psychiatrist and my driving instructor morphed into the same person. God knows what Freud would have made of that. My fortnightly visits over the next six months essentially involved me emptying all my stuff out on top of him, him asking me if I would be interested in taking antidepressants and me saying that I would have my degree in psychology ripped from my hand should I ever consider the psychotropic route.

We finally went our separate ways. I passed my driving test first time. God knows why the psychiatrist and I finished.

Psychotherapy was all the more entertaining. Having sat on the waiting list for considerable time, I finally met the psychotherapist fellow. We met in the corridor outside the room where all the action was to take place. It was there he told me his name. He ushered me into the large, high ceilinged, Victorian looking room. He indicated, without speaking, that I should sit on a comfortable, velveteen padded kitchen chair. He sat down on a similar chair, about five metres away. He looked at me intensely and said nothing.

I said nothing. He said nothing. I reciprocated.

It felt like this went on for about ten hours. In reality it was probably five minutes. I could feel my anxiety rising. What did he want? What was his plan? What did he want me to say?

I cracked. I would have been a really shite prisoner of war. I told him everything. Rank, serial number, and then everything that had ever happened in my life. He asked me one question. 'Did you have any thoughts before coming here today?'

'Not really. I didn't know what to expect.'

'Really?'

'Well, actually, I did have a dream where all my teeth were broken and falling out.'

'Interesting. That means you're afraid of something happening to your head.'

Profound. It all felt a little like the touchy-feely pages of Cosmopolitan.

At the end of the meeting he told me that the NHS was paying for one psychotherapy session a week. He felt that I would benefit from at least two sessions per week. He asked me how much I would be able to pay towards that.

I had no idea. This was my first professional job. I'd been a student for seven years, on and off. I was wealthy beyond my wildest dreams! What would I pay for my sanity? We agreed that I'd get back to him on that.

Was this an abuse of power? Was he allowed to sell his private wares alongside his NHS stuff? What the hell was that all about? What should I have done? What should I have said?

After about a week of quiet reflection, I decided that I could survive without his particular brand of psychotherapy. I dropped him and my GP a polite note stating as much. For the time being at least, psychological services and I agreed that a trial separation was for the best.

Three months later I was back at work. I had to return really; I was about to be put on half pay and I had a wife, a son, and several debts to support.

In the summer of 1994, my good friend and fellow social worker, Mark, told me that he had arranged a football match against some hospital or other.

'Can you remember which one?' I asked, thinking No, it couldn't possibly be.

'Er, no,' he said. 'I'll get back to you on that.'

Closer to the day of the big match, I contacted Mark again. 'Any idea which hospital?'

'Er, yeah ... ' Silence.

'Well?'

'It's er, one of the wards from the Royal Ed.' A bit more silence.

'You wouldn't happen to know which one?'

'No.'

'It wouldn't happen to be Ward 6, would it?'

'I'm not sure. It might be.'

Of course it fucking was! I was playing a friendly football match against the ward where I had been "resting" only a few months before. You couldn't make this stuff up.

What is the social etiquette for situations such as these? I gave everyone, including the guy who'd admitted me, the generic, 'Hi, how's it going?'

I knew. They knew. I knew that they knew. They knew that I knew.

It was arse-clenchingly uncomfortable.

No, I don't remember what the score was. But I do remember making some darting runs down the wing, splitting their defence asunder. Which, of course, answered my question. If I had legged it from the ward, this bunch hadn't a hope in hell of catching me.

CHAPTER 3

CHRISTOPHER

I was born on the 6th March 1965, exactly one year, one month, and one day after my big brother Jim. I was dragged into the world in my parent's bedroom, under the gaze of our very close family friend, Louise. Louise, being only 16 at the time, told me she had expected me to spring, *Alien*-style, out of Mum's belly button.

Apparently, she almost fainted when my head started to come out of the other place instead.

My dad's memory of it all was pretty sketchy. For a while he thought I was two months premature. Since the world of midwifery and gynaecology was still black and white at that point, it is likely that if I *had* been so premature, I wouldn't be tapping on the keyboard today.

I grew up in a wonderful, magical world. Dad, a five feet four Scotsman from Paisley, and Mum, a five feet four Scots girl from Wick, endeavoured to provide me with all the necessary goodies to ensure that I grew up feeling loved, with the capacity to become a well-rounded citizen. They had my oldest brother, Stuart, before having me and Jim some years later.

Louise left the area so early on in my life, I can't really remember it. She married Keith, a bus driver from Kettering. He'd been to the grammar school – a fact that impressed anyone who was willing to listen. They provided me with a young friend, Michael – four years my junior – to torture. Quite generously, Stuart provided me with a nephew, Stephen, a few months later.

Dad was born and brought up in Paisley. My memory is a little vague, but I think he was the oldest of 43 (give or take 30). He was a bit of a legend among his family – he was seen as a real hard man. All of his brothers (some nearly a foot taller than him) feared him unconditionally. The story from the mists of time was that he used to be a bit of a street fighter who became a semi-pro boxer. He stopped boxing, he told me, because he was a smoker and he couldn't give up. It's amazing how, as a child, I accepted that as an unalienable truth.

Isn't false memory syndrome a fabulous thing? There's a rumour / story that I can almost believe I was witness to – to the same extent that I believe I saw Santa and his reindeer flying across the sky one Christmas. Stuart had been taking boxing lessons. He returned home – all six feet of him (I'm not obsessed with heights, it's just that I'm amazed at the physical size of my dad compared to his legend) – and said something along the lines of, 'C'mon Dad, try to hit me.'

As the story goes, Stuart frolicked around, protecting his face as he Ali-shuffled about the place. Dad calmly walked up to him and simply touched his left ear. This is only a boxing myth when it doesn't work. Stuart obliged Dad with the expected reflex. Both his hands went to cover his ears, leaving his face free to be thumped. Dad punched him squarely on the chin, knocking him clean out.

Interestingly, Mum didn't take this terribly well and offered to leave him. Dad vowed he would never lay a hand on any of the children again.

There was no way Dad would jeopardise what he had with Mum. By all accounts he'd had a hell of a life. He was a bit of a crazy and angry man when they met. He'd fought in the war, but had spent a significant part of his time in the army in military prison, having thumped an officer who'd had the audacity to call his sister ugly after seeing her photo. He decided to remedy the situation by stealing a jeep with a variety of weapons and heading (inadvertently, he tells me), into enemy territory. Having realised his heinous error of judgement, he deserted said vehicle and returned to camp to have his testicles roasted over the fire.

He met Mum in Wick. He'd worked on Dounray, the nuclear power plant, and was now working as a cook on a trawler. Not an easy picture for me to imagine. Dad, cook? Surely not.

They got married and went to live in the Gorbals – Glasgow's finest slum. That's where they had Stuart. Times were hard. But hell, they weren't my times! They moved to Corby when the steel manufacturer, Stuarts and Lloyds, stated that they would give work to the men of Glasgow, their sons, and their son's sons. Poverty or steel working? Tricky choice.

Dad moved to Corby first to get the council house. In the meantime, Jim was born in Wick – which meant that when I was born, I was 'the only Englishman in the family.' These were my nana's words. She kind of spat them out in a way that suggested that she had just accidentally eaten one of her corns.

They all piled down: Mum, Dad, Jim and Stuart. This must have been a dream come true for them all. A three-bedroomed, newly built council house with a front and back garden.

I was born into a relatively affluent household. Both Mum and Dad worked. I shared a room with Jim. Stuart, being the eldest, had his own room.

Our days weren't exactly halcyon. They were normal. We were fed, watered and taken on Butlins holidays. We had a roast on Sundays and tinned pears and custard for pudding. Jim and I would play horsy-back with Dad. Dad would help me build a variety of cardboard cut-out things from comics. I remember once he and I were kneeling, making a play theatre. He suddenly shouted out in pain and collapsed onto the floor – deliberately falling in such a way as to not go crashing into our wonderful creation. Or so I thought. Isn't the child's mind a wonderful thing? Turns out he had a perforated stomach ulcer.

I remember getting a colour television, a new carpet and central heating. We even got a new three-piece suite that looked all space-agey, like something out of Space 1999. I remember that magical moment, walking through the door and seeing it for the first time. Jim and I had stayed at Louise's for a week while all the refurbishment was going on. It was like a completely new house!

I remember hugs and cuddles aplenty. If you're willing to share a secret, I was Mum's favourite. Things just didn't appear to be my fault – ever. Okay, I'm overplaying that – I ended up with a red arse more than once at my mum's hand. That said, if I cried I tended to get what I wanted.

I remember I'd only eat my mince and tatties off my poor dad's plate, and only then if he'd mash it up and make it into a castle first. And only then if he'd take all the onions out. Me, spoilt? Surely not!

Both Jim and I were seen as real brainy boys at school. We both found it all a bit easy. That's not terribly surprising, since comprehensive education had just been invented and all lessons felt like they were pitched at the lowest common denominator. It left a large number of us feeling like we were educationally gifted.

It was a similar world with sport. I had my dad's fast running genes. They had obviously helped him with fleeing the scene of the crime – those same legs helped me outrun most folk on the football pitch.

Those same legs helped me win the variety of summer holiday games in the square round the back of our house. We played Tig, Kick the Can, Hide and Seek, and British Bulldog, along with Japs & Commandos and Cowboys & Indians.

Added to all this was my gigantic ego that Mum furnished me with. She told me that I was a great storyteller with a great imagination. With this piece of information safely tucked away, I would stand in front of my class, my year, my school – anyone who would have me really – and make up long stories about foxes and rabbits and bears. My memory is that my audience loved me. They adored me. They would scream for more.

There again, maybe I gave the teachers time to do their marking. Maybe my fellow pupils thought, 'Well, it's better than maths.'

My imagination served me well throughout my school life. No matter which part of my school report went tits up, I could usually rely on comments such as, 'Christopher has a wonderful imagination,' or 'Christopher is a lovely boy. If he could stop day-dreaming, he'd do much better in maths' to see me through.

It always felt a bit like cheating. I could see the most wonderful stories in my mind's eye – all I had to do was report on them and copy them down. I thought this is what everyone did.

One of the problems with living in a town with thousands of Glaswegians was that many of us schoolkids were exposed to that great Glaswegian hobby – sectarianism. We had a number of songs that we sung on our bus to school. 'Double Decker 282, hurry up and get your shoe,' is branded forever in my memory. When this got a bit too much, we reverted to chanting, 'We hate the Catholics. We hate the Catholics.' Well, it was easy to remember.

One day it struck me that a good friend of mine, Paul McIlvany, was a Catholic. I didn't know why I hadn't considered that before. He lived up my street, but didn't go to my school. He once split my head open when he hurled a quarter brick at it – but really, you can't hold that against a chap. Suddenly I was struck by the duplicitous nature of my existence. I couldn't hate Catholics and still play with Paul. Something had to be done.

I stood up on the bus and explained my plight to anyone willing to listen –which was really everyone, given the poor quality of the songs. I said I couldn't sing the 'We hate the Catholics' song anymore because I actually had a friend who was a Catholic. Simple really. And it was. Everyone stopped singing that song, which left us with 'Double

Decker 282' for the rest of my infant school existence. Sorry folks. I suppose this experience, and others like it, helped me to realise that life didn't have to be a certain way just because someone else said so. No matter who they were.

Like many children of my era, I had a plastic revolver that I used to pretend to be James Bond. Like many parents, my mum was very safety conscious. These two facts led to her taking me aside one day and saying the fateful words, 'Don't stick those plastic bullets up your nose.'

Unsurprisingly, the thought had never crossed my mind. Until now. So, up it went. Why not? What harm could it do?

Further and further it went until I realised I couldn't actually reach it any more. And so we went to the doctors. They didn't have an implement to deal with such a tricky problem – I had to go to hospital. We appeared at Kettering General Hospital casualty department. This was the first time I'd ever been to hospital and – far more interestingly – it was the first time I'd ever met an Asian person.

He was the doctor on call that day and my mum told him my sorry tale. He produced a shiny silver widget that was just right for the job. They were a cross between pliers and scissors and he brandished them with great expertise. Almost 40 years on, I'm buggered if I can think of any other use for this particular tool. Did the hospital meet up with someone from Generic Toy Gun Producers Inc., noting that it would be in both their interests to produce such a gadget?

You can see the presentation: a middle-aged man in an ill-fitting suit, waving a plastic gun and rolling the toy bullets meaningfully on the desk in front of him. 'Small boys up and down the country will be jamming these things up their noses. Something must be done. The Proboscis 2000 is the tool for the job.'

Anyway, he plucked the bullet from my nose with ease. I have a wonderful false memory (please let it be true) of him standing on the steps of the hospital, happily waving to me and my mum as we wandered off – another pair of satisfied customers.

When I was about three years old, Mum and Dad decided it was about time that I started drinking water from a glass rather than a plastic beaker, just like the rest of the population. Unfortunately, I had a bit of a habit of sinking my teeth into my drinking receptacles. No matter. I'd learn. Anyway, what kind of lunatic would start biting chunks out of a glass?

Jesus Christ. I remember Mum and Dad standing there looking at me earnestly, shouting, 'Don't chew, don't chew!' And then, 'Spit it out!' But my problem has always been that I regard rules as discretionary and, in most cases, really for someone else.

My friend, Andrew Bruno Something Something Muirhead Munro, was also a bit of a rule breaker. A maverick. We called him Bruno and I thought he was fabulous. He had a zest and passion for life like no one else I'd ever met. Everything was exciting to him. He was funny and witty and imaginative – everything I believed myself to be, just cranked up a little.

Bruno also used to spit on his arm. He would spit a small, measured dose of saliva, administered on his sleeve, usually at one-minute intervals. Being a curious and somewhat disinhibited child, I asked him one day, 'Bruno, why do you spit on your arm?'

Quick as a flash, he replied, 'It's better than spitting on you.' What else did I need to know?

Bruno also barked and jumped up in the air apropos of nothing. In retrospect, he probably had Tourette's syndrome. At the time though, I didn't think about it. He was just Bruno and he was fantastic. We did drama together and we would walk endlessly around the woods in the centre of Corby, going over our lines and the lines of everyone else in the play. At these times he didn't bark, spit, or jump in the air. Likewise, when we were on the stage, he was perfect with his words and actions.

He lived right next to Corby's woods, a huge expanse of trees plonked unceremoniously in the middle of the new town. Now that was a magical place to be. I loved everything about it, from the wind rushing through the trees, to the birds getting a bit overexcited in spring, to being able to see the passing of the seasons in such vibrant colours. Bruno and I shared that passion for the woods, and that meant we knew our way around them better than most.

We loved the glue sniffers. They were, I believe, an entertainment service provided by Corby District Council for those people who didn't have a television. Some days they were like zombies from *Dawn of the Dead*. For me and Bruno, they were an endless source of entertainment. In the woods there was a crab apple tree. This was probably the easiest tree to climb in the world, ever. We'd spend hours in its branches, pretending it was anything from the Starship Enterprise to a part of the rainforest in Equatorial Guinea. Our tree was very close to one of the main paths through the woods. A path that was frequented by the glue sniffers. Oh, the fun we had.

The reason I know it was a crab apple tree is because it provided us with seemingly endless ammunition to fire at the unsuspecting, intoxicated individuals below. The tree had a kind of two-tier effect – in the upper branches we were completely invisible, and in the lower branches, if we were careful, we could collect more projectiles without being noticed.

We'd spend many a happy hour waiting for, then torturing, our victims – giggling silently at the suffering of the bemused individuals who couldn't quite work out why there were apples ricocheting off their heads.

When we were 11, Bruno and I went off to different senior schools. We never kept in touch.

So, games in the street, bullets up the nose, glass eating, and zombies. Sounds like any normal childhood really.

CHAPTER 4

MUM

It pisses me off that we've discovered the simple, sneaky, bastard virus that could, in many women, lead to cervical cancer. It pisses me off even more that we now have a procedure that could potentially make this brutal illness a thing of the past.

Yes, you read that right. I'm pissed off. Pissed off that, had the researchers *really* pulled their fingers out and figured all this out much earlier, cervical cancer would not have destroyed my mother – all too quickly and all too slowly.

I'm pissed off that this initially invisible intruder didn't choose to take someone else's mum. Not mine. I was still using her, thank you very much. Then I would still have had someone to hide behind on the sofa with when we were watching the *Hammer House of Horrors*, someone to tell me what a big strong boy I was, and someone who loved me unconditionally. Someone else could suffer the absolute black hole of despair of watching their mother die instead of me.

I was nine or ten when we first found out that Mum had cancer. I later found out that they had attacked it aggressively, using a combination of radiotherapy and surgery to remove anything that wasn't completely welcome. Her symptoms, I remember, were general fatigue and a bit of a limp. She came out of hospital with cotton wool and gauze aplenty. She'd been an auxiliary nurse for a while, so she'd easily convinced the ward that she was more than able to tend to herself. And I'm sure she was.

1976 was the hottest summer I can remember. We went on a caravan holiday to Lowestoft. We turned up – me, Mum, Dad, and Jim – and gazed upon the splendour of all the beautiful shiny caravans there. In among these homes of beauty were two tired-looking chocolate brown and cream six-berth behemoths. Jim and I laughed at the thought of which poor sod was going to be holidaying in these less than deluxe lovelies.

The short answer was *us*. We had our week in a shit-coloured caravan. As soon as we took one step inside, Mum set about it with every cleaning utensil known to humanity. By the time she'd finished on that first day it was damn nearly habitable.

It was a great holiday, and seriously hot. I remember my shoulders actually becoming crunchy. Jumping and cavorting in the sea proved somewhat problematic as the salt invaded every sun-scoured lesion on my back. Mum put butter on these wounds – I think she was probably planning to eat me later.

We didn't know about that sort of stuff in 1976. Crunchy skin leading to cancer? Ridiculous! Perish the thought. Put some butter on it and everything will be lovely. Global warming hadn't been invented yet. How could the lovely, warm sun cause anything really bad?

So far, I have had no repercussions.

It was a holiday we felt we deserved. The stress of Mum's cancer scare was put to one side as we all had that typical British seaside holiday. Lovely. Great. Pity about what was waiting for us on our return home though.

'It's great that Mum's going back into hospital,' Dad appealed to me as I cried into my pears and custard. 'That means they're going to make her better.' I was sitting miserably at our little blue Formica kitchen table, glaring at him miserably.

No, sorry, I just wasn't buying that. I had already been told she was better – why on earth would she need to go back into hospital to make her even more better?

Mum went into Wellingborough Hospital at first. Things continued as normal. Jim and I carried on going to school. Dad went to work and visited her regularly. At this time, Stuart and Carol had gone to live in South Africa. We didn't have a phone, so Dad kept Stuart up to date with all that was going on using the phone in Mr and Mrs Miller's house across the street.

Nothing much was said about Mum's illness / road to recovery until she was transferred to Northampton Hospital. Suddenly Dad wasn't going to work anymore. Suddenly (and altogether more exciting) Jim and I weren't going to school any more either. We all trooped into Northampton most days. Jim and I chatted to Mum for a bit during each visit, bestowing her with kisses and cuddles.

Cuddling and kissing were all very well, but with us not going to school and Mum being confined to her own room in hospital, conversation was a bit limited. Dad invariably chucked some money at us, and so Jim and I wandered around Northampton town centre. I had Subbuteo – the international edition – and it was obviously essential that I got the Luton away team so they could clash with the mighty Brazil when I got home.

These didn't feel like scary times. It just felt like more of the same from last time. Mum would come home with a wide range of pharmaceuticals and life would go on.

One day though, that all changed. Jim and I were playing the sacred Subbuteo at the back of the living room, just under the window. This gave us sufficient light to ascertain exactly who had knelt on Pele and what should be done about it. He had now been glued back onto his base so many times he just had a couple of translucent blobs sticking out the bottom of his shorts where his legs used to be.

Dad came in. He was wearing his denim jacket and looked tired and pale. Looking back on it, he'd obviously been rehearsing what to say in the car on the way home.

'We've always been honest with each other,' he said. There then came an outpouring of words that included, 'Your mum's coming home. There's nothing more they can do for her. We can look after her here. Stuart's coming back from South Africa.'

The wonderful thing about denial is that it kicks in automatically without you having to do anything. Sure, I heard all of the words, but the ones I chose to attend to were, 'Your mum's coming home,' and 'Stuart's coming back from South Africa.'

Stuart did indeed come back from South Africa. He arrived at Louise's house while we were there. I can still see him coming through the garden gate in my mind's eye, with Louise rushing up the path to greet him, shouting, 'Stuart!' She did that laugh / cry thing that only grown-ups can. He ran straight past her and threw his arms around her husband, Keith. He gave him a big kiss, laughed at his own comedy genius and then demanded a Scotch pie. 'The greasier, the better!'

He stayed with us while preparations were made for Mum's return home. I felt young and a bit excluded as Jim showed great interest in his incredibly interesting older brother, who had tales of black servants and car crashes. Stuart was some manner of technician out in South Africa. Doing manly stuff on a day-to-day basis carried with it a level of risk that being an author, as I was going to be, just didn't have. A colleague of his had had an accident in the work place. My youthful mind slotted it under 'Manly Accident' in the memory-storage part of my brain, so it could have been anything from an electrocution to a shark attack. Stuart, being the man's friend, colleague, boss, or just a plain old nosy parker, was chosen to accompany him to the hospital in an ambulance.

It turned out that the man's injuries were pretty superficial. He was back at work almost immediately. Unlike Stuart, who suffered a shattered collar bone when the ambulance crashed due to driver error. It turned out that the ambulance driver had been banned from driving tractors because of his erratic style. Someone somewhere obviously thought he'd be better suited to transporting sick people in a far faster vehicle, rather than maize.

Stuart particularly enjoyed showing us his scars and the place where the metal pins had gone in. He also enjoyed telling us about the black servants he had. I must have said something along the lines of, 'Isn't that a symbol of white man's oppression in a country that has already been raped and plundered?' but in 11-year-old speak. He told us it was okay, because everyone had servants in South Africa. It suited everyone.

Lovely.

Stuart went to visit Mum in Northampton General. She was delighted to see him. The nurses were delighted to see him. He looked like one of the Beatles and he knew it. The main thing he spotted was that Mum was without a television in this horrible hospital. So, he set about remedying that. A black-and-white portable TV was duly delivered. In the eyes of the world, this made him an irresistible mix of Paul McCartney and Mother Theresa.

Please take time to pause with me as we fully appreciate that image.

Stuart was distressed when he saw her. He came home and declared, 'That's not my mum.' We had obviously grown accustomed to Mum's appearance as she gradually deteriorated, losing a third of her body weight over a few months. For Stuart, it was altogether a bigger shock.

Stuart said that if Mum came home, he'd move out. I remember thinking how bizarre this was, given the fact that he'd travelled half way around the world to be with her. Mum did, in fact, come home. Stuart did, in fact, move out and lived with his mother-in-law for the rest of his time in England. As I sit here now, with the benefit of 20 / 20 hindsight, I realise that his move was a sensible one – to make more space for Mum's return home. But in my confused, 11-year-old mind, I convinced myself that he was abandoning us.

So, Mum was delivered home to her newly bought orthopaedic bed in her new vibrant blue dressing gown with the sacred portable TV. She didn't look that ill. She actually looked really happy. I was puzzled at the time. Had they made some kind of mistake? Was some other poor sod waiting to die? Then I asked myself the question that no 11-year-old boy should have to ask himself: 'Does *she* know she's dying?'

It all felt terribly normal. She seemed fine. It was the same old Mum back home.

After Stuart moved out I moved back into sleeping in a double bed with Jim. This was right next to Mum and Dad's room. Being 11 and 12-year-old brothers, Jim and I had a hobby that is shared by siblings around the world. We would merrily batter shit out of each other and then go to sleep. Mum's tolerance for such behaviour was low – being terminally ill and all. She had always been the administrator of corporal punishment in the Young household and this was to continue now she was home. Still thumping each other, we'd hear as the bedroom door opened. We'd have some awareness of her making her way downstairs to the kitchen. We could even vaguely hear as the drawer where she kept her whippy sticks was angrily pulled open and slammed shut. We didn't stop fighting even when we heard her coming back up the stairs with the whippy sticks. But we did stop trying to kill each other once we had received a few stingy whips.

One day, I decided that I was a bit fed up of the stingy whip. I decided that no more would I suffer the sudden appearance of red stripes on my legs in the name of discipline. Knowing that she kept the whippy sticks in one of the kitchen drawers, I set about remedying the matter once and for all. For which, dear Jim, I can only apologise. I opened the drawer, took out the whippy sticks, and broke them into uniform, one-inch pieces. Then I put them back. A stroke of genius. My membership of MENSA was assured.

One night, soon afterwards, Jim and I were tenderly beating each other to sleep. The bedroom door opened, and there were sounds of footsteps downstairs … still I didn't register. Then there was the rattling of the kitchen drawer. Was there a flicker of realisation? No, probably not just yet. Then came the almighty slam of that same drawer and the thundering of feet upstairs. She moved bloody quickly for someone who was supposed to be dying. Finally, it dawned on me. I disengaged from the superficial thumping of Jim and gazed at the door silently. Jim carried on, obviously wondering why the fight had taken such a one-sided appearance.

What followed is best described as shock and awe. Stories are still told, and songs still sung, of that rain of arse-reddening slaps that fell upon Jim and I that night. Jim's small mind must have been searching for the answer to two simple questions:

1. Why is my terminally ill mother mashing me into a pulp, and

2. Where did those sticks go?

Jim, dear brother, now you know.

The above battering acted as a kind of nuclear deterrent for the rest of Mum's time on earth. Jim's behaviour altered incredibly. In a matter of days Jim stopped beating me senseless and started telling me bedtime stories. False memory syndrome – possibly.

Mum gradually began to deteriorate. The cancer spread to her brain. Her mind played tricks on her and, to some extent, on us.

March 6th, 1977. My 12th birthday. Mum had got it into her head that she had arranged for a surprise present for me. Only she couldn't remember where she'd put it. She and I spent a wonderful afternoon shifting the sideboard – nope, nothing there. Shifting the sofa – nope. The dining room table and chairs – no, nothing. Just to make sure, we looked all over again.

I'd been driven by a desire for Mum to be right. She'd been a bit forgetful recently. I so wanted her to be right. To be fair, I also wanted a bloody birthday present. Dad had been a bit preoccupied with other stuff. We were both a bit upset – that said, we still managed to laugh about it.

A week or so later, Jim and I were slapped in the face with the reality of Mum's illness. We'd come careering into the house. I'd obviously done something sneaky and horrible to Jim and I was running away from the consequences. We were both laughing as he promised my immediate demise.

Mum laughed too. 'Who's your friend, Jim?'

We both stopped dead in our tracks. I gasped for air like a recently landed halibut (other brands of fish are available). I was her favourite blue-eyed boy. I wasn't Jim's friend. I don't think I cried. I was too shocked.

Fade out …

Fade back to a woman writhing in agony on a bed in the living room. The bed came down when she could no longer climb the stairs. She groaned and moaned incoherently. She didn't seem to know where she was. She used a bedpan now. Dad would sensitively usher us out to change her pad and pants.

Only once did he fail. I was looking at her groaning and writhing and she pushed the duvet off. There was a pervasive smell of shit and, before I could look away, I saw her vagina. It's funny, the shit didn't seem to bother me. It was the fact that she'd always been a very private woman who didn't want other people knowing, never mind seeing, her business. The views and opinions of other folk mattered to her. Dad rushed in and pulled the duvet over her, cooing gently that she really should cover herself up. He spoke to her in the same way that parents speak to their newly born babies. He didn't expect a response – he just wanted her to know that she was loved and that he was there.

The period of totally caring for Mum was mercifully short for Dad. He only had to wash, dress, change, and monitor her, 24 hours a day, for about two weeks. April 6th 1977 – exactly one month after the birthday present fiasco – I came downstairs to find Dad sitting next to her bed with his head in his hands. He was 54 and he looked like he'd aged 20 years overnight. He wasn't crying – he just sounded desperately sad.

'Your mum died at about six this morning,' he said so quietly and so gently. I remembered the talk the previous night about the "death rattle" and how it wouldn't be long now. I hadn't heard the rattle – it was more of a deathly wheeze. It was like the very act of clinging on was becoming impossible. Clearly it was.

'Can you go upstairs and tell your brother?' The effort of telling me had obviously been huge.

I duly went back upstairs. Jim was awake. I uttered two simple and devastating words that no 13-year-old should have to hear. 'Mum's dead.'

His response was unexpected. 'You're joking!'

What? Yes, I know I have always had a wayward and occasionally questionable sense of humour, but surely ... He came downstairs, saw Dad's devastated form, and told him, 'I thought he was joking!' What a laugh, eh?

The rest of the day was hardly a blur of activity. We may have had breakfast, we may have had dinner – who knows?

Mrs Murie came round. She was a workmate of Mum's at Golden Wonder. We hadn't seen her for a while. To be fair, we hadn't seen anyone for a while. She had been Mum's best friend at the mighty crisp factory. This had been the year that her daughter, Sandra, and I had gone to the same senior school. All Mum wanted was for me to do better at school than her. Mrs Murie said that she'd been 'drawn' to the house. She felt that something had happened. The drawn curtains at three in the afternoon would have given her a clue ... She mumbled some platitudes and left.

Dad didn't really do socialising at the best of times. I imagine he wasn't at his most talkative. I can't imagine what was going through his head that day. I'm sure that somewhere he was thinking that his dream of marrying his girl, having a little white fence, and laughing had all turned to shit.

The funeral was a strange old affair. A whole bunch of folk who'd been conspicuous by their absence all piled into our living room to hear the beginning of the vague platitudes from a minister I'd never seen in my life. They all looked suitably sad, listening attentively to what the man of the cloth had to say.

'You don't have to come to the funeral,' Dad had said.

So I didn't. Jim did – I didn't. Instead, I lay on my bed, wrestling with a black tie, really thinking about very little.

CHAPTER 5

DAD

So, he'd married his girl. They'd had three (varying markedly in degrees of loveliness) children and bought a lovely house with a front and back garden – the back garden even had a little gate.

But now he found himself throwing a handful of soil on top of a wooden box that contained all of his hopes and dreams. Fuck.

In retrospect it was clear he was beginning to fall to bits when he asked me to tell Jim that Mum had died. His was a gradual decline at first. After Mum died, he bought a family tent and we went off to explore Scotland.

We packed up the old Morris Marina Coupe with everything we'd need for our three-week adventure. That meant the tent, the gas stove, the biggest water container in the world, and some bedding. Oh, and all the clothes we thought we'd need which, in my case, was my purple Y-fronts and my Spider-Man T-shirt.

We got as far as Grantham.

The clutch had gone. It took the fine people at the garage two days to fix it. In the meantime, Dad had decided that, even though we were only 30 miles from Corby, we would stay in a bed and breakfast.

The woman who ran it looked exactly the way landladies are supposed to look: permed hair, horn-rimmed glasses, an Embassy

King Size dangling from the corner of her mouth and her arms folded across her ample bosom.

'Where's your mother?' she asked, clearly a complete stranger to tact.

'She's dead,' I said. And then by way of explanation, 'She died of cancer last week.'

She told us what a terrible shame that was. She asked about Dad. I wondered if she was going to apply for the now vacant post of my mum.

'He looks really old,' she said, in such a way that meant that he shouldn't.

'Yeah, but he's a really fast runner.' I thought that this was a top asset for a potential husband. Jim told me to shut up.

The car was fixed and Dad never did marry the landlady.

The weather was great to begin with. But when we got to Fort Augustus, just near the banks of Loch Ness, the weather turned decidedly Scottish and I first noticed that Dad was becoming more and more conspicuous by his various absences.

'I'm just going into town,' was a euphemism for 'I'm going to the pub.'

He'd leave Jim and me to our own devices. Already he was giving Jim more responsibility than he was able to cope with. Already Jim and I had nearly managed to kill ourselves without Dad noticing a few times.

One night Dad went 'into town' again. Town was about two miles away. The rain was pissing down. He didn't have a waterproof anything. He vanished for about four hours. Jim read me Jabberwocky (The Monty Python book of the film) while he was gone using the camping gas light. Dad returned at about one in the morning, pissed and soaking. He'd never done that before.

We had a whistle stop tour of Wick and John O'Groats and Thurso and Scrabster – seeing all the folk that we'd visited with Mum just two years before. Jim and I were made to feel really special. 'You poor boys,' appeared to be the general theme. We were festooned with hugs and cuddles, soft words and love.

Dad's vague, life-threatening neglect continued.

Scrabster was a small fishing town on the northern tip of Scotland. It had the most fantastic rock pools you have ever seen, with crabs and shrimps and starfish and anemonies. The rock pools were inaccessible to most sensible folk. They were situated on top of the various rocky stacks and stumps that marched out into the North Sea. With the tide out, these rocky outcrops stood as high as 15 feet out of the frothing waters below.

Those of you with weak hearts, high blood pressure or questionable continence should look away now.

Jim and I saw these outcrops as stepping-stones. Neither of us took much notice of the fact that we couldn't swim as we jumped from pillar of rock to pillar of rock. We scraped our feet against the jagged edges and the barnacles as we sought the ultimate rock pool. God, it was worth it!

There, on top of one of the largest rocks, was a pool that looked like it had been designed purely for my delight. The water was warm, about six feet deep and teaming with wildlife. It was wide enough for us to launch ourselves across, giving us the sensation of swimming but without having to wave our arms and legs about. It was fantastic.

We looked back at the danger of the rocks below and the fact that we couldn't swim. We couldn't blame it on the twilight, or that we couldn't see the wider picture. We concluded that we must both be fucking stupid. We didn't tell Dad about that adventure either.

The world had taken on a kind of surreal quality as we drove around the Scottish Highlands without a care in the world.

For my dad, returning to work meant more misery. He had been in charge of his section of the tube works at the steel works. He had been told that he should take off all the time he needed to look after his wife and two boys. He was told that his job was safe.

When he got back, he was handed a brush and was told that sweeping the warehouse was now his job. I imagine he was less than delighted at his new position.

Having not been at school for most of the year, I found I was behind in most subjects. It was English that upset me the most. I had been one of the top in my year. I now found myself in the bottom 25%.

While I flunked out at school, Dad fell further and further into himself. He spent more and more time in the pub. He passed more and more financial responsibilities onto Jim. Jim was in charge of the groceries. Jim was in charge of clothes shopping.

Over that first year without Mum, a few things were rapidly becoming apparent: it was no one's responsibility to do the housework. It was no one's responsibility to do the garden. My clothes and shoes weren't being replaced. There was no toothpaste. Or soap. Or shampoo. Or food.

Added to this, Dad was now drinking at home. He kept his bottle of Bell's whisky under the kitchen sink. One day Dad had drunk his first bottle of Bell's and was about to start on his second. Jim and I were more than a little alarmed at this. So we decided to challenge him and told him he wasn't allowed to have it.

'Right then,' he said, while taking off the suit jacket he wore all the time. This was Glaswegian non-verbal communication for, 'If you even try to take that whisky off me, I'll tear your leg off and hit you over the head with the wet end.'

We were both aware of Dad's crazy history. We quickly assessed that taking him on, even in his inebriated state, would not be wise. Being somewhat averse to being dismembered, we negotiated with

Dad to try to work out an amicable resolution to this tricky situation. He told us he wouldn't drink all the whisky if we had a drink with him.

Cue two Tupperware beakers.

Jim and I glugged down the vast majority of that bottle of Bell's. I think I had a pink beaker and Jim's was blue. I remember lying there on the sofa, 12 years old and pissed out of my face, with the room spinning around me. I might have been thinking that this hadn't been the best solution to this particular problem. I might well have been thinking that Martians had landed in the garden.

These were the dark times. Dad wasn't all bad. Really.

Things gradually got worse for Dad and for us. Quite remarkably he managed to keep his job. The house that he and Mum had invested a lot of time and money into gradually deteriorated around us.

Dad smoked his roll-ups and the living room reflected that. The ceiling yellowed. The wallpaper on the walls began to look like something found in some fusty programme about how the Victorians used to live. The cats, Ginger and Suzie (Jim later claimed her name was spelled Siouxie – as in Siouxie and the Banshees, to demonstrate just how cool he was), started to live a slightly lawless existence. They would shit and piss really where they fancied and also bring in their latest kills, including mice and sundry garden birds. The house was dotted with their little corpses – and their smells.

Ginger was notorious for being insane. Anyone – *anything* that approached her was liable to lose blood. This psychotic creature was happily stinking up the house without any comeback or punishment.

The house was smelly and dirty. I was smelly and dirty. We were all smelly and dirty.

Dad told us and anyone who was willing to listen that it was his boys that kept him going. When we were alone in the house and he'd had a few whiskies, he told us that once we were grown up and away from the house he would kill himself. No pressure there then.

I got to the point where it all got a bit much for me. I finally cracked and told Dad that I needed him around. I didn't want to be alone night after night in my smelly house, in my smelly and ill-fitting clothes. I asked him time after time not to go out, to just stay at home with me for once. 'I'll be back at half eleven,' he'd say, gently and not unkindly.

Getting pissed all the time is not without its risks. No, I don't mean liver disease. Falling. He fell more than a few times, sustaining fairly serious injuries and knocking himself unconscious. One night, Dad arrived home startlingly pissed. I lay in bed as I heard him bounce around the kitchen, dropping glasses and plates as he prepared a little something just before bed. Finally, I heard him make his way, falteringly, up the stairs.

Quite close to the top, he missed his step. Had he been sober he'd have just stumbled. However, he wasn't sober and so he fell all the way down the stairs. There is a sound that only flesh and bones bouncing off stairs can make. He made that sound. When he reached the bottom, there was a moment of silence. It probably lasted no more than five seconds. It was in that time, though, that my thoughts began.

Die, you cunt. Just die.

I felt a lurch of disappointment when he started to groan. It was a gargling, moaning groan. It sounded vaguely like he was calling for Jim. *Just fucking die.*

I lay in bed, not moving, my breathing shallow in case someone could hear me.

Die!

After 20 minutes of this almost inhuman noise, Jim finally heard him. He rushed downstairs to find Dad's small and twisted form. Jim phoned the ambulance and Dad was duly rescued.

I got up the following morning and feigned my surprise at Dad being in hospital. 'Really? What happened?'

Dad had found himself very close to death that night. He had managed to break his neck. That said, he only had minimal injuries to his spinal cord, which meant he never felt his fingers properly again.

He was delivered back from hospital a couple of days later. He improved over the following weeks and was soon able to go back upstairs to sleep. Before we knew it, he was well enough to get back to the pub and the off-licence. Finally, he returned to work.

I became angrier and angrier. At school I must have been a teacher's nightmare. I'd stopped doing homework. I was also getting into more and more fights at school – venting my anger and frustration on a variety of unsuspecting victims.

Although I appeared to have a number of crunch times, one of my biggest occurred one sunny day in the summer of 1979. I'd walked home from school as usual, but was still fizzing from anger over something and nothing. I was about 50 yards from home when I saw Anthony Hutchison. Hutch.

Hutch was a bit of a nutter. He was completely lawless and, because of this was one of the hardest guys in our year. He was also one of the fastest runners. 'Hutch, you're a wanker!' I shouted. Bravely, I ran away.

He caught me about ten yards from my house. In retrospect, he probably wishes he hadn't. Hutch caught me and I exploded with anger. Mum dying, Dad drinking, me being smelly and not having any food in the house – it all made me furious and he got the lot. I don't think he hit me once.

He was quite a mess when he finally extricated himself and ran away. Word got round pretty quickly that 'Chris Young has beaten up Hutch.' So now I was weird, smelly, and a nutter. Folk began to keep their distance.

Had he been paying attention, Dad would have been proud. Had he been paying attention, Dad would have noticed that there were days and nights when I just didn't come home. The thing about rebelling or acting out is that it's all a bit meaningless if no one notices.

In 1980, the shit really hit the fan. Word was out that the quality of the iron ore in Corby was not great. As a result, it would be cheaper to have it dragged out of the ground elsewhere. This meant that a huge part of the steelworks was due to close. The men of Corby went on strike.

The sons of the strikers marched with them as they chanted, 'No steel closure! We want the right to work!' Some of my friends got to appear on local radio and TV. It was all very exciting. It was also dazzlingly shit.

We had even less food than we'd had before. Men in suits would come to our door and we'd refuse to answer. If we saw them, we'd pretend to live elsewhere. Once, they managed to get in and they put a pre-payment metre on the TV. 50 pence would get you two hours of quality viewing.

This added insult to injury. As if life wasn't fucking hard enough, the telly would go off half way through *The Sweeny, Trumpton, Match of the Day*, and / or *Coronation Street*.

The main problem at the time, though, was lack of food. I remember the excitement I felt when one day the Salvation Army came round with a small, yet significant, box of food. It included tins of beans and meat, but best of all a small box of Kellogg's cornflakes. Imagine how my joy turned to dismay when I realised we didn't have any milk. No matter, I had them dry. I was past caring.

To this day I still think someone's posh if they've got Kellogg's cornflakes in their cupboard.

Apart from this box of food and my friend's parents, there was another reason I didn't die of starvation during these hard times. Our local fish and chip shop gave away batter bits for free. I still drool at the memory of the crunchy, greasy fare drowned in salt and vinegar.

My problem was that I was still the son of my mother. As such, I couldn't get this free stuff every day. My pride wouldn't allow it. I'd rather go hungry.

In that same year – 1981 – Dad's mum died. I was in the bath and I heard Dad shouting for me to come downstairs. These days he was only really assertive when there was someone else around – so when he demanded that I came down the stairs 'now' I guessed that he had a family member with him. I obediently played along with his game and duly made coffee for him and Uncle Jimmy as they told me of the demise of their loving mother.

Uncle Jimmy finally made his excuses and left, leaving me with Dad. He was distraught. Inconsolable. I thought about his shite parenting, how he'd become self-absorbed over these short and terribly long four years.

My mate, Kev came round. I told dad I was going out. Dad became frantic.

'Where are you going?'

'Out,' I said, not terribly gently. 'It's okay, I'll be back at 11.30.'

At that moment I really hated him. I hated the way he'd fucked everything up. I hated the way he only cared about himself and his suffering. I hated the way he'd turned his back on me. And now? Fuck, I hated the way this situation – my world – had made me react to his pain. I was punishing him in the way he'd punished me.

'It's okay, I'll be back at 11.30.'

His words.

At that moment, I hated myself too. You reap what you sow.

In 1981, Dad accepted a redundancy package from the works. For 16 years of his life, they gave him approximately £10,000. You could buy an awful lot of whisky in 1981 for £10,000.

Jim kept his head down and managed to get the A levels required to enable him to escape to the University of Surrey in sunny Guildford.

In that same year, I spoke to Mr Haig, our sixth form tutor, about my academic future. He told me that the best thing I could do was leave school and get a job.

The fucking steelworks had just closed. Unemployment was running at about 25%! Great advice, Mr Haig.

My mates, who had the same discussions with Mr Haig, were advised to knuckle down and concentrate on their work, and that everything would be okay. Interestingly, I was the only one out of this bunch to procure a degree. Bitter? Me? Too fucking right.

This left me at home with Dad. I felt the weight of the world on my shoulders. I knew that if I left home, Dad was likely to fulfil his suicidal ambition. Jim was keen to reinforce that and told me regularly that I couldn't leave home. In 1982, Dad took some of his well-earned drinking money and paid for a holiday to the Costa-del-Sol with me and Louise. On a coach.

I think the holiday lasted ten days – two full days of which were travelling on this 'luxury' coach. At the time there was no such thing as a luxury coach. A coach became luxury purely by virtue of the fact that it had the word 'luxury' written on the window at the back.

I remember devouring peaches the size of my head as we left sunny Spain. Imagine the joy I felt when we were told that there was no running water on the bus. My hands and face attracted flies from all over Europe for the rest of the journey.

Dad promised he wouldn't get drunk. Then he promised he wouldn't get drunk all the time. Then he said he had had a bet with one of his friends back in Corby that he couldn't get drunk on Spanish vodka (If there is such a thing). That was it really. He was shitfaced for the rest of the holiday.

After a year of living alone with Dad, my wits could take it no longer and I moved out. We were all terribly concerned about Dad on a day-to-day basis. Would he drink too much? Of course he bloody would! Would he eat properly? Did he ever?

Dad remained on his liquid diet until he died in November 1990.

I moved around a bit until I went to college at the North East London Polytechnic. Here, I was roughly 80 miles from home. As such, I regularly visited Dad on the Corby Flier (my name for it), a coach that travelled twice a day from Marylebone to Corby. I told him it was so I could pinch his meals on wheels. He'd started getting these because of the pressure he'd received from Stuart. He never ate them. I'd eat the jam roly-poly and custard. Other than that, I left well alone.

One lovely summer's day, I came home unannounced from college, asking Dad if he had anything to eat. 'Yes,' he said. 'There's some meatloaf in the oven.'

Knowing Dad's history and his somewhat laissez-faire approach to sophisticated dining, I asked, 'How long has it been in there?'

'Oh, I just made it yesterday.'

That was good enough for me. I was a student and a man in my early twenties. I seemed to be in an almost permanent state of hunger. I cut a bit off. I think I might have had it in a sandwich. It was a bit bland – but hey, it was food.

I knew Dad would be unlikely to put this nutritional product in the fridge, so I thought I'd do that for him. I picked up the meatloaf from the baking tray to put it onto a plate. I've got to say I wasn't overly happy when I saw the happy family of maggots, who had been hanging out in meatloaf city, just maggoting about on the plate.

Mental note to self – make Dad a meatloaf sandwich. I threw the nasty product away. It was clear though that Dad's voyage of self-destruction was continuing, albeit in a sad and passive way.

Over time, thoughts of Dad's threats to top himself became a bit of a distant memory. Until one day.

As usual I arrived home, unannounced. As usual I came in the front door. Unusually, there was a smell of gas circulating the house.

I walked into the kitchen to find Dad sitting on the floor. He'd turned on all the gas rings on the cooker without lighting them and, not surprisingly, the room was full of gas. In his left hand was a box of Swan Vesta matches. In his right was a Swan Vesta match, which he was striking repeatedly against the sandpaper on the side. He was crying his heart out. 'I'll take those, I think,' I said as I took the nasty, dangerous, sparky things from his hands.

There it was. His one and only suicide attempt – thwarted by me arriving home unannounced. Fuck. It would have been an impressive exit.

We talked about it at some length. Jim and I had left home. The cats had both died. Mum was still dead. Dad had just had enough. This was the one and only time where he'd plucked up the courage to do it, albeit in a drunken stupor, and I'd fucked it up for him. I didn't talk to Jim or Stuart about it. It just didn't seem right.

And that's the way it was. Dad gradually deteriorated through poor diet, smoking, lack of exercise, and his old mate, whisky. We all visited him through guilt, concern, and curiosity. How was he still alive?

In the summer of 1990, all of Dad's Christmases came at once. He had been blessed with lung cancer. The GP told him that, although it was essentially inoperable, he could lengthen Dad's life with a whole variety of potions and radioactive therapies. I think his exact words were 'Bugger that.' He did ask the doctor if he could carry on drinking and smoking though. He was told that that would have little impact on his remaining months.

I was living in Scotland now. I came down by train every second weekend to see how he was doing. It's funny, when I received the diagnosis I raced down to Corby expecting Dad to look somehow different. Nope – he was the same old, skinny, bald 68-year-old man.

We talked a little about his life. We talked a bit about Mum, the cats, Jim, and Dad's cancer. I'd get him a whisky. I'd make him a snack. All gentle and quiet stuff. No wailing, no gnashing of teeth. 'It's funny,'

I said to him one day. 'You're the one who's dying, but it's the rest of us who are falling to bits.'

It was true. Here we all were, approaching this inevitable day. I felt I was racing backwards and forwards from Scotland. I didn't know whether to love him or hate him. After all he'd put me through. But he was still my dad.

Louise and Stuart appeared to be on the scene almost continuously. Was there a feeling of guilt because of their absence at the time of Mum dying and the aftermath? Who knows? Jim, as was his way, dealt with his grief quietly and privately.

At this point I had already met and married Poppy. In October, we found out that Poppy was pregnant. She was reluctant to tell folk because it was still early days. That said, we agreed that Dad should be the first person I should tell. So I did. About one month before he died, I told Dad that he was going to have a grandchild. He was really happy – but sad that he'd never get to meet them. He never had the audacity to offer me any words of wisdom about parenting. Just as bloody well.

That day finally arrived. I got a phone call one Friday morning from Keith, Louise's husband. Dad had died that morning. Seemingly it had been a peaceful affair and he hadn't been in too much pain at the end.

When I spoke to Louise afterwards, she told me that she'd continuously pumped him full of Oramorph – a morphine based medicine. She was worried that it had been this, and not the cancer, that had taken him. We agreed that he was on his way anyway and if she did something to accelerate it, albeit unwittingly, it was probably for the best.

I remember that day quite well. I didn't collapse in a wailing lump of tears. I didn't scream about how unfair life was. I went to work. I worked in a day centre for people with physical disabilities in Prestonpans, a mining town not far from Edinburgh. I got the 129 bus there from Edinburgh and I went swimming with a bunch of folk with a variety of disabilities at a pool in Tranent – another mining town. All very surreal. All very quiet.

I told my managers about Dad. They asked me what the hell I was doing there, and to come back to work when I was ready. It was all very lovely.

I arrived in Corby on the following day. It was fucking odd to visit the house and to find Dad just not there. I spoke with Louise, who was still reeling from the death.

On the Monday, Jim and Stuart and I went to visit Dad at the funeral parlour. Interestingly, lying there in the casket, Dad reminded me of a shuttlecock. Some joker had dressed him in a white robe thing that I never remembered him wearing to the pub. His little bald head, decorated with the scars from a fall off an escalator, poked out the top.

The day of his funeral arrived. My memory of this auspicious day is sketchy. This was due to my good friend Derek, who I'd known since I was five. Every time I opened my mouth, he poured Southern Comfort into it.

The graveside is where things first started happening for me. There was a host of folk from Dad's side of the family who I'd never laid eyes on before. There was a minister who I'd never laid eyes on before. And there was a piper, who I'd never laid eyes on before, playing A Scottish Soldier.

That did it. I wailed. I cried uncontrollably. I was crying for Mum, for my cats, for Dad, for my home now gone, for my childhood, for my fucking life. Stuart, Jim, Louise, Poppy and Derek had no idea what to do with me. One of Dad's sisters grabbed hold of me and held my ribs together as I completely lost control. I have no idea how long I cried for.

When I woke up the next morning I was struck with the stark realisation. I was 25, I had a child on the way and I was an orphan without a home. I felt so very alone.

CHAPTER 6

JIM

It was awful. Horrific. I watched, open-mouthed, as Jim staggered through the garden gate, his hands clutching his abdomen. It soon became clear what was going on. The knife handle protruded from his stomach, and there was blood all over his hands.

'Muuuuuuum ...' he called out as he finally made it to the back door.

She rushed to him, a look of horror on her face as she looked at the crippled form of her ten-year-old boy. 'Jim, what's happened?' she cried, as he fell into her arms.

'I ... I found this knife handle in the street.' Jim showed Mum the knife handle and the tomato ketchup he'd smothered his hands with, grinning like a loon.

She was bound to find it funny. Eventually. There was probably a point where Jim must have thought *shit, I wish I'd really impaled myself on a knife*, as Mum beat him to within an inch of his life.

I thought it was funny. I didn't tell her I thought it was funny. But inwardly, I was laughing my rocks off.

Jim and I had the typical sibling relationship for brothers who were separated by a year. He'd play with me if his mates weren't around. I'd be obnoxious and get him into trouble as and when I could. That said, there was a solidarity there. It was okay for Jim to beat and torture me indiscriminately, but woe betide anyone else who had a go.

I was in the square round the back of our house. No surprise there really, that's where I spent the vast majority of my early years. The Colgates were a family relatively new to our street. This meant that the existing and well-established pecking order had to be er … renegotiated. Brian was a year older than Jim and Shaun was a year younger than me. I had already demonstrated to Shaun, nonverbally, that his place in the food chain was substantially lower than mine.

Brian had not taken exception to the placings, just at how strongly I might have put my point to his younger brother. He was now explaining to me, through the medium of a good kicking, that he'd rather I hadn't been quite so vehement in putting forward my views to Shaun. He had me cornered between a car and a wall in the street and I had reached the point where I was hoping he was going to tire a little.

It was then Jim noticed my plight. Being a mathematical sort, he swiftly calculated that the sum of the force of the Young brothers would be greater than that of a single Brian. With this in mind, he joined the fray.

Being a mathematician and not a psychologist, he had not taken all extraneous variables into account. The most important of these variables was that I'd had quite enough physical activity that day, thanks, and decided to bravely leg it. Thus leaving Jim to enjoy Brian Colgate's full wrath.

That isn't entirely accurate. It became clear to me as I fled that the Colgate boy had found reserves of anger and energy he didn't realise he had, borne of the fury and indignation of the attempted rescue. I think Jim got a bigger beating than the one originally intended for me.

I'm sure we all learned a valuable lesson that day. 'He who fights and runs away – and leaves his brother to get a good pasting – lives to, er … '

On top of this, Jim also suffered the indignation of me cuddling him every night as we shared a bed. I had some notion that I'd fall off the earth or, at the very least, everyone else would bugger off and leave me if I didn't have at least one hand on someone all through the night.

As we grew, Jim's ability to misread situations continued to get the better of him.

There had been a fair at West Glebe Park – a large swathe of greenery containing a number of copses, a pitch-and-putt golf course, and a bunch of football pitches. Jim and I had spent our fair money really quickly on a variety of shitty rides and stalls. We still had ages to play so we went to the play park at the edge of West Glebe.

We were magically drawn to the monument that was an old steam train. It was painted bright green in some local authority attempt to make it look like fun. It was fun. We would spend hours playing train tig.

You would be correct in your assumption that I am going to use two tried-and-tested phrases here: 'Had I been paying attention', and 'Look away now.'

Train tig involved clambering all over said train while playing tig. If you were tug, then you'd give the tigger five seconds to get away.

Hutch had suffered the same fate as us. He'd run out of money and didn't want to go home yet. At this tender age – eight or nine – Hutch had not yet become a fully-fledged nutter and was still a fun guy to hang out with. He joined in with the train tig session.

Look away now.

Hutch had been tigged and was looking for revenge. Had I been paying attention, I'd have noticed that standing with the funnel of the train's chimney behind me was not the wisest thing for me to do. Hutch stood on top of the train, facing me.

Which way should I go? I hadn't really thought this out. If I moved too quickly I'd fall off the train and onto the concrete below. I was just putting this down to experience – thinking something along the lines of, 'I don't think I'll stand here again' when Hutch lunged at me, shouting in his broad Scots accent. 'Tig!'

I remember nothing after that. Jim went home. The walk from West Glebe to our house took about half an hour, so it gave Jim some time to think as to what he should tell Mum.

In a Bruce Forsyth, 'What's on the conveyor belt tonight?' style, Jim exclaimed, 'Guess where Christopher is.'

Mum went through a variety of friends' houses and places where I could have been, until Jim got bored with his game and called out the answer. 'No – he's in hospital!'

I woke up in the ambulance to find Hutch staring at my prone form. Even when he sounded concerned it still sounded like he wanted to do me some damage, so I chose unconsciousness again. When I finally came round properly a day or so later, Hutch told me how he'd watched as I'd vanished backwards over the chimney after the impact of his somewhat firm tig. Both he and Jim went round to the front of the train, fearing the worst.

It was okay – I'd landed on my head. I bled a lot and had a most splendid wound on my left cheek. The good news is that they replaced the concrete around the train with sand. It was great to know my sacrifice had not been in vain.

Why am I telling you all this? Why do you need to know about Jim the Impaled, Jim the Colgate Slayer (Not), and Jim the Comedic Deliverer of Messages?

It's because, dear reader, after Mum died, we lost an awful lot of that boy. Sure, there was the usual sibling rivalry stuff – the, 'Christopher, why don't you just fuck off, can't you see I'm playing with my friends?' moments, and the racing-each-other-up-the-street-to-the-house-so-we-could-get-to-the-toilet-first stuff going on. There was nothing out of the ordinary until ...

After we got back from our Scottish holiday, Dad absolved himself of all housekeeping duties by giving Jim a sum of money plus the family allowance (now called child benefit) to get the groceries. Dad would pay the rent and the gas and electric bills. Sorted.

Well … not really.

One week, Jim had been unable to get the shopping in and had put this responsibility onto my youthful and eager shoulders. 'I usually just spend £6 on the shopping,' he said, handing me the rather small wad. I went to the shops and bought the small amount of food that this meagre amount would buy. Gradually it became clear that this was why we never had anything to eat in the house.

In home economics, the teacher ran a class experiment. We were all to find out how many calories we ate in a day, how many sweets and sugary drinks we had, and how much we spent on the week's shopping. There was much excitement as we compared and contrasted our calorific intakes. Some folk in the class appeared to live purely on chocolate; some folk ate a medium amount of shite. I ate none.

This, I felt, immediately put me on the moral high ground. All these folk were eating things that were bad for them – and I didn't.

It was the comparative cost of the groceries that was of most interest to me in this little bit of research.

'Martin?'

'£20.'

'Tracey?'

'£25.'

'Paul?'

'£30.'

And so it continued around the class. The highest was about £30 and the lowest around £20.

Until it got to me …

'Christopher?'

'£6.'

And then, by way of explanation, I said, 'We eat really well.' Which wasn't remotely true – unless of course you took into account all the food I got from a variety of friends' houses. Derek's mum, Willie Irvine's mum, Kev's mum and Gary Ilko's mum all got the same treatment: 'Oh, I'm sorry – are you having your tea? Oh really? That would be lovely, if you're sure it's not too much trouble. In retrospect I'm sure they all knew what was going on – it was a wonderful conspiracy of silence where I flattered them mercilessly in return for a meal.

Oh, and of course I had the infamous batter bits. But none of that cost any money.

There was a bit of murmuring and the teacher quizzed me on everything from the accuracy of my accounting to the size of my family. She concluded that I must be mistaken.

When I recount my sorry tale to friends and professionals a common question bubbles to the surface. 'What did the teachers do?'

Well I guess the word 'nothing' kind of covers it. What should they have done? They'd been presented with a child who'd been a real high flier in primary school. He'd come to senior school, hardly attended at all in his first year and had, unsurprisingly, academically fallen on his face. By second year he was back on course and was put in the top class for the rest of his school career. He could have tried a bit harder though.

Maybe they just didn't know. I assumed Dad would have informed the school – certainly, a couple of the teachers appeared to know, but no one really said anything or did anything about it.

Mr Booth, the woodwork teacher, was the delightful master of this craft. To say I wasn't particularly good with my hands is a bit of an understatement. It seemed that every week I took it upon myself to break a hacksaw blade. Mr Booth rewarded me for this by whacking me across the arse with a small cricket bat that he'd lovingly made for the purpose. This week, Mr Booth was demonstrating some tricky task on a jigsaw or some such thing. We all stood around the wonderful machine, enjoying the banter with our mentor, when I demonstrated my love for his art by passing out.

Mr Booth rushed me outside where I duly came round and puked up on the pavement outside the craft block. I remember I hadn't eaten for a while so it was mainly yellow bile and water that came up. Being a curious sort, Mr Booth asked me what I'd had for breakfast.

My mind raced. If I said 'Nothing', he might get concerned and ask Dad to come into school. Then they might realise just how shit things were for me and put me into care.

If I said, 'Bacon, eggs, sausages, fried bread, baked beans and black pudding, all washed down with fresh orange juice' he might have noticed that none of these items were in my vomit, realise I was trying to cover up and ... put me into care.

I said 'Cornflakes and a glass of milk,' thinking this might keep him off the scent. He paused. He didn't believe me. What was he thinking? He got me to go back inside and sit quietly for the rest of the class.

Nothing happened. He didn't say anything about it again.

And that was the pattern of it all. At some point, Jim and I had got our small heads together and concluded that if anyone were to discover too much about our situation, we'd find ourselves in care. Whatever 'care' might be.

So we covered up, lied and fabricated our way through school. Which takes us back to the question, 'What did the teachers do?'

What could they do if, apart from a few subtle clues here and there, they didn't know anything?

While Jim was doing a pretty good job of looking after himself in challenging circumstances, I was developing some pretty strange behaviours. Some of them were harmless. I released my pent-up anger and testosterone by masturbating, which was only fun when Jim or my dad didn't walk in unexpectedly and catch me in the act. Some were less harmless. Suffice it to say, I threw myself into the task of pugilism with great gusto. I don't think this served to endear me to many folk.

As time passed I became more and more introspective. I think I was being attacked by a particularly effective two-pronged assault.

There was the assault from the outside world. The people around me must have seen a change from the happy-go-lucky eccentric in training, to an unkempt, ill-disciplined, angry young man.

Then there was my inside world. I hated what I had become. I felt like an outsider. I relished this label that I'd given myself, but at the same time I despised it. When I was using my wit and charm, it was great to be me. I could see humorous opportunities where others saw nothing. Using my imagination, I could take people to some of the fine places I frequented. Gradually though, I became less keen to share. I'd go to my little inner spaces on my own.

The first time I really remember doing this was on a school trip to Edale Youth Hostel in Derbyshire. This was essentially a rambling holiday where we were to explore the many and varied walks in and around the start of the Pennine way. I loved the hills. The feeling of freedom, of vast openness, filled my teenage heart with joy. Being fitter and abundantly more enthusiastic than many of my schoolmates, I was always involving myself by helping others at the back, by joining the leading pack, by showing great interest in the route, and so on. God, I must have been a pain in the arse.

It was on one of these excursions that something a little odd happened. We'd stopped by a river to enjoy our packed lunches of damp sandwiches, squashed up fruit, and a hot beverage that tasted like whatever had been in the thermos on the last trip. I took myself to a spot along the bank to eat mine. I remember feeling a little sad and that I found the sound of the river soothing, possibly even therapeutic.

Then *nothing*.

I was suddenly surrounded by the teacher, Mr Long, and a few of my friends looking quizzically at me. Where had I been?

The troops had all moved off, en masse, on the way to some fine hill or other. Because I was so involved with a variety of folk on the way, everyone assumed I was with someone else – until the coin finally dropped. No one had seen me since lunch – and that was an hour ago. So, the above folk retraced their steps and found me where they had left me.

I was sitting on the riverbank, staring into the middle distance. I had vanished into my own inner world. When asked, I had absolutely no recollection of what I'd been thinking about or whether or not I'd heard everyone go off. I hadn't been asleep. This was to be start of me 'zoning out'.

It took me a little while to refocus – to fully appreciate what was going on around me. Folk were nervously laughing. Perhaps someone said, 'What's wrong with him?' but I'm not all that sure. I re-joined the throng and rambling recommenced. No further questioning. No further comment. It all served to reinforce the view that I was a little odd.

On that same school break things got even weirder. We'd been marauding around outside the youth hostel playing a game that was a hybrid of football and *Terminator 2*. We'd been asked to come in because it was late and we had an early start.

Gary Ilko and I chose the hiding option. We legged it around the back and waited for our hiding place to be sprung. We were both panting and laughing. I remember my skin felt cold in the evening air. While we were looking at each other, Gary suddenly sounded alarmed. 'Chris, what's wrong?'

He told me later that the colour had drained out of my face and I'd lost all expression as I gazed straight through him. From my perspective, something altogether stranger was happening.

Gary Ilko's head changed into my mum's.

It was absolutely shocking. I felt light-headed; my mouth dry. She was vaguely smiling. I was terrified.

She vanished as quickly as she'd appeared. I think the whole experience lasted for about 30 seconds. Shit, now I was really bonkers.

I told Gary what had happened. He was great. He was just concerned about me. Was I okay now? Was I scared? Should we tell someone? No, that was it. We never told anyone.

Years later I discovered that this was probably a hypnogogic hallucination. When I say 'probably', I mean 'definitely'. I mean, if Gary Ilko had really developed the skill to morph his head into heads of his friends' deceased parents, we'd have seen him doing it on TV by now. A hypnogogic hallucination is borne out of stress, combined with an incredible desire for that person to be there.

Now that was a really odd school trip. I returned home and life went on.

I spent more and more time on my own. I hated to be alone and yet, in many cases, I was choosing to exclude myself from the world. I felt terrible about my appearance – about my clothes mainly. This gradually spilled over to other areas of my appearance; my face, my hair, my body. All this gave me a heightened state of arousal. I felt anxious and angry so much of the time.

I hid myself away. I started to display my 'polar bear trapped in the zoo' behaviours.

I would take one of the chairs from next to the dinner table and put it in the corner of the room, the front legs of the chair facing out into the room. I then took a tennis ball and would bounce it off the wall and header it between the chair legs. Every time I did this it was a goal.

I drew up a list of every team in the English first division. I set up league and cup games. I would choose a team and start scoring goals. When I missed, that meant it was time to start racking up the score for the other team. Yes, as you can imagine, there were some most interesting scores like West Ham 1 – Chelsea 72. The thing was, I documented everything. I used every bit of paper in the house, including my sports day certificates, to keep an accurate account of how all the teams were doing in my own fantasy league.

Hour upon hour. Day after day. Thankfully, I never thought to record top goal scorers or I'm sure I'd still be scribbling my records today.

In a similar vein, I raced small round sweets called Wordies. Our coffee table had a slight incline in it. I would release two sweets at the top of the incline and the first one past Dad's coffee cup would be the winner. For those of you who are concerned about the rainforests, you'll be delighted to hear I didn't document these races.

There was one Wordie that stood (bloody hell, I nearly wrote 'who stood' – no unresolved issues there then) above all of the others. It was lime green and had 'Cat' printed on it in purple letters. Cat won everything. Other Wordies would come and go – but Cat was there for good.

Oh god, this sounds really loopy.

As time passed I had less and less to eat and spent a lot of my time hungry. It was okay to eat the others – but Cat endured. About two years after this all started, Cat was the only Wordie left. It was tatty and frayed around the edges. The once bold lettering had faded now; only some of the purple colouring was left.

Jim's shopping regime had been in place for some time. The cupboards and the fridge were empty. There wasn't even a margarine and mustard sandwich to be had.

I was so hungry. So hungry.

I ate Cat.

I was devastated. I remembered all the times we'd had, all the races he'd won. Sure, I'd contrived to help him win a few, but he was head and shoulders above the rest. But now, at my hand, he was gone. I'd become attached to a sweet for fuck's sake!

I *did* have a real cat that I was also pretty attached to. Ginger the dog slayer would give me the love and affection I needed. (I've just had a thought. We *always* had food for the cats. Clearly Jim felt that it was more important to keep them fed – *and* they could catch mice and birds and the occasional mole.)

Even when I was angry, this (well-fed) furry friend would come and see me and purr. She'd fetch little paper balls that I threw for her. She'd sleep on my bed. She was just *there*.

One day I came home from school – angry and alone. As usual she'd come to see me. Everything would be okay. Not this time. Fuck.

I took hold of that little cat and threw her. She had no idea what was going on. I caught up with her and hit her around the body, then around her head. I grabbed her and shook her. I threw her onto one of the armchairs. It was there she had a seizure.

My anger vanished immediately. What had I done? I'd just battered the one thing in the world that showed me love. There in front of me her eyes rolled and her legs kicked out at some unseen assailant. 'I'm sorry, I'm sorry,' I repeated again and again as I stroked that same body and head that I'd been beating only seconds before.

After what seemed hours she came out of it – dazed, but happy to see me. She purred as I stroked her and tickled her under her chin. She sat on my knee for pretty much the rest of that evening. We both sat in a kind of shock. What the fuck was going on?

It never happened again.

In the world of psychology, there's a belief held by many that you can't just get rid of a behaviour – you have to change it. You need to replace it with something else. At 13, I wasn't terribly aware of any psychological theories. That said, at 13 I was going some way to proving these fine people right.

It's a bit like trying to squash an unburstable balloon. Every time you squeeze it tight, another bit pops up through your fingers.

My anger was still alive and well. In my mind, it was still okay to fight with – and threaten and aggressively posture towards – people at school and people I played football with. They were sentient, thinking beings who were more than able to look after themselves – or work out ways to not piss me off. For some, this proved impossible. For some, simply breathing and existing were attributes sufficient to cause me to fly into a rage. I'd work on that later.

With beating up Ginger there came guilt. With guilt, there came self-hatred. With self-hatred, there came inwardly turned anger. With inwardly turned anger, there came self-harming.

It wasn't quite as simple as that though. The self-harming actually provided me with respite from the psychological turmoil in my head.

It started one day with pins. At school in needlework, many of the boys (including me) thought it would be an absolute hoot to push a needle or a pin through the dead part of the skin of our fingers. The result? A finger that had the appearance of the old 'arrow-through-the-head' illusion. Girls would scream and boys would cackle evilly.

I was practising this at home one day when I accidentally pushed the pin into some living flesh. Not being someone who ordinarily relishes pain, I guess I must have hopped about manfully, running my finger under the cold tap until the bleeding subsided. It was here the two-pronged attack of my wonky thinking came into play.

First of all – this was pain *I deserved*. I was horrible. I had done an awful thing to my cat. Once I put my mind to it, I could find loads of reasons as to why I deserved to hurt myself. Hitting people did eventually come into it – but that came after not doing my homework and hating my dad.

Secondly ... secondly ... fuck, how do I describe this without sounding completely bananas?

At the tender age of 13, I had more nasty stuff going on in my head than I could easily tolerate. My mum had died of cancer. My dad had revealed his alcoholic credentials. Everyone – that is, all the other grown-ups in my life – had vanished without a trace and Jim was spending the family fortune. The mixture of isolation, upset, anger, and just plain old sadness filled my thoughts so much of the time.

I found that sticking needles into my fingertips took away some of the focus from the psychological pain.

The dense gathering of nerves there provided just the right amount of distraction at the right time. Momentarily, the clutter in my mind cleared. All the competing thoughts fell by the wayside as the white-hot pain came to the front of my mind, screaming for attention.

I felt calmer after the pain subsided. I became hyper-aware of my surroundings and I drank it in.

The problem with finger-stabbing is that the pain goes on for much longer than you would want it to. After the sensory heightening moments of watching the blood blob and flow along the contours of the ridges and whorls of my fingertips had passed, I was left with bloody sore fingers. I found it hard to write or pick my nose.

No, this just wouldn't do.

We had a black comb that had a long and pointed metal handle. I decided that this would do the job. Self-harm is one thing, but dying of some horrible infection borne out of sticking a metal spike into my arm was not high on my agenda. I sterilised the comb handle by holding it in the beautifully cleansing flame of our gas cooker.

It wasn't terribly sharp, so pushing the handle into my left forearm took quite some force. The first time I did it, the pain was fantastic. I could feel my breath shorten, my eyes water, my nose stream. My mouth was wide open as I silently pushed the full four inches in, then through, my arm. I clenched my teeth as I saw my skin whiten and bulge at the promise of the point breaking through.

All the shit in my head just evaporated. I was addicted. I couldn't do it all the time – someone might notice. How do you explain *this* away? As far as I can remember I was unaware that this was practised by others. I was alone in the world in my little world of minor self-mutilation.

There was hardly ever any blood. There were times when there was hardly any pain. Very occasionally I'd have another shot. This was rare because it took a lot for me to build up to the point of the assault. That said, there were strange experimental times when I wasn't stressed, when I didn't have the driving belief that I was worthy of punishment. I just did it out of boredom, curiosity ... I'm not sure what. I just did it.

No one ever found out. It was my little secret.

As Jim grew through his teenage years, he developed that cruel egocentric streak sometimes exhibited by this group of humanity. Dad had given Jim some money to buy me some trousers. Why he didn't give the money to me is anyone's guess – he gave it to Jim.

Jim went for the cheap option: a pair of the most ludicrous brown flares that I'd ever seen. Added to that, they were about three inches too long for me. No matter, I had nothing else to wear for school club, so I wore them.

I spent my evenings playing table football and then going on to play five-a-side football in the gym hall with my mates. As you can imagine, playing table football with clown's trousers on didn't pose much of a problem. Me and Shaun Hannah continued to defeat everyone who stood in our path.

The five-a-side was altogether different. Football was something from which I gained my little bit of kudos. I fell all over the place, tripping over the hems, my feet and the ball. It was awful. I remember looking across and seeing my brother and his mate, Andy Hadden, laughing uncontrollably at my plight.

What could I do? I didn't do anything. I had some childish notion of dignity and I took all my upset and anger home with me and put it in a box for later. I'm still not terribly good at being laughed at.

Jim was a very popular boy in the sixth form. He was a bit of a bully with a caustic tongue that he used to belittle everyone. So perhaps for popular, read 'feared', with folk being nice to him because they didn't want to look like an arse.

Yes, I'm being bitter. That probably wasn't the case. There were folk who liked him for who he was.

I was different from Jim. Over the years I'd become a little crazy and folk appeared to enjoy my slightly offbeat humour. I liked to be liked. I liked to be the centre of fun and frivolity.

Jim and I were having a bit of a public argument in the common room. I can't remember what it was about – but I *do* remember that he wasn't faring terribly well.

He stopped the argument dead by stating, 'At least I wasn't voted *the* most hated person in the sixth form.'

I can still feel that lump in my throat, that lurch in my stomach accompanied with a complete inability to speak.

I didn't cry until I got home. I spent all my time trying to fit in with normal folk in my crazy fucking world. And now ... and now I'd discovered for what? For some bunch of bastards to democratically vote me in as ... Fuck!

Dad, unusually for him, spotted that something was wrong. 'What's wrong?'

That said, it wouldn't have taken the most gifted of counsellors to spot my distress. I was crying uncontrollably. 'Ask him,' I blurted as I pointed at my loving brother.

I took an emotionally charged swing at him – hitting him in the face. It was a bit shit and floppy. I felt defeated.

'He's not going to be happy until he's beaten me up!' Jim declared in his defence.

Dad explained that there wasn't going to be any beating up. I told him what had happened and it all dissipated without blame and without further incident. Unresolved.

Jim threw himself into his A Levels and vanished away into Dad's bedroom for hours on end. He'd complain if I sang while I was cooking, doing the dishes or tidying the house. I'd either been, or was about to be, chucked out of school. Just another thing to add to the growing pile of shite that was my life.

Don't worry, this self-pitying diatribe finishes shortly.

Jim and I were standing in the kitchen. We were probably chatting about nothing much. He had his back to me. Suddenly he turned round and punched me squarely in the face. I hit the ground like a felled tree. Jim, upon realising that I wasn't unconscious or dead or paralysed from the neck down, took the only sensible course of action available to him. He ran upstairs and locked himself in the toilet.

I lay on the checked linoleum, staring at the variety of brown stains on the ceiling. I could have been there for hours. I was probably only lying there for a couple of minutes. I felt wonderfully calm, almost serene.

I got up, walked upstairs and knocked on the toilet door. 'It's okay, Jim, you can come out now. I'm not going to do anything.'

Silence. 'Come on, we're grown up – we can talk about it.'

The door opened. I didn't wait for second thoughts. I grabbed hold of Jim and dragged him out. I punched him in the head and face all the way down the stairs. I pushed him through the door of the living room and up against the sideboard. The sideboard that me and Mum had wrestled with all those years before.

I didn't feel any anger. I didn't feel anything. I was vaguely aware of Jim shouting and crying out as I repeatedly punched his face. He held up his arms to protect himself. I pulled them down with my left hand while I continued to punch him with my right.

In all my experiences of fighting – of being in them or seeing them – the participants make a noise, grunting and shouting as they trade punches. I was completely silent, quietly splitting his lip, chipping his teeth, making his nose bleed and giving him black eyes. I felt like an observer passively watching this scene of unfeeling violence.

Dad sprang up out of nowhere. Suddenly he was standing between us. He was shouting as well. It took a while for me to reconnect with it all. I felt nothing. I looked at the mess I'd made of my brother and I felt nothing.

I was aware of something horrible as I came back to reality. Had it not been for Dad throwing himself between us, I would still be hitting Jim today. I would have killed him. I would have continued in that silent trance until he was no longer moving.

That realisation really struck home, because I never chose the pugilistic option with anyone after that day.

CHAPTER 7

DEREK

'You fucking bastard!'

It was New Year's Day, 1982. I had been sitting with Derek's mum in their living room, sipping tea, and chatting pleasantly about the events the night before. New Year's Eve. Hogmanay.

Derek's heartfelt verbal attack on me made me realise, in no uncertain terms, that when telling me what had happened, his mum may have kindly censored some of the events that had unfolded following my simple swig of a can of lager the night before. I was now sitting on the same brown, velour-esque sofa. There were no signs of blood and / or vomit. What could I have done?

'You fucking bastard!' Less aggressive now. More a kind of, 'How *could* you?' statement.

The events of the previous evening, as *I remembered them*, had been as follows:

Derek and I, at the tender age of 16, had decided to fully embrace our Scottish heritage. This, of course, involved the noble art of 'first-footing'.

Apparently, according to Scottish tradition, it's lucky to have a tall, dark stranger (there were few stranger than me) bearing gifts (usually alcohol or coal) to be the first person to step over the threshold of your castle in the New Year. Derek and I decided that the coal option was not really for us and, as such, he furnished himself with a litre bottle of Bacardi and I chose a similar amount of Teacher's Whisky.

I fully believed that, since Corby was often referred to as 'Little Scotland', most folk would take a drink of my whisky as we clattered into their homes, leaving me more than able to push Derek back home in a wheelbarrow. However, had I been paying attention (you can look away now), *no one* appeared to want to drink my whisky. *Everyone* wanted Derek's Bacardi. I took a swig of whisky in every house we ventured into.

Okay, I'll cut to the chase. By the end of the evening I was waving around an empty bottle of whisky. I was sitting on the sofa in Derek's house telling anyone who was willing to listen that I had drunk a litre of whisky and that I was still able to string a sentence together. I was a medical marvel!

A 16-year-old boy drinking a bottle of whisky? I imagine you might have a few different words for me.

Delighted with my drinking prowess thus far, I decided that a can of lager would probably have a therapeutic affect or would be unlikely to make any difference to my state. I was clearly impervious to alcohol. I took one swig of that can of lager then, BOOF! I was miraculously transported in time and space to my bed, eight hours later.

Derek recounted the story as calmly as he could. He did become a bit hysterical in places but, in general, I thought he did rather well.

When I took the now famous swig of the lager I had been sitting next to Derek's auntie. I think she and her husband had come down from Scotland to Corby to enjoy the festive period. She was 50.

My memory states that her husband was sitting opposite her. This would have placed him on top of the McLachlan TV. Beautiful and state-of-the-art I'm sure it was – it wasn't a seat. My synapses had already become a bit trigger-happy. So there she was – a laughing, round-faced and perm-haired woman from the north – sitting next to me, finding humour in all I had to say. Apparently I was a picture of charm and wit.

At some point she decided it would be nice to share in the joy of Hogmanay with her children who were roughly my age and were, in all probability, destroying their family home with a party of their own in the absence of their parents.

Derek's dad had just got to the point of the evening where he claimed that, between them, he, Derek, and Derek's brother, Richard, had every record ever scratched into vinyl. It was at this point, quite understandably, that I chose to follow Derek's auntie to the foot of the stairs where the phone resided. As the legend goes she was in the middle of Happy-New-Yearing her family when I took the phone from her. Obviously I had far more interesting things to tell them than she would. I'm sure what followed was a kind of cultural exchange between Corby and the West of Scotland. Anyway, it was far more entertaining than taunting Derek's dad with a variety of made up bands and songs and watching him rifling in vain through piles of LP's in an attempt to find the non-existent song.

So, we all said our goodbyes to the nice Scottish folk living down the other end of the phone. Lots of ostentatiously loud festive phone kisses were exchanged as the receiver was returned to its rightful place. But all this kissing and whatnot had clearly put an idea into my misfiring, festive, youthful and testosterone-laden mind. Here in front of me was a beautiful woman who required a New Year kiss that she would remember for all time.

It started off well. That kind of sealed-up kiss reserved for aunties, parents, cousins and rampant 16-year-old boys who thought their luck was in.

To cut a painful story short, I lobbed my tongue down her throat (god, I hope those were her own teeth) and held her in a passionate embrace. So passionate was the embrace that even her husband had considerable difficulty in extricating me from his lovely wife.

At some stage my primal brain must have realised that my type of entertainment was no longer required. The suction was broken from her face and I ricocheted through the house, leaving without so much as a, 'Happy New Year!' I had clearly decided it was time to go home to die. Obviously, not before urinating the length of their back garden.

My brother, Jim, found me in the living room. I was still fully dressed, wearing my ancient parka, lying face down on the carpet. The hood of my coat was up, over my head, and full of vomit. I really hope it was mine ...

I stopped drinking for two years after that. Derek's auntie always asked after me after that fateful night, telling anyone who was willing to listen what a lovely boy I was.

I first met Derek McLachlan when I was five. We both went to the centre of excellence that was Studfall Infant School and we both were seen as brainy boys. Although, in truth, he was substantially brainier than me.

We went to Studfall Junior School, where we found ourselves in the same class. We made it to the fourth year of Studfall Juniors without really colliding too much – knowing about each other's existence, but that was really it. We were in the chess team together though. Derek was board one and I, er, wasn't. Board ten was important as well. So Mr Davis had said.

Up until first year of senior school, Derek and I lived parallel lives – travelling in the same direction but with little going on between us. Gradually, almost imperceptibly, things began to change. We began walking to school together. Nothing much out of the ordinary there; he lived on my way to school. There again, so did a hundred other folk.

I think he really came into his own after Mum died. While my life was in turmoil, my head spinning and people feeling sorry for me and avoiding me in equal measures, Derek was developing an approach to life which has served him well to this very day. He did nothing. He didn't treat me any differently. Whereas I have the habit of wanting to analyse every facet of every relationship, he just lets them happen. When I see something wrong between folk, I have to fiddle with it, become involved, try to make it better. Derek always chose the *do nothing* approach.

So by doing nothing and not judging me, young Derek gained my trust and friendship. By being the funniest human alive and being off-the-wall, I gained Derek's curiosity. My unpredictability made me kind of interesting.

About four years ago, Derek phoned me. He was in a similar flutter to the time he recounted the auntie snog fiasco. He had remembered a time where my off-the-wall thinking, combined with his practical ability to make things happen, had nearly brought about our untimely demise. I think he hoped I'd say something along the lines of, 'No, don't be ridiculous, Derek. You've made this up. This, my friend, is false memory syndrome at its very worst.'

Instead, I simply said, 'Oh, fuck!'

By third year at senior school, Derek and I were both in the 'A' class. We were two of Lodge Park Comprehensive's finest minds. Our class, we were told, taught us the equivalent of grammar school education. Please bear this in mind as the story unfolds.

While all the other boys were playing with their gat guns, Derek's dad got him a crossbow. A crossbow. Now this was a real fuck-off kind of a weapon. For fuck's sake, what is a 14-year-old boy who lives in a council estate in Corby going to do with a bloody crossbow? At first we shot the fence and sundry targets.

But then we hatched a plan that led to that phone call all those years later. It was summertime. Derek and I set ourselves the most simple of tasks. Collect all the coats we could and we would meet up in the field an hour later. The coats were for the purposes of health and safety.

So, there we were, two of Lodge Park Comprehensives finest minds, in the middle of a field with a crossbow and a pile of coats. We took turns. Well you would, wouldn't you? One of us would put on all the coats while the other one shot them with the crossbow.

Great phrases from the afternoon included, "Wow, great shot Derek. That would have definitely killed me!" Oh my fucking god!

We spent the whole afternoon entertaining ourselves that way. We never did it again. Interestingly, no one asked where all the holes in their coats had come from.

After many years working in social work, I haven't come across a 'trust game' that comes anywhere near to our little crossbow in the field affair. God, it was stupid – but more trusting than anything I have ever done.

Derek and I spent a lot of time playing football, throwing a boomerang, and latterly videoing our golf swings.

As a couple – don't get me wrong, we weren't that way inclined (although there was a day when Derek's brother came in to find us *manfully* wrestling on the sofa) – of hale and hearty young men, Derek and I moved around different social circles in search of entertainment.

For example, hanging out with John Beech and Gary Ilko gave us the *Famous Five* kind of lifestyle where we'd go on adventures – swim in the river, frighten ourselves with snake skins and bravely run away when Gary accidentally set fire to the door of the sports centre.

I know what you're thinking. What lovely stories. Chris and Derek against the world. When all the world had turned to shit, Chris could rely on his best mate, Derek. And, of course, Derek could rely on Chris. Fantastic. Isn't that just great?

Well no. Not at all, really. Something was rotten. And that rotten thing was me. So twisted and angry was I that, at times, on quite a regular basis, I would beat Derek up. Anger would well up inside me apropos of nothing. I was completely unpredictable. When the anger became intolerable then I'd hit him. I punched him at the zoo. I kicked him hard when we were out playing in the square. I really beat him up once for playing *Turning Japanese* by the Vapors once too many times on his record player.

In later years, Derek was able to tell me about the fear he felt when the veins on my forehead stood out. He just knew pain was soon to follow my silent display of inner fury.

'Why did you hang out with me?' I asked him once, hoping for an earth-shattering reply.

'Because you were really funny.'

It made me think of those comedians who talked about how they used their razor sharp wit to stop them from being beaten up by the big nasty boys. I was the big nasty boys. Only I made folk laugh afterwards.

One day in Religious Studies with Reverend Long, we were discussing personality types. Some people were introverts and some people were extroverts. Some were something in between. Mr Long was randomly asking the folk in the class if, by and large, they enjoyed their own company or the company of others. Imagine my shock, horror, and dismay when Derek declared he enjoyed his own company. I suddenly felt desperately lonely. In my small juvenile mind I had believed that, apart from Derek, there was little else in my world.

Fuck.

Looking back on it, it reads like a typical wife-beating, insecure husband scenario. I'd like to say that this was a moment of enlightenment for me – but that was still a few years away. For now, we still hung out together, although for a while I was more insecure than usual.

While Derek's dad was bestowing him with a substantial arsenal with which to protect himself, I was still yet to discover the genetic defence mechanism that my father had passed on to me.

One day, in English, I was happily sitting next to Gordon Simpson. He played football and basketball in the school teams with me. Nigel Morris, a wonderfully camp youth, minced by our desk. Being the mischievous youth that I was, I felt that it would have been a slight on his character had I allowed him to walk past without me sticking a maths compass in his arse. Unfortunately that day Nigel was mincing slightly quicker than normal and, as such, I missed him completely with my first swipe. Not to be put off with this, I chased after him and, with an energetic lunge, I successfully impaled him.

During the chase I managed to kick myself on my left heel. I only had a momentary experience of the full joy of harpooning the lovely Nigel before the whole world began to go warm and fuzzy – and then black.

I woke up at my desk sitting next to Gordon. My head was resting on my forearms on the desk. I felt really tired and a bit confused. 'That was fantastic!' said Gordon, far more enthusiastically than I felt.

'What?' I might have said. The whole world felt just a little disconnected.

'That was just like an epileptic fit!'

'Oh?' I wasn't terribly conversational.

A few days later, Mr Long approached me in one of the many school corridors. 'I heard you might have had a seizure in your English class?' He looked concerned. My mind raced. If I told him that I had had a seizure then the authorities might get involved and I might have to go into care. If I had epilepsy, in my mind I wouldn't be able to play football or basketball ever again.

'No,' I said flatly.

'Because Gordon Simpson said— '

'I was just mucking around.' Equally as flat.

'Oh, I see. You might want to tell him because he was a bit worried.'

In later years I finally discovered that I suffered from a strange old condition called a Reflex Anoxic Seizure. My body reacts to pain that is also a shock, in a bit of a whacky way. My heart stops for anything up to a minute and then the whole system is booted back into action by a seizure. Apparently, while I'm waiting for my heart to restart, I go horribly pale.

Well that's fucking useful! I think of it as an extreme form of playing possum. I wonder how many Youngs have been passed by on the battlefield, believed to be dead, only to snap back into action a minute or so later. The nice thing about the condition is that it gives me a warning before I lose consciousness. Usually, I have about 30 seconds to find myself a comfortable place before I pass out.

It's passed on through the male of the species. At the time it was just one more thing for me to hate my father for. In a world where I just wanted to fit in, to blend in unnoticed, here was another glaring thing for me to come to terms with.

In the meantime, my sporting career was going from strength to strength in spite of any obscure cardio / neurological conditions I might have. I played for both the school football and basketball teams. The football season covered the winter months while basketball filled my summer. So for those of you that were thinking a bit of sport would have sorted this young man out, you might want to reconsider.

For the first four years of senior school our football team was, without putting too fine a point on it, shite. Why we were shite was always a bit of a puzzle. Individually we were all competent with the ball, reasonably fit, and passionate about the game.

Nevertheless, I loved playing football. I was a defender. I enjoyed the release of aggression that I got out of the crunching tackles that I merrily threw at any unsuspecting forward. I loved the thrill of the chase, the exhilaration of it all. More than anything I loved the feeling of being part of a team. A shite team, but a team nonetheless. I wore my brother's boots and the rest of the kit was provided. I was just like everyone else. I just blended in.

I wonder how violent I'd have been without sport?

I loved basketball. I thought it was singularly the most boring game in the world to watch. But to play? Well, that was a different matter altogether. Lodge Park Comprehensive had been blessed with a massive, all-mod-cons-included sports centre. I spent every lunchtime there playing basketball with different members of the team. What a luxury! Looking back, it was little wonder we devastated teams from miles around. We were untouchable for my first three years at school.

The problem was that my brother Jim didn't play basketball. This meant that I couldn't borrow his basketball boots. This would have been a problem had it not been for a piece of genius on my part.

Dad, in a fit of generosity one day, decided that I would benefit from new shoes. The soles of my current ones had long since gone and I think he had become aware that I had been cutting out bits of cardboard to use as insoles, to prevent too much water coming in.

He gave me £8 for this task. He allowed me the independence of thought and deed to do this myself. And there they were. The basketball boots of my dreams, retailing at a very reasonable £7.99. It was a no-brainer. I got myself the beautiful boots.

The biggest problem for me was that I now had to wear them as my school shoes. It was in an era where that sort of thing just wasn't done. Children wore black shoes to school. There'd be none of that crazy 'wearing sports shoes' malarkey for a number of years. But I didn't care. Well, I did a bit. Especially when I had to put up with the daily whine of Fiona McKenzie: 'Chris, why are you wearing basketball boots to school?' For someone who just wanted to fit in there were times when I just didn't do terribly well!

Basketball also gave me the kudos I required when the rest of my life was falling to bits. When it came to the fourth year, the world of school basketball changed. We were still the finest team in the land, but god we had to fight for it. No more crazy antics for us. No more trying to score by bouncing the ball backwards through your legs, a manoeuvre that was fucking painful when executed badly. No, we'd become far more serious about our game.

And so it was that we arrived at the last game of the season. We had to win. We'd won everything so far, but the evil Pope Jim had scored more points than us. If we lost, then the championship was theirs.

Southfield was a typical Corby school, with a small school gym with wooden floorboards, attached absent-mindedly to the rest of the school. Almost as a kind of afterthought.

There we were, ten of Lodge Park's finest, anxiously anticipating the match ahead. There wasn't much in the way of chat, just quiet reflection as we waited for the start of the game.

To be frank, Southfield weren't very good. However, what they lacked in skill, they more than made up for in mindless aggression. Very early on in the game, Mr Walker, our games teacher, decided that we needed to match that physical presence. I was usually part of that presence – but today he had decided I wasn't enough. We were winning, but not as comfortably as we might have been.

On came the mighty Mick Thompson. Off I came. Pissed off? Me? You bet.

Had cage fighting been invented back in the day, I'm sure that young Mick would have held every belt and crown there was to win. Not only was he physically and mentally strong, he also exuded an aura that said, 'Touch me and you're gonna die.'

It was Mr Walker's plan to scare Southfield into submission.

If we'd gone for the 'outsmarting them with our dazzling skills' approach, I think we'd have won comfortably. As it was, it was like a toe-to-toe slog between two aging heavyweight boxers. Little thought going in as they hoped to gradually grind down their opponent.

Suddenly, Southfield edged ahead. They were winning by one point. The seconds were ticking ever closer to the end of the game – actually, the seconds were ticking really quickly towards the end of the game because the little bastard Southfield timekeepers, sensing victory was in sight, kept on pushing the time on by a minute here, and a few seconds there.

Equally suddenly, Mick Thompson reached his five-foul limit and had to come off. Mr Walker brought me on.

There were 30 seconds to go, and we were one point behind. I was really pissed off at having been kept on the bench for most of the game. I was at the halfway line when the ball came to me. I was aware of all my teammates screaming for the ball. I looked at the clock – there was no time to pass. The Southfield timekeepers were sitting hunched, cackling between themselves. They were going to win.

The smell of schoolboy sweat and dusty floorboards were thick in my nostrils as I shot from what seemed like miles from the basket. False memory syndrome has increased that distance over the years … I thought if I missed then the tall and unfeasibly intelligent Graham Martin would get the rebound and finish the game for us.

We didn't need him though. The ball went straight through the hoop without touching the sides. My shot was punctuated by that satisfying swish as I won us the game and the league …

My greatest sporting memory – as alive today as it's ever been. I still use that memory in times of adversity today. Even now the sights, sounds and smells are beautifully vivid. I can feel the hairs rise up on the back of my neck as I write.

When I moved onto to the 5th year, I had to put all things sporting to one side. Our O Levels were seen as vastly more important than all that silly running about.

We still played a bit to keep our hands in though. We were in some cup game or other, playing against Kingswood school. By now we all had the bodies of men with the minds of seven-year-olds, and we all threw ourselves around the court accordingly. During this particular game, one of the Kingswood man-children ran into me, giving me a dead leg. I hobbled about manfully for a bit, but ultimately had to come off.

After the game Mr Walker put his hand on my shoulder and said, 'That looked like a sore one, Chris.'

In my recent life, I was completely unaccustomed to public displays of affection. I burst into tears and cried uncontrollably. Mr Walker had no idea what to do. He was a real man's man. I was one of the tough guys in the team; I wasn't supposed to behave like this. He looked acutely embarrassed. To remedy this, I affected a heavy limp to demonstrate that I was suffering terrible pain and that my unfortunate loss of control had nothing to do with emotions whatsoever.

My dad hadn't touched me since my mum had died. Not in anger nor affection. It was something he just didn't do. That one gentle touch from this seemingly unfeeling man had brought all this home to me. My social façade had crumbled for just a moment.

My teammates looked at me incredulously. Jesus! I just wanted to be the same as everyone else, and now here I was affecting a limp in some futile attempt to cover up what was going on in my head.

That year we were also to be presented with the county basketball cup on the school stage. Oh, the glory of it all. This great moment was slightly tarnished for me when Mr Walker took me aside one day and said, 'Chris, you're getting the cup on the stage next week. Could you wear some proper shoes while you're up there?'

Well, no. I couldn't. I didn't have any. I'd just have to wear my basketball boots and he'd have to be happy with that. Bastard.

The glamour of sport aside, I busied myself at school with bringing my academic career to its knees. I was cheeky. Violent. Obnoxious. Disobedient. Unlikely to do my homework. Likely to lose my schoolbooks. A teacher's dream, really.

And so, with my sporting career over, it was no great surprise to anyone when Mr Haig and I had the 'leaving the sixth form' conversation.

*

Derek finally left school and got himself a job in computing. With this, his first job, Derek bought himself a white Ford Fiesta XR2. Yes, it was a boy racer car.

I was still farting about generally in life. I was probably one of the first people ever to experience a feeling of relative wealth when I went on the dole. Jim had got himself a place at Surrey University. He was studying chemical engineering and was currently living in halls of residence.

It was Jim's birthday. Derek drove me down to Guildford to allow me to celebrate that auspicious occasion. Apart from being fed liver curry (don't try it – don't even feel tempted) there was nothing particularly remarkable about the visit. It was on the journey home that something strange happened. An epiphany.

It started to snow. Heavily. Snow in February in the home counties? Who'd have thought? We were listening to Prefab Sprout's album, *Steve McQueen*. It was light, poppy and beautifully sentimental in places. Derek was demonstrating to me the detrimental effect that the snow was having on his ability to steer.

'Look, I've turned right and nothing's happened!' It was true. But as long as the road remained straight, I thought, we'd be fine.

As all this was going on, I took some time to really look at Derek. He was the same height as me at five-ten, although he had a slighter build. His hair was a similar colour (light brown) but his was straighter, shorter and thicker than mine. Where my face is roundish, his is longish. Where my eyes are blue so is one of his. The other is distinctly greenish. Just like his favourite singer at the time, David Bowie, Derek had different coloured eyes. But it wasn't all that physical stuff that hit me.

It was at that moment as we careered out of control in the snow – the smell and taste of liver curry still in my mouth and the dulcet tones of Paddy McAloon washing over me – that I realised that I was completely and utterly in love with this man sitting next to me. I didn't tell him – it's not the sort of thing we did back in those days.

He had always been there. Through thick and thin, sickness and health, for better and worse, in richness and in … what am I talking about? He was there through some fucking trying times.

I was just struck by the fact that this handsomish, funnyish, stupidly intelligent guy was everything to me. To this day I can't fully explain it. As long as I know that Derek is in the world, I've a feeling I'm going to be okay.

CHAPTER 8

STUART

There now follows a public information film on behalf of the Department of Education regarding the potential pitfalls of fucking around at school.

I'd left school. Fuck! I'd left school. Now what?

Before leaving school, I'd met with the careers advisor. For some reason I'd told him I was interested in engineering. He confidently told me that there would be a lot of opportunities out there for an intelligent chap like myself to get on in the world. He told me he'd be in touch.

True to his word, he contacted me three months after leaving school. He had an opening for me. I called him from the phone box at the bottom of my street. I'd lost myself in the fantasy world of future employment. Why bother staying on at school when here, after three months, I found myself being offered the job of my dreams? Sure there'd be an interview, but with my flannel I'd be given the job in seconds.

'A garage forecourt attendant? What exactly does that entail?' It didn't sound as glamorous or exciting as I'd imagined.

'Filling cars with petrol, handling money ...'

Oh dear. The reality of leaving school with O Levels in English language, geography and physics was becoming all too clear to me. How the job could be construed as engineering is anyone's guess.

It was a Youth Opportunities Programme. I worked from 8.00am until 5.00pm, five days a week, for the generous sum of £25. Thank god for my glass collecting job at the Silver Band Club, a working men's club quite close to home. For three nights a week, they gave me £16.

£41 per week. My wealth knew no bounds.

With Derek still at school at the time and with no income of his own, I would take him out usually once a week to get us both bladdered. Occasionally, we would indulge in the cocktail bar at the Strathclyde Hotel. Five cocktails for £5. Only if you drank them at lunchtime on a Saturday though. I still remember the harsh glare of the Corby sky as we staggered out to see what the rest of the day had in store.

This wasn't as altruistic as it sounded. It felt like payback. He'd spent all these years looking after me, the least I could do was help him to destroy some of his brain cells through alcohol abuse.

I bought myself clothes and shoes and pants and soap and shampoo and toothpaste – all kinds of luxury items that I'd lived without for so many years. It was great to have money in my pocket and to feel independent.

That said, both my jobs were just a little bit shit. The phrase 'no future' sprang to mind more than once. Both jobs did, however, provide an impressive level of entertainment.

I loved working in the Silver Band Club. As with all working men's clubs, the Silver Band had a committee. On the committee was a particularly effeminate fellow – we'll call him George because that was his name – who liked to stand at the exit to the bar, to ensure that we glass collectors had to squeeze by him a number of times every evening. It wasn't a problem really, we all had a bit of a laugh about him. We all felt he was harmless.

One night though, I'd been collecting the glasses in the lounge. George saw me and asked me to collect the glasses in the committee room. Realising he was up to no good – especially since the committee room was empty and it only had one door that could be easily blocked – I said something along the lines of 'I'll just get these glasses back to the bar ...'

'Go and collect the glasses in the committee room or I'll have you sacked.'

I didn't want to be sacked. I quite liked my £41 per week. Without a word, I went into the committee room to collect the glasses. As expected, George followed me into the room. Unexpectedly, though, he locked the door behind him and declared in his softly spoken, West of Scotland accent: 'Chris, I love you!'

There then followed a Benny Hill-esque chase scene, where George ran round the large table in the middle of the room in pursuit of my lithe 16-year-old form. In no time, he was red-faced and panting. Knackered though he was, it looked like I wouldn't be going home that night.

Thankfully one of the other committee men unlocked the door and bellowed, 'What's going on in here?'

George shook his head and panted, 'Nothing.'

And I squeaked, 'Nothing,' as I danced out of the room.

Now *that* was a story to tell anyone who was willing to listen ...

Even after that episode I think I could still be described as a bit naïve. I loved to skip around, collecting glasses, and chatting with anyone who'd listen to my nonsense. Davy was an older man who came to the club regularly with his mate who was of a similar age. We'd all laugh and joke. It was all very nice.

One day, Davy's friend didn't come in. Through the grapevine I found out that he'd died of a heart attack. I hadn't realised just how much Davy had relied on him. They were both clearly very sociable men, but after days and weeks, Davy continued to sit on his own. Being a carey-sharey type, I thought it would be the right thing to do to give old Davy a bit more of my time. Occasionally during my break I'd sit and chat with him. He obviously appreciated the time I gave him because one day he said, 'Chris, I wonder if you'd like to come back to my place for lunch – you know, after you've finished your shift?'

The word 'homosexual' sprang immediately into my mind. And then, as quickly as it had jumped in, it jumped out again. Davy, gay? Absolutely not.

So the day came along when I would go back to his place. I had doubts, but they felt completely unfounded. I was being silly. This was a poor old lonely man who craved company. He didn't look gay. He was shortish, plumpish, had slicked back grey hair and wore jam-jar bottomed glasses. He wasn't gay.

After my shift I walked into the Lodge Park Estate and found his flat. I knocked on the door and he let me in. I was struck by an overwhelming sense of isolation. He had a couch and an armchair. There was a small TV in the corner. There were no photos or pictures anywhere. I became aware that there was no smell or sound of lunch being prepared.

'Cup of tea?' he asked in that friendly manner of his. We chatted about folk at the club while he pottered about in his kitchen preparing the drinks. He came back through to the lounge, stumbled and poured my tea over my trousers.

'They'll have to come off. I'll dry them on the heater.'

'No, I'll be okay. I'll just keep them on. '

I was still aware that no food was being made. I remember scolding myself for being so judgemental. *He's an old man. He lives on his own. His best mate's just died. He just wants a bit of company ...*

True enough, he started talking about his time in the RAF and the great friends he made there. The talked about the bastard sergeants who made them clean the toilets with toothbrushes. We were laughing and joking together. All thoughts of homosexuality had gone.

'Have you got a big cock?' Davy asked me out of the blue.

I might have said, 'Er ... '

'Can I see it?' He was obviously encouraged by my vague answer.

'Er ... no.' Shaky, but firm. Or so I thought.

'If I can't see it, can I feel it?'

'No.' I got up and left, still feeling somewhat aggrieved that I still hadn't been given anything to eat.

The next day I saw Davy in the club, still sitting on his own. He still had the same friendly banter. I decided to stop spending my breaks with him though. I didn't want him to get the wrong idea.

*

Meanwhile, back in the world of the garage forecourt attendant, things were pretty dull. My days were filled with monotony. The only entertainment I had was when I melted plastic pens with the petrol I'd got onto my fingers. The highlight of my day was when Derek and Willie Irvine went past on the bus on their way to college in the town. They'd wave enthusiastically and I'd reciprocate maniacally, trying to show them what a fine time I was having.

Since the job was only vaguely more interesting than counting the grains of sand in, er, a bucket of sand, I would set myself little challenges throughout the day. For example, could I get the man with the most ludicrous wig in the world to come out of his car on a windy day? Tragically, no I couldn't.

Could I break my own personal record for the amount of cars I could fill with petrol at the same time? Well, I'd give it a try.

Back in the good old days of garage forecourt attendants, the petrol nozzles could be stuck into cars in the safe knowledge that it would click itself off when the tank was full. Also, you'd be in the safe knowledge that you were able to fill your tank without having to sell your kidneys to some unscrupulous surgeon.

I was filling four cars at the same time. I'd equalled my best as I jumped over the hoses from the petrol pumps, ensuring a prompt and friendly service to all my customers.

Unfortunately, I miscalculated one of my jumps. I tripped on the hose and the nozzle flew out the side of the car. Petrol continued to spray out as I rushed to switch the pump off. I wasn't quick enough and the petrol sprayed up my nose, in my eyes and in my ears. It also soaked my body. I managed to switch the pump off though.

I was aware that the whole world was going a little woozy. I had to get back inside. I had to get this petrol off me. I had to wash my face and ... Not surprisingly, I passed out. I lay unconscious across the threshold of my little office for a couple of minutes until the decision was made for one of the mechanics to take me to Kettering General Hospital.

I started to wake up as my friend and colleague drove like a maniac up the grass verge to avoid the traffic. I sort of passed out for the rest of the journey, waking up in A&E with my fellow patients looking at me with great concern. My skin was burning and my eyes and ears were stinging.

There now follows two of the greatest experiences of my life.

A tired-looking doctor emerged from one of the cubicles. After a very short consultation he decided my ears had to be syringed. He went away and returned with the largest syringe I'd ever seen in my life. He squirted warm water (?) a saline solution (?) won ton soup (?) into each ear. The feeling of satisfaction I felt as my ears were emptied of residual petrol and wax was almost orgasmic.

He explained that we'd have to use calamine lotion to help with the burning sensation on my skin. He vanished and into my cubicle there came three young female nurses. Now, I'm sure this isn't some kind of fantasy caused by the petrol vapour. They *all* rubbed the calamine lotion all over my body. I thanked God for the NHS. I'm not sure what they did with my eyes. For all I care they could have taken them out and washed them in the sink. As far as I was concerned, my life was complete.

The loony mechanic drove me back home. The decision had been made that I should have the rest of the day off.

*

After the Davy incident things at the old Silver Band quietened down for a bit. Same old glasses. Same old banter. Same old folk getting up on the stage thinking they were Barry Manilow.

One evening, there was a bit of a hoo-ha. A definite kafuffle.

As usual, a couple of the other glass collectors and I took the 20-metre journey across the road to get ourselves something from the Pytchly Court Chippy. I was a connoisseur of the potato fritter. Theirs was a particularly fine example of this tasty tuber.

Did I really just write 'tasty tuber'? No matter, it's in black and white now – moving on …

While I was waiting in the queue to be served, I was approached by a young guy, just a few years older than me, who had a faraway look in his eyes. He was looking at my army jacket (very fashionable at the time – no, really). 'What does the C and A on your jacket stand for?'

'Captain America.' I grinned back.

He walked off. I thought nothing more about it and bought myself a good fistful of fritters. I was walking between two of my friends when I heard a shout. 'Captain America's a wanker!'

I turned round just in time to see my assailant – the guy from the queue – as he smacked me over the head with a large glass bottle.

In my mind, fighting was something I was pretty good at. However, after being hit by the bottle everything seemed to be, I don't know, sort of faraway ...

Roy Tait – the guy who had taken terrible umbrage at my witty riposte to his earlier question – set about the task of knocking me over. This he achieved with a few punches to the head. I found it so hard to protect myself. I just didn't feel terribly coordinated. Having got me just where he wanted me, Roy, a peripheral member of the notorious Fisher Mob who were named after the Kingfisher Pub just along the road, felt that kicking me in the head would help him in his quest. Whatever that quest was.

Still conscious and realising I was going to have to put this one down to experience, I curled up tightly in a ball in some hope that he'd get bored. 'Look over there,' said Roy.

You'd like to think that all my instincts of self-preservation would have helped me out here. Unfortunately, you'd be wrong. I stuck my head out to see where he might be pointing. He kicked me in the face. 'I won't be falling for that one again,' I thought to myself.

Yes I did. I fell for the 'Look over there,' trick three times. Well, I was a bit woozy.

At one point, I got up and grabbed him, threw him over my shoulder and wandered about for a bit. I didn't really know what to do with him. My head wasn't working. I dropped him, then fell over. Roy took this as an opportunity to jump up and down on my head.

Years later, I would recount this incident to my psychiatrist, asking if she felt that the assault might have had some organic effect on my mental health. 'Well, it wouldn't have done any good,' she replied. All those years training for that.

I found myself slipping in and out of consciousness. Not with the psychiatrist – we're back at Roy Tait. Try to keep up! I was suddenly aware that the steady thumping on my head had stopped. I looked out of my foetal position in time to see Laz – another member of the Fisher Mob – grab hold of Mr Tait and throw him into space.

Yes, I am fully aware that it is very unlikely that Laz was able to generate the forces required to help Roy escape Earth's atmosphere. My mind was a little mushy, so give me a break.

The cavalry, in the form of several men from the Silver Band, arrived just a little late. They took my pulped form back into the club. One of the committee men had been a boxer. He was keen to see if I had concussion. 'How many fingers am I holding up?'

'Four, and one thumb.' I felt drunk.

'How many now?'

'Four, and one thumb.' I felt great.

'How many now?'

'Four and … ' I keeled over and lost consciousness. I woke up at about one in the morning on a trolley in A&E. A young house doctor told me that they'd done all the necessary tests on me and that I was fine. I could go home.

I remember thinking this was all a bit strange. I was eight miles from home. I'd just had my head kicked in. Public transport had long since stopped. I had nobody with me. Would it have been such a huge jump of the imagination to allow me to stay over for the night?

I asked the doctor and he explained it wasn't hospital policy to keep folk in my position in hospital overnight. Then by way of explanation he said, 'Is this some kind of gang uniform?' He was looking at my jacket. He thought I'd brought this on myself.

Great.

I stalked off into the night, trying to remember where Louise lived. She had stayed in Kettering, on the other side of town. As I neared her house, it suddenly dawned on me that I might not be particularly welcome at this time of night. I knew her husband, Keith, slept on the sofa some nights so I knocked on the door gently in an attempt not to wake the whole house up.

Keith, carefully at first, began to open the door. Upon seeing it was me, he opened the door wide, letting the light from the house show him my face. Then he screamed. I know I had a bit of a head injury – but that was under my hairline. I couldn't work out what all the fuss was about.

Keith let me in. We were both babbling incoherently. He, about the mess of my face, and me about what had happened and the mess of the fucking NHS. I went upstairs to the bathroom to take a look in the mirror at what all the fuss was about. Those bastards at the hospital hadn't cleaned my face or the wound up. In my dazed state I wasn't aware that the blood had poured down the right side of my face, congealing to make it look like I had a huge gash from the top of my head to my chin. It looked like I'd been hit with a fucking axe.

I thought Keith did rather well. He really doesn't like blood.

The aftermath of my beating was all terribly interesting. First of all, Dad told Jim that he wanted to hunt down this Roy Tait character and do some horrible things to him. Funny, he never mentioned it to me. Strangely, he never mentioned it to Roy Tait either. No, he just wanted to vent his injured masculinity.

It had been a Thursday when I'd received my lesson in keeping my gob shut from Mr Tait. I made an executive decision not to go back to work the following day, since I was still pretty shaken up. That said, I decided to go back and work at the Silver Band Club on the Saturday – I felt it was wise to get right back on that horse. Everyone there was fantastic. I didn't have proper black eyes; instead it looked like I'd put eyeliner on. As such, my sexuality was light-heartedly questioned throughout the evening.

As I went home that night, I felt kind of proud of myself, thinking that lesser mortals may have chosen never to darken the doors of the club again. I did think twice about buying potato fritters though.

Monday came and I returned to the garage. My facial scars were spectacularly multicoloured. Shades of blue and green melted into gentle yellows across my cheeks and eyes. My boss, Mr-I'm-Still-In-Touch-With-The-Masses, was furious. He told me I'd been 'spotted' working at the club on Saturday. If I was able to work for them, then I should have been in on Friday. He told me he wouldn't have the wool pulled over his eyes.

I didn't say anything. I just quietly thought to myself, 'You cock.'

A couple of months later, my good old friend Barney told me about a 'proper job' in the factory where he worked. Brandishing my three O Levels and my wit and charm, I managed to cruise into my first properly paid position. I was a labourer for a company that pressed paper onto chipboard for people who couldn't afford proper wood. Our major clients were the manufacturers of cheap(ish) coffins.

I told both my lovely bosses that it was time for me to move on to develop my career in the, er, forestry business.

Barney was famous in our year at school for sitting his English literature O Level and writing something along the lines of, 'This subject is a pile of shite and it was taught to us by a fucking lunatic,' give or take a few expletives. He also introduced me to cannabis.

The artificial wood factory looked much as I expected. It was a long production line housed inside a huge warehouse. It was all very new and shiny. The large panels of chipboard went in at one end, along to the glue rollers, along to the guillotine, along to the press, and finally along to the inspection section. Little did I know that as I walked onto the factory floor that day, I was walking into Dickensian England.

For 95p an hour, I initially lugged bits of wood and cardboard around for a living. I had no responsibility whatsoever and essentially did what I was told. Well, there's a first time for everything.

Since I showed an aptitude for not making an arse of such simple instructions as, 'Take this over there', promotion was never far away.

Within a month, I rocketed to the highly responsible position of Inspector. With this came a huge increase in pay. I was now getting £1.25 per hour. I was giddy with my new-found riches.

My new job involved looking at the bits of wood at the end of the production line. The 2-by-3-metre panels rolled up in front of me so that I could look at one side. Then they were picked up by big suckers so that I could look at the underside as well. If the panel had no bubbles or creases in the pressed-on paper, then I'd press a button and the board would be added to a pile in front of me. If it was defective in any way, then I'd press a button and the suckers would carry the synthetic wood over my head and put it in a pile behind me.

Well that's simple enough. What could go wrong with that?

Hmmm. When I rejected a bit of wood it wouldn't always pass over my head without incident. Often, because the paper hadn't been stuck to the chipboard properly, it would fall on my head. These were weighty objects, but to be fair, I was only nearly killed the first time it happened. After that I was prepared and fended off the tumbling wood with my hands and forearms.

I thought this was okay. I thought this was normal. It was just an occupational hazard. Well, what doesn't kill you makes you stronger. Onwards and upwards.

One day, the manager came to the workers and explained we had got a new order. Nothing strange about that. The problem was that this was particularly thin wood for wood panelling for walls. Delicious. What home would be complete without synthetic beech boards on its walls?

The problem with wood this thin is that our production line couldn't deal with it properly. When the huge conveyor belt that was attached to the press moved forward, it pushed the panels underneath the rollers that were supposed to carry them off to the inspection section. This caused the panels to bend and crack and occasionally snap.

But you don't really want to know about that. You want to know how Dickensian England had come to Corby, don't you?

The press exerts tonnes of pressure on the wood, glue and paper sandwich, effectively setting and drying the glue at the same time as imprinting an 'authentic' wood grain onto the board. The key words here are 'tonnes of pressure'.

We had to stop these small boards from being destroyed by our production line. How did I do that? Easy, I put my hand *inside* the press and pulled the board out.

Wasn't that a little dangerous? No! No, of course not. We had five seconds between board squashings. Plenty of time.

There was another problem. The boards in the press were a little out of reach, so I had to stand on something to help. A stepladder? A chair? Barney's shoulders?

No, we had a much more lunatic thing to stand on.

As mentioned earlier, the boards were pulled into and pushed out of the press on a big conveyor belt. The big conveyor belt was driven round by a great big chain. The chain was driven round, in turn, by a great big cog – roughly the size of your average bike wheel. The cog was held in place by a bolt about an inch wide.

You're right! I stood on the toes of one foot on that nut with the chain and the cog whizzing round while I pulled the burning hot boards out of the press. Not Dickensian enough for you? Okay, let's move along to the glue rollers.

Ordinarily, it was Barney's job to deal with all things gluey in the factory. It was his job to make sure the right mixture of sticky stuff and the setting stuff were poured onto the rollers. This was a tricky old job and was dependent upon things like the type and density of the wood and paper, the ambient temperature in the factory, and how much Barney had had to drink the night before.

Occasionally the glue would set on the rollers. This meant that the whole production line was brought crashing to a halt while Barney and I scraped the glue off the still revolving rollers with some water and four inch pieces of metal banding strap. We then used tissue paper to ensure it was dry.

Once, I accidentally let go of a wad of tissue paper and listened to the grinding noise it made as it was dragged through the rollers and spat out at the other side. The gap between the main rollers was 15mm.

The whole of the production line was run by a somewhat tetchy and borderline alcoholic electrician called Chas. He was an impatient individual who was keen to keep the line going, whatever the cost. On this particular day, Chas had decided that I was just not cleaning the rollers fast enough. So, with a flick of a switch, he doubled the speed of the rollers while I was working on them.

Sure enough, there was that strange grinding sound again. I looked around for the tissue paper – but I couldn't see any. What I could see was that my right arm had been dragged into the rollers. Thankfully shock had kicked in immediately, so, at the time, I couldn't feel anything.

Pain receptors aside, the rest of my brain was functioning normally, albeit in a somewhat accelerated fashion due to the amount of adrenaline coursing through it. I braced my feet against the bottom of the machine as I realised that I was unable to reach the cut-off switch that would have stopped the whole of me being pulled through the rollers.

I took the only course of action available to me. I screamed, 'Heeeeeeellllppp!' at the top of my voice.

Quick as a flash, Barney ran across the factory floor and pulled the switch that I'd been only able to flail my left arm at. The rollers stopped and he wound them apart to allow me to pull my arm out.

Norman, the somewhat hapless and neurotic lorry driver ambled over and said, 'God Chris, you really shouldn't shout like that, you gave me quite a fright.'

Twat.

Me and Barney looked at my right hand and forearm. They were completely hairless and comedically flat. I was taken off to have a cup of sweet tea while we all considered the best course of action to take after an arm-squashing incident.

Unemployment was rife in Corby. The men who I worked with, Norman, Chas, Steve, and Barney were all happy that they had a job in the current climate. We knew that if I reported this, the factory would probably be investigated for this and its other shonky practices – and ultimately be shut down. Five more folk to add to Corby's already vast army of unemployed.

I also had the notion that if I went to hospital with it, they might ask some compromising questions which may have led us all along a similar route. Fuck.

What would *you* do?

Well, I took a week off work. None of my bones appeared to be broken. There was a slice in the index finger of my right hand where the metal strap I'd been holding had cut into me. I couldn't use my right arm at all for two full weeks. Even now it's significantly weaker than my left arm.

I came back to work to perform one-armed duties for a while. All my workmates seemed to respect me for not reporting it. Looking back, I'm gobsmacked at my stupidity. What about all the other potential Chris's who could get their arms pulled in and squashed up? The factory bosses would just continue on their merry way. As long as they were up to speed with their orders, then they didn't need to worry about a few minor casualties.

So there I was, back at work. After a time, I was put back on full duties and I was, once again, allowed the freedom to risk life and limb, all in the cause of the synthetic wood industry. What else could happen?

Oh yes, the guillotine.

The guillotine, as the name would suggest, was used for cutting stuff. In this case it cut the paper after it had been stuck onto the wood. The guillotine made two noises. Firstly it made an electrical buzzing noise lasting about half a second before it went, 'Kerchunk!' as its razor sharp teeth did their job.

From time to time we had to change the rolls of paper that went onto the wood, giving different wood effects like pine, beech and mahogany. This was a potentially dangerous job because the person replacing the paper had to put both their arms fully between the blades of the guillotine to pull it through. Normally, the whole production line was switched off while this took place. On this particular day in September 1982, I was the person responsible for changing the rolls.

Over the past couple of weeks, the production line had been playing up a bit. The company had flown over a German fellow to muck about with the electrics. Barney and I tactfully called him Herman the German, but other than that, we paid him no heed.

So, both my arms were through the guillotine with Herman the German playing about with the electrics – the stage was set. If the guillotine had not made a buzzing sound prior to a kerchunk, then I would be typing this today with my nose or my feet or by blinking or some such thing.

As I grasped the paper on the other side of the guillotine I heard the familiar buzzing noise. If I had taken the time to think at all then I would have fulfilled the expectations of my colleagues as they expected to see my severed arms zipping along the conveyor belt on their way to the press.

Fortunately I didn't think. I just pulled my arms out as quickly as I could in time to watch the blades bite harmlessly at thin air. I took this opportunity to turn to my German colleague and call him a stupid fucking cunt. As I did so, the director of the company wandered in with some prospective clients. Delighted as I was at my ability to call people names in my stressed condition, I told him he could stick his fucking job up his arse.

And so my employment with this idiot company came to an end.

Even after all this, I still told the dole that I'd given up my job voluntarily. I was still worried that my colleagues might lose their jobs if I reported this company to anybody. As a result, I didn't get any unemployment benefit for 12 weeks.

At least I still had two arms and that strange thumping feeling in my head had stopped.

Thankfully Dad still had a chunk of that £10,000 that he'd been given when he left the works. Equally thankfully, he kept a significant part of that money underneath his mattress. To complete the hat-trick of thankfullies, he spent so much of his time pissed that he wasn't terribly aware when I helped myself to a few quid here and there.

*

Oh my fucking god, I was unemployed! I was under-qualified and I was unemployable. I sat at home for what seemed like months. Barney came round a few times and asked me if I was going to come back to work. Each time I told him I thought I'd made myself quite clear. This company clearly had no notion of health and safety. They knew they had a workforce that was terrified of unemployment and they believed they could do anything they wanted. Well, they weren't going to do what they wanted with me.

But I was unemployed! I lived at home with my drunken father in a shit hole for a home. In contrast to this, Jim had got the qualifications he needed and was about to fuck off to university.

After Jim had left, Dad suggested he would supplement my unemployment benefit if I did some work around the house – decorating, gardening, shopping, and the like. The thing was, I was mentally on my knees. I'd had enough. My past was shite and my future was non-existent. I just ground to a halt.

Sure, I did a bit of gardening. I even did a bit of decorating, but really, I'd just had enough. I went through the motions of going out with my mates at the weekend. We'd have a few laughs and a few drinks, but now I was completely lost. For almost a year I wandered about in this limbo – this non-life.

One day I bumped into an old friend of mine, Mark Maglone. He was like a member of the Beatles – only in my year at school. He was kind and always ready with a smile. 'Society's failed you, Chris,' he said.

It sounded so clichéd, 'Society's failed you.'

I remember thinking it was nice of him to say, but at the end of the day it was me who'd fucked up. It had been me who hadn't done my homework, who'd lost his books, who'd arsed about in class, who'd spent all his time fighting, who'd – fuck – given up his sport. This was me. I had done this.

For a chapter entitled, 'Stuart,' you must be wondering when he's going to turn up. Well, dear reader, wonder no more, because here he comes.

Stuart had continued to follow work around the country. He, his wife Carol, and their three children Stephen, Amy, and Jennifer had moved to Guisborough, a small town in Cleveland, while Stuart worked in one of the chemical plants in nearby Teeside.

Bless him, he must have seen that I'd hit the buffers. In his mind, I'd always been a happy-go-lucky child who always saw the positive, the humour, in everything. He was shocked at this inert, introspective thing I'd become. 'Come and live with me,' he said. 'Just until you get back on your feet.'

I summed up the pros and cons in moments. I could live with my alcoholic dad and watch him and me gradually deteriorate into god knows what, or I could live a relatively affluent life living with a 'normal' family, albeit miles from any of my friends.

'Okay.' It seemed like the lesser of two evils. I could get myself back on my feet, return to Corby and live happily ever after. Anyway, my friends could visit me – hell, I could visit Corby; if you look at the map it's not really that far. In a couple of months I was going to discover that the 'short coach trip' between Corby and Middlesbrough would take eight hours.

When I arrived, I was welcomed into their home. I was moved into a room with Stephen. I was fed and watered. It was all terribly nice. I'd moved from a world where there was no dinner on the table to a world where children said, 'Thank you for a lovely meal. May I get down from the table?'

Stuart took me on tours of the local hostelries, and I began to get a flavour of what Guisborough was about. It was scarily like Corby, an ex-steel town. Unemployment was high when I moved there and the general mood of the place was pretty low.

I also experienced gratuitous red tape for the first time. Every week I would visit the nice lady at the unemployment office and every week she would tell me, with a huge smile, that my papers had not yet arrived from Corby. If I'd really had to rely on them I'd have died of starvation.

What did I expect? My first experience with the DHSS, as it was back in the day, had been ridiculous. Back in Corby, the lovely administrators had ensured I was paid promptly and regularly – up until the day when they stopped paying me at all. 'Why aren't you paying me?' I asked politely. I thought this was a perfectly reasonable question.

Instead of answering me, a strange question and answer session followed. 'When's your birthday?' the attractive woman behind the counter had asked me.

'6th March, 1965,' I answered promptly and courteously.

'No it's not – it's the 12th, isn't it?'

Try this with one on your friends and family. Take something that they know to be true and tell them that it's not. You could change their name, their date of birth, Christmas, their sex ... think of the fun you could have. 'Er ... no, it's the 6th.'

'We know that you're claiming benefits in Sunderland as well.'

If you look at a map and reflected momentarily on the shit transport system at the time, you'd realise that it would actually cost me more than the pissy £17 they gave me every week to get there and back to claim it. You will be amazed, if not astounded, that after four weeks they finally had to concede that there was another Chris Young living in Sunderland, whose birthday was the 12th of March 1965.

So I wasn't terribly shocked nor indeed stunned when I found that it was taking months for my details to be passed from their offices in Corby to Guisborough. Dozy bastards.

Eventually though, I did get my benefits. I was also ensconced on a number of courses at Redcar College for further education. First of all there was the communication studies A Level– this was a strange hybrid of English, the most vague hint of psychology, and an unnecessarily large chunk of secretarial work without the typing. The lecturer, Steve, was the most enthusiastic man in the history of human kind. He spent much of his time telling the woman next to me that she should chuck her fiancé and go out with me instead. This caused me to blush to the point of facial explosion. I wasn't terribly confident around people of the opposite gender.

Secondly, I revisited my maths O Level. This was really odd. This guy stood in front of us and told me about things I thought I already knew. If I already knew it, why did I fail in the first place?

Finally, I was introduced to the wonderful world of sociology. Now this opened my eyes to a whole new world. A world of 'why?' and 'did it really happen that way?' This ignited a little light in my head that I hadn't realised was there.

I'd been at college for a month or so when Carol told me that she and Stuart thought I should go out there into the big wide world and get a job. As with Corby, the only jobs around for your lowly qualified fuckwit were ones that had been made up by the government to make the unemployment figures look good. In no time at all, I found myself on a gardening project in Stokesley. The great outdoors and hard physical graft, that's what I needed.

I had never been a big fan of gardening, but I just wanted to fit in. So I got on with it. The day started with a number of us sweaty oiks being jammed into the back of a Ford transit with no windows. We were then driven around, at what felt like break neck speeds, for about 45 minutes. We were then decanted out into the barren space of wasteland and told to get on with it.

This all got my youthful mind a-wondering. It made me think of sailors in a submarine. *Sure* we were driven about for 45 minutes, but for all I knew, this bit of wasteland could have been a five-minute walk from Stuart's house. With the closed-in transit van, they were giving us the illusion of going to work. I think sociology was beginning to play tricks on my mind.

At least we definitely ended up somewhere else in the transit. Once we arrived at said wasteland, we were handed pick-axes and told to batter our way through the Stokesley permafrost. After two weeks of this, I had stretch marks on my biceps.

It never really felt like gardening – it was more like *The Great Escape*. Instead of Donald Pleasance pretending he could see a pin on the floor, we had a somewhat flowery gentleman who looked not unlike a scarecrow. It was his occupation to tend to his pigeons in a shed next to our "garden" and then come along and shout at us. The phrase that will stay with me forever is 'You're a bunch of fucking arse-'oles, you've got nowt in your 'ouses.'

Whatever he meant by that, he was probably right. We weren't gardeners. We were the flotsam and jetsam of life that had been washed up on this little patch of waste ground just to batter shit out of it. This wasn't a job with a great future.

Back at college, I was soon to realise that Redcar bus station was officially the coldest place on the face of the earth. As I stood there waiting for the erratic Guisborough service, I'd see explorers and husky teams arrive and plant their flags, knowing that they wouldn't have enough provisions for the journey back. But they knew that they'd managed to conquer one of the last untamed wildernesses of the world that was Redcar bus station.

I might be overplaying just a little.

The great thing about mum dying was that, while I was growing up, my time was very much my own. I could stay out all night and do pretty much as I pleased. The problem with living with Stuart and Carol was that suddenly my carefree days had come to an end. I had to eat at regular times. I had to say 'excuse me' when I left the table. Instead of valuing the beauty and tranquillity of sitting around and doing nothing, Stuart would fill my time with chores – or, worse still, watching him doing manly chores on his car.

Because I'd started the A level in computer studies prior to being unceremoniously punted from school, I still enjoyed tampering with the family computer. They had a BBC micro and I would program little routines to keep my mind stimulated, to keep me entertained.

Stuart and Carol were taking on more of a parental role, so they took me aside and explained that they felt that all this computing stuff wasn't a very good use of my time – maybe I should focus on socialising? Maybe I should think about what I was going to do once I'd finished the courses of freezing my bollocks off at Redcar College. I could still stay with them while I studied to become a social worker at Middlesbrough Poly ... or while I studied to become a nurse (?) or while I trained to become a policeman. I was beginning to feel a little swamped. I'd only planned to move in with them for a bit, and now here they were planning all the intricacies of my foreseeable future.

Looking back at it, I think Stuart felt I was ill-disciplined – bright, but lacking focus. He saw it as his role to bring me back into line. One day, while we were all sitting around the dinner table, Stuart stressed to Stephen, 'If you don't study at school, you'll end up like your uncle Christopher.'

At last I'd achieved something in life. I was a good bad example. How did he think that was going to make me feel?

A further nail in the coffin of my little holiday up North was when Carol confronted me with some of the somewhat dark poetry I'd been writing at the time. As I recall, the general theme was my death and the impending end of the world as I knew it.

'I found your poetry, Chris,' Carol looked genuinely worried. 'Do you want to talk about it?' It was all good open questioning type stuff.

'No, it's just something I'm trying out.' I just wanted to fit in – the last thing I wanted to do was discuss my mental innards with someone I hardly knew. I was also pretty pissed off because I felt she was looking into my private stuff. I'd been writing my poetry on a pad that I kept under my pillow. Carol must have thought, 'Aww, that's nice, Chris is writing some poetry, let's just have a little … Oh my god!'

That was it. The end. No further questions. The stress of challenging me must have been immense. Any answer that I gave that didn't imply I was going to kill myself and them, probably tomorrow, must have come as a great relief.

In a somewhat vitriolic tirade, I offloaded all my concerns over the phone to Louise. I told her all about my worries, about them wanting me to start three different professions at the same time, and Carol reading my private stuff. All I wanted to do was see the courses at college through. If nothing else, I wanted to demonstrate to myself that I was able to move on. I asked Louise not to tell Stuart or Carol about any of this.

What the fuck was I thinking? The following day I was confronted by Stuart. He was in tears. Louise had told him everything. I was completely overwhelmed. I just wanted to fit in. It wasn't too much to ask, surely? I cried. Suddenly it all felt untenable. I felt betrayed. I'm sure Stuart felt betrayed – all they wanted was what they thought was best for me. He thought I needed discipline when all I really needed was love.

Bugger.

I manfully fled back to Corby straight into the waiting arms of my poor old dad. He was so glad to have me back. I, however, was less delighted. I was back where I'd started. Same old drunk Dad, same old disgusting house, same old unemployment and same old lack of prospects.

Things really had to change. This was not the way it was going to be. I was going to get my A Levels. I was going to go to college to qualify as a social worker. First though, I had to get the ball rolling. I had to move out again.

A friend of mine was renting out a couple of rooms in his house. He thought it would be a great idea if I moved in with him while I gathered up the qualifications to get me on my way. I thought that sounded like a most splendid idea. And it was.

Over the next two years, I got the qualifications required to get me to that citadel of learning that is North East London Polytechnic. Tresham College was situated in Corby Town Centre and it was here my life started taking a turn for the normal.

Sure, I did the falling out with my landlord and my other housemates kind of stuff, but we always kissed and made up again. On Saturdays, me and Derek would go and get Dad's shopping in and would lug it back to his house. Only after eating the cold Chinese chicken wings in Market Square, gazing upon the glory of the fountains and any beautiful Corby girls that had the decency to wander by.

I was astonished at the amount of food I could buy with the money Dad gave me for his shopping – roughly half the amount that he'd ever given Jim.

Somehow I fell into the role of treasurer of the student union. I found myself at the centre of all of the social events that Tresham had to offer. Okay, it wasn't quite Carnaby Street in the sixties but, fuck, my life had taken a distinctly upward turn.

I got a girlfriend. Granted, she didn't particularly like me, but hell, it still counted. Lisa chucked me on a fortnightly basis. Just to keep me on my toes I guess. I suppose these mini-breaks allowed me the space to snog a variety of other women of the student persuasion at the social events that I felt vaguely responsible for.

So, my life appeared to be back on track. All thoughts of having my arms pulled and / or cut off were rapidly becoming a distant memory. I was gradually coming to believe that I wasn't a failure and that things were going to be okay.

In 1986, with my A Levels in sociology and psychology tucked under my arm, I fled to London to make my fortune.

CHAPTER 9

LOUISE

'Get in the house!' Louise yelled, almost screaming at us.

'What's wrong?' I shouted as we safely dragged Mary, Louise's four-year-old daughter, back inside.

We were all panting, our eyes popping out of our heads. Louise was bordering on the hysterical. The dog, Shep – half border collie, half god knows what – barked defiantly at the window overlooking the back garden as the scene unfolded before us.

'What's wrong?' I repeated to Louise, the only grown-up available for sensible comment. 'What is it?'

'There's a snake in the garden. And it's fighting with Blackie.'

We all looked out to see the imaginatively named cat wrestling with *something*. Blackie stood up on her hind legs, scratching at this unknown assailant. She rolled about with it, biting it and giving it those bunny kicks that only cats can. Then she'd run away only to turn again to face this monster of the back garden.

We all climbed over each other, standing on the living room sofa to get a better, and safe, view of what was going on. 'It looks like a short snake,' someone, possibly me, shouted.

'A snake? I'll phone the police!' Louise cried.

Being a nerdy, animal loving, inquisitive sort of soul, I knew that it was very unlikely that Blackie was having some kind of life and death struggle with an adder, the UK's only poisonous snake. I thought, at the very worst, we could be dealing with a grass snake. A small, non-venomous creature that lived mainly on insects and very small mammals – of which Blackie wasn't one.

Having bravely caught a lizard in my back garden with a table spoon and a jam jar a couple of years before, I felt I was more than suitably qualified to deal with whatever Blackie was sinking her teeth into.

In a true Captain Oates style, I stood at the back door and, in as manly a voice as my 11-year-old pre-pubescent form could muster, I said, 'I'm going out there. Keep the door closed.'

To be brutally honest, Blackie was infinitely scarier than the beast I finally managed to catch using the coffee jar and bit of card that I'd been provided with. She had decided that since she was getting the upper hand, this thing she had in her vice-like grip was hers to eat. After a great deal of growling, scratching and hissing I finally managed to rescue the poor, now clearly defenceless, creature.

It was a caterpillar. Granted it was a fucking huge caterpillar – the biggest I've seen outside of London zoo – but it was a caterpillar nonetheless. It *did* have a big spike growing out of its rear end, but that was more decorative than offensive. For those of you who are interested, it was probably the caterpillar of the humming bird hawk moth.

So that was Louise and her family.

Histrionic. Dramatic. Working as a family unit in an 'all for one and one for all' kind of style. I think she liked the image of the mother bear looking after her cubs.

Although she was always around, helping out, popping in, doing this and that, making her an invaluable member of our world, I have no memory of Louise in my early years – she left the area when I was two or three. Not to worry though, I'm sure she was delighted that her babysitting duties would follow her wherever she went. Mum seemed to decant Jim and I on a regular basis. Louise didn't work at the time; she was busy looking after child number one. This meant that Mum had a regular, cheap, not terribly handy (being eight miles away) childcare service.

Already though, I was developing my 'normal rules need not apply' approach to life. Louise had a large free-standing cabinet in her kitchen. It held all the cutlery and crockery necessary for normal domestic life. Being an independent sort, I liked to get my own cup when I was thirsty. Louise had a vast array of Tupperware, so the likelihood of me chewing up one of her tumblers and bleeding to death was fairly slim.

Since the taps were out of reach to the young Christopher, Louise felt it only reasonable to keep the cups on the top shelf of the cabinet so that she could be in charge of the whole drink-getting process.

So – cup, top shelf, and an independent, and some say spoilt, four-year-old in need of a drink. Now is probably a good time to mention that Louise didn't have the best of relationships with Mum. With this in mind, she was always keen to please Mum, trying to demonstrate she was capable in all things domestic. How Mum laughed when she found her little boy just as he had managed to climb to the top shelf of the cabinet. I'm sure her sides were fairly splitting with mirth as it toppled over, the top crashing into the opposite wall of the kitchen, all of Louise's plates, glasses, knives and forks whizzing past my poor little head. I think if the kitchen had been a foot wider, the cabinet wouldn't have been stopped in its fall and I would have been squashed flat.

Okay, you've got me – no one was laughing. Least of all me. I obviously felt that this was a golden opportunity to demonstrate to everyone around me that, in spite of my trauma, my lungs were still in perfect working order.

And so it was. The more poor Louise tried to impress Mum, the more I would contrive to make things go completely tits up. As time went by, I think Louise gradually decided that there was absolutely no pleasing Mum. So she began to rebel in her own little way. Not terribly overtly – no, Louise chose a more surreptitious way to kick back at Mum. She found she could be a little bit naughty through Jim and me.

For example, having been taught the beauty of French nursery rhymes by my darling carer, it came as a complete surprise to me at school when nobody else finished the song Frere Jaques with the line, '*Shit and Piss Marie.*'

Louise's crazed revenge didn't stop there. Oh no. Although Mum was happy for me to watch horror films with her while curled up on the sofa with her, she made sure that my youthful mind was not overly terrorised by inappropriate nasties. She limited my exposure to horror to *The Hammer House of Horror* – namely films where you could tell that the bad guy was someone dressed up and where the only truly horrific thing was the acting.

Louise introduced us to films like *Children of the Damned* and a variety of horror books that kept my youthful imagination going for hours. It all felt wonderfully conspiratorial. Louise would allow us access to these forbidden fruits in return for our silence. Mum didn't need to know a thing. So, over the years we saw Louise as someone who was a little whacky – Bohemian even – who understood us kids and our needs to be just a little bit off-the-rails.

At times, it became a little dull for me in the Young household, you know, having to be the youngest and everything. At Louise's I wasn't. At Louise's I could coerce and drag her son Michael around, getting him to do the things that I wanted to do, play the games I wanted to play, and generally push him around. Michael and I would spend hours digging about in the dirt, finding all kinds of creepy crawlies to examine.

We noticed that, occasionally, when an ant from one nest wandered into the territory of another nest, then battle would commence. Now *this* was better than telly. One-on-one was all terribly interesting, but what happens when you get a few ants from each side to square up to each other? What happens when, say for example, we were to dig up one nest and move a whole bunch of ants next door to another? The problem with pitting black ant against black ant was that it was tricky, unless you were an ant, to work out who was on whose side. We solved that problem by moving a red ant nest in with a mountain of black ants.

See what happens when you leave me to my own devices? When you put me in charge? It's like *Lord of the Flies* – well, kind of.

Time flew while we were having fun. Louise marked the years by measuring us and scoring lines on the wall next to her pantry. I remember that some weeks there'd be frenzied measuring activity when I was sure, absolutely positive that I was due a growth spurt. We'd listen to sixties music. The Beach Boys, Bread, the Kinks, the Beatles, Herman's Hermits and The Tremeloes were all common currency. Occasionally Louise would let Keith put something on the stereo that he liked, but it was invariably some heavy metal shite that didn't make any reference to falling in or out of love whatsoever.

Louise had whacky friends – her wild and crazy parties were spoken about in hushed tones with knowing winks and snorting laughter. In short, Louise was fun.

And then Mum died.

For a long time, Louise ceased to exist. I just assumed she had her own family to look after. She was busy with her own stuff. But after two or three years of homemade misery, I gradually decided that it was time to have Louise back in my life. At 14, I was more than able to use public transport and, if Keith, or one of his friends was driving the bus, I could get to travel for free. I had the passport to Northamptonshire.

It was still the same. Fun and a little conspiratorial. Since Michael was four years younger than me, I suddenly felt that I was in on the 'in jokes'. I was involved in the grown-up giggles and nods. This was great fun – and it felt like growing up.

Since my home was a complete pigsty, Louise's house offered me a place to bring my mates. Derek, Colin and Barney all had a sample of my new surrogate mother's somewhat irreverent lifestyle. Much of the time though, it was just me who climbed on the 265 bus to Kettering to get away from it all.

The more I visited Louise though, the more I gradually became aware that not everything was as it seemed. Louise suffered from something she and her family referred to as her 'funnies'. At these times, she would take to her bed and take a blue (bomber) or yellow (peril) tablet as the occasion would demand. At particularly bad times, she'd take both.

Over a couple of months, Louise started to become a little more serious. She told me intimate information about her life and family and that she was sexually abused from a young age. Somewhere deep down I felt that I had heard somewhere that Louise was prone to making up stories, and so internally I questioned her history.

My mind raced. What would she have to gain by lying? She must be telling the truth. I made this conclusion purely based on the fact that, at the time, I liked Louise. She'd looked after me, cared for me – filling that awful vacuum following Mum's death. I didn't ask any of the obvious questions – When? Where? Who? How long has this been going on? How old were you when they first did it? Was it still going on?

Almost 30 years later, Louise would tell me that it had been going on since she was six years old and that it had continued well into her adulthood. Fucking hell.

I continued to visit Louise. We spent more and more time together – somehow, we were brought closer by this awful secret she'd shared. In my normal, everyday life I continued to struggle with my relationships with other people. I was still aggressive towards boys and, because of my complete lack of fashionable clothing I felt that I wasn't even on the starting grid in my race to win the heart of a girl. As I grew though, I came to realise that I was quite handsome, if you caught me in a particular light and if I didn't smile too broadly. Linda Reid, a girl in my class at school, had stopped a small discussion group we were having in English to tell me what stunning blue eyes I had. Although I'd wanted to die on the spot it did make me think, *D'you know, you might just have something there.*

One day I was standing in the kitchen at Louise's house. She had a mirror just next to the sink. I looked at my face, thinking that there might be some hope for me, when Louise walked past and said, 'You *are* really handsome.'

I felt great. It put a bit of a skip in my step. But then, as a kind of surrogate mother she was meant to say things like that, wasn't she?

In a world that had been bereft of physical contact except for the occasional punch-up, Louise made me feel warm and happy again with the occasional hug, telling me that she loved me and I was funny.

It was while I was admiring myself in that same mirror (had I become a bit self-obsessed?) that Louise said something slightly unusual. She told me that she really liked the way I blew gently into her ear.

I had *never* blown into Louise's ear, gale force or otherwise. I had never even thought of doing it. Why would she say that? And yet it still made me smile. There I was, 15 years old with the body of a man, the mental age of a six-year-old, and the emotional age of an infant. Of course it made me smile.

She began to look at me differently. There was prolonged eye contact. There was an altogether new kind of smile when she looked at me. She acted all twitterpated every time I was around her. She touched me more and more. She'd stroke my head, run her hands over my shoulders, and occasionally she'd cheekily pinch my bum and giggle.

I really liked this new-found attention. I'd look forward to my visits to Louise's. I found myself hoping that I'd catch her at times when Keith was on a late shift and the kids were in bed. We'd listen to *our* sixties music together. We'd talk about everything and nothing.

I was round Louise's one afternoon when I'd bunked off school. She didn't mind that sort of thing, being a free thinker. Keith was at work and the kids were at school. We'd been talking about relationships. I had explained that, even though I'd gone out with Theresa Paton for a couple of weeks and had kissed her with tongues, I wasn't really ready for that girlfriend / boyfriend kind of nonsense.

I was sitting in my usual place next to the stereo and Louise was sitting on the sofa opposite. She looked at me very intensely and said, 'Here, let me help you with that.'

She walked across the room and sat next to me on the floor. She undid my trousers, took out my cock and began to wank me slowly at the same time as kissing my mouth deeply. She stopped kissing me and concentrated on my cock.

My mind was swimming. Suddenly my legs felt terribly far away. The room, my cock, Louise – everything was miles away. I found myself fixing my gaze on a round glass picture on the wall. It had a kind of three-dimensional effect – a stag had been painted (badly) on the glass in the foreground and a scene from the Scottish Highlands had been printed on the paper in the background. Dad had bought it for Louise when we'd gone up to Scotland after Mum had died.

Suddenly she stopped, 'Shit, Michael will be home from school in a minute. You'd better do yourself up.'

I was back into the world of reality again. I hurriedly did up my trousers. What the fuck had just happened? Michael did come home from school; Mary came home too and we all had tea.

A week or so later Louise and I went out for a drink at the pub across the road. Getting served with alcohol wasn't really a problem since, at 15, I looked about 47. I hadn't stopped thinking about what happened. I couldn't speak to anyone about it –except Louise.

On the way home we walked arm in arm as we chatted about nothing. Then we stopped in a secluded spot just under some trees and she kissed me. I was so confused, but turned on. I kissed her back. Louise started to cry. My head was spinning – my mind and body were completely out of control. I wanted to kiss her – shit, I wanted to fuck her – and here she was crying.

When we got back to the house we told Keith that we were going upstairs to talk. This was nothing particularly unusual for him, since Louise and I appeared pretty close and we did spend a lot of time talking. Keith wasn't a terribly big fan of chatting so it kind of let him off the hook. Louise and I went upstairs, undressed each other and I lost my virginity. I came inside her very quickly with her shouting, 'There – there – there!' with Keith watching the television downstairs.

We went back downstairs and watched television with Keith for a while. We might have had a bacon roll, we might have had some hot chocolate – who knows? I went to bed in Michael's room and she went back to bed with Keith.

I lay awake for hours listening to Michael's gentle snoring. What the fuck had I done? What the fuck had *we* done? This had to stop and it had to stop now.

The following day I got up with Michael, Mary, and Keith and I waved them all off to school and work promising that, at some point during the day, I would wash the breakfast dishes. Later that morning I heard Louise in the shower. I decided I would confront her with my decision – nipping it in the bud before we really fucked things up.

I met her coming out of the shower and we kissed. We went into the bedroom and we rolled about on the bed for a bit. I pulled away. 'This has got to stop,' I said, 'It's wrong.'

Louise's response came a bit as a surprise, 'You fucking wimp!' I'll never forget that derisory look on her face as she sneered at me. 'Fuck off.'

So I did. I fucked off. I broke my promise to Keith and the kids.

For the following week, my mind was in complete turmoil. It was wrong – it was right. I thought that she, as the adult, would've agreed with me. I thought she would have said something along the lines of, 'You're absolutely right Christopher, we've made a terrible mistake. Let's just try and get our relationship back to where it was.'

I had to go back and talk to her about it. 'Fuck off' was not a good way to leave things. I went back. We went out for a drink and we talked about it. 'I'm in love with you, Christopher,' she said. This wasn't fucking helping! I was 15 years old and she was in her early thirties. It shouldn't have been down to me to be saying, 'You can't be – you're like my mum.' And she was. Ever since I'd sought out the shelter of her family, she'd done all the things that I'd imagine my mum would have done for me.

'But I'm not.' She stressed the word 'not' like that made it all okay. 'I want to be with you.'

This emotional table tennis continued throughout the evening. I went to bed as soon as we got back and left early in the morning. What if she told Keith? Or Dad? Or anyone? Oh my fucking god – what a mess.

I let a few weeks go by without seeing her again. Life went on as normal. Dad was still shit, the house was still a dump, I still relied on my friends' parents to feed me.

What about Derek? Fuck, I couldn't even tell my best friend about what had happened. Surely this would stretch the boundaries of friendship even for us. I remember when we'd been about 12, he and I sat ourselves down and vowed to tell each other our most terrible secrets. I can't remember Derek's. Shit. We'd built all that stress and nonsense around it, and I can't even remember what his terrible truth was.

In case Derek has forgotten I told him that, as a young child, I really liked Tuc biscuits. Not a crime in itself, I hear you cry. The horrible thing was that I liked to chew up one Tuc biscuit and gob it out onto another, placing another on top and then devouring it. I invented the Tuc sandwich – don't let anyone tell you otherwise.

The Louise thing though – god, that was just unchartered territory. I had to go back and talk to Louise again. She was the only person in the world that I could discuss this with. And so I went back again and we went for a drink.

'I'm pregnant.' She stated this in the same bland way that she'd said, 'I was sexually abused when I was younger.'

Being unaccustomed to women saying such things to me, I blurted out, 'How do you know?'

'A woman just knows these kinds of things. You forget, I've had two children already.'

This couldn't get any worse. I asked her about abortion and she said that there was absolutely no way that she would consider such a thing. Fuck. It wasn't meant to be like this. I was 15 years old and the woman I thought of as my surrogate mother was going to have my baby.

I went home again. I didn't go back to Louise's for about a month. In the meantime, I wandered about in a shocked daze. What the fuck was I going to do? This was no good. I couldn't avoid her. I couldn't avoid the situation any longer. I had to be responsible.

In time-honoured tradition, I went round to Louise's house and we went out for a drink. 'What are we going to do about this baby?' I said, taking the bull by the horns.

'Oh,' she began nonchalantly, 'I'm not pregnant. There isn't going to be a baby.'

I had to get away from her. She was dangerous. She seemed to have absolutely no insight into what all this was doing to me. My whole world was spinning uncontrollably. Nothing was real.

30 years later Louise asked me, 'If things were so terrible at home, why didn't you come to me?'

I wish, I wish, I wish I'd said the first thing that came into my mind. 'Because, Louise, when I did, you fucked me.'

*

I had almost no contact with Louise for the next two years. Dad, Jim and Stuart felt I was being ridiculous. 'Surely nothing is worth destroying your relationship with her?' appeared to be the recurring theme. If someone had said, 'Why don't you just kiss and make up?' one more time, I swear I would fucking kill them.

I couldn't tell anyone. I had to hold this inside until the day I died. I thought I had taken the whole messy business, folded it up and stuck it in the cupboard under the stairs in my mind never to see the light of day again. But things just don't work that way, do they?

About six years later, after I'd flunked out of school, nearly lost both my arms, fallen out with Stuart after starting to talk to Louise again, only to find she'd broken all my confidences to put me right in the shit (I wondered what she would have thought if I'd broken some of her confidences?); after I'd got my A levels and finally, finally found myself at college – something strange happened.

I was doing physiology as part of my degree in psychology. We were looking at the body's responses to stressful stimuli. We were looking at the good old 'flight or fight' response. The plan was to measure my response to having my bare foot plunged into a bucket of ice. To this end I was plugged into a heart rate monitor and a galvanic skin response thingy. The pupil of my left eye would be videoed.

It was all pretty straightforward, first-year psychology stuff. As all my fellow students expected, my heart rate rapidly increased, my sweat glands caused the GSR monitor to go off the scale and my pupils dilated to their maximum size.

The problem was I hadn't actually put my foot in the ice bucket. No – what all the gizmos and gadgets were actually measuring was my response to seeing my own face on the video monitor. I bluffed my way out of this by saying that I wasn't feeling very well.

It was then that I realised that I hadn't looked at myself for six years. After what had happened with Louise, I was unable to look myself in the eye. I avoided looking at mirrors and my reflection in shop windows. Looking at photographs of myself made me feel physically sick.

Over those years I had decided that I was every bit as culpable for what had happened between me and Louise as she was. I saw it as tantamount to incest – as two consenting people choosing to break one of the most fundamental family rules. I was despicable and disgusting and I'd spent six years denying my own physical existence.

*

Fast forward with me to 1995 again. I'm back in Deacon Brodie's Tavern with Jim. The Hungarian man has come and gone. It was 25 years after the incident with Louise. I really felt it was time he knew.

'I'm not really sure how to deliver this, so I'm going to be short and sweet,' I'd clearly been skirting around something all evening. It must have been a relief to him that I was finally getting down to it.

'I lost my virginity to Louise when I was 17.' I just couldn't bring myself to tell him I'd been 15. Would he have jumped to my defence? Called the police? Encouraged me to use the full force of the law against this heinous child abuser?

If this had a massive emotional effect on Jim, he certainly didn't show it. After a short pause for thought he said, 'This makes no difference in the way I feel about you. You're still the kind of guy I'd like to go out for a drink with.'

And that was it. I felt kind of thankful that he didn't slap my face and leave, screaming things like, 'You're no brother of mine!' I was also relieved that he didn't say, 'She did exactly the same with me.'

Mum dying of cancer; Dad becoming an alcoholic; abject fucking poverty and then shagging my surrogate mother – it all felt like it had happened yesterday.

CHAPTER 10

SQUARE PEGS

'You killed my father, and you're not going to get away with it!'

This wasn't going terribly well.

To complement the academic knowledge I was gathering at the North East London Poly, I'd got myself a job as a nursing assistant on a secure ward in a large psychiatric hospital during the summer break. This helped me in two ways. First of all, it gave me some real money to play with (having mindlessly blown most of my grant in approximately ten minutes) and secondly, it gave me the chance to fully assess whether or not I was really cut out for working in this area.

As time went by, the hospital managers gave me a wide range of experiences – working with older people, working with younger people and now, working with people with whom society wouldn't be completely happy if they were wandering the streets.

The charge nurse, Declan, an authoritative, red-haired Irishman, had stressed that although this ward was great to work on, it was still full of risks. The role of the ward staff was to minimise that risk to both the patients and the staff. We were taught control and restraint.

'The aim of the control and restraint procedure is to stop the second punch landing,' Declan told me. Given the unpredictable nature of some of the patients on the ward, he couldn't guarantee that control and restraint could do anything about the first punch.

The basic rules were: don't put yourself into risky situations – for example, always work in the eyeshot of a colleague, making sure you know where all the panic buttons are – and 'get to know as much as you can about the person you're working with', so that you knew which triggers to look out for.

As per ward procedure, I had read all about Ryan prior to working with him. He was a giant of a man with minor learning disabilities and some manner of schizophrenic-type illness. He had no history of violence.

The ward was arranged in such a way that the day living area was downstairs and the sleeping dormitories and the bathrooms were upstairs. Ryan, as usual, had been taking his time to get dressed that morning. He was lovely to work with because he was friendly and jovial and it was easy to cajole him into action with the promise of food. I constantly chatted with him about the weather and what was for breakfast as he had his shower, dried himself and then put his clothes on – all with the minimum of verbal prompting.

And then he got back into bed. 'You cheeky bugger!' I laughed. 'Come on Ryan, there's a cooked breakfast with your name on it downstairs.' I smiled as I gently tugged at the duvet.

He grinned, apparently getting the joke, and pulled back. In no time at all we were having a tug-of-war with the duvet. What a laugh. There was no one else on the upper level as we continued, grunting and groaning – becoming slightly flushed with exertion. All the other staff and patients were downstairs digging into their breakfasts.

Suddenly, Ryan flew out of his bed, grabbed hold of my shirt and pushed me hard up against the wall. 'You killed my father and you're not going to get away with it."

My feet weren't touching the floor. I'm a big guy, I thought to myself. This really shouldn't be happening. I looked around for the panic buttons. The closest was about ten metres away. Marvellous. I found myself babbling. 'Don't be silly Ryan, I couldn't possibly have killed your father. I've never met him.'

Rule number one of working on a secure ward in a psychiatric hospital – minimise risk to yourself and the patients.

Ryan had no history of violence.

Rule number two is slightly more vague, but roughly states that if you are stupid enough to find yourself in a situation like this, don't waste your time by trying to rationalise with someone whose idea of reality is completely different from yours.

Ryan pulled his right fist back.

I was still dangling from his left hand, pressed up against the wall. I put both of my hands around his fist. I quietly thought to myself, If he hits me with that then there isn't going to be much left.

'Help! Heeeeeellllpppp!' I shouted as loud as I could. Unsurprisingly, nobody came.

I babbled for a little longer and then kicked him hard in the balls. I struggled and squirmed until I managed to get free. Manfully, I ran like hell. I got downstairs to the nurses station, panting. 'Ryan ... I killed his father ... No history of violence ... I called for help ... '

I wasn't being terribly eloquent or coherent.

'You called for help?' Alan, one of the staff nurses, sounded a little scornful. 'You actually reinforced his behaviour?'

Wanker.

He and the rest of my male nursing colleagues trooped upstairs, took Ryan by the wrists and put him in 'Time Out'. This was a small, darkened room that would allow him the space and time to calm down and also to reflect on what he'd done.

Surprisingly, this actually worked with many patients. The staff would wrestle and battle with this Tasmanian devil to get them into the Time Out room – five minutes later the door would be opened, and out would step an altogether happier individual.

It still felt a bit archaic though.

The problem with doing this to Ryan was that he had absolutely no recollection of what he'd just done. The whole process was completely meaningless to him.

To the whole world and their dog, it appeared obvious as to why I had chosen to study psychology. Similarly, one would think it was patently obvious that, by looking at the mental health troubles of others in the psychiatric hospital, I was actually looking at myself.

I was doing all this because it made me feel comfortable. I guess I knew I was different from the population at large; I just chose not to look at me too closely.

*

I arrived at college in London to find that I had nowhere to sleep. I met a guy in a pub called Everton (the guy, not the pub) who was doing applied physics and I slept with him in his car for a couple of nights while I tried to accommodate myself somewhere altogether more suitable.

I eventually moved into a shared flat in Manor Park, having been approached by a bloke, while I was having a piss in the urinal of a local pub, who uttered the unforgettable line, 'Are you a good fun kind of guy to be with?'

I explained that I was, at no point believing that his intentions could be anything other than honourable. He then offered me a place in a shared student flat where we both demonstrated to each other that we were good fun kind of guys. Just to demonstrate how hardened and rock and roll we were, we sang Rolf Harris's 'Two Little Boys' from start to finish in the nearby chip shop on the way home.

I'd like to think that single performance gave us a kind of legendary status.

Was the world a different place then? Was it really okay to sleep in cars with people you'd just met or go home with men who ask you if you're a good fun kind of guy while taking a waz? Oh god, if any child of mine ...

I moved in with Paul (toilet boy) and it turned out he was on the same course as me. We frequented the local pub which, it turned out, was nestled nicely in the middle of the East End's gangland.

I got in with a fine bunch of folk on my course who were situated half way between the nerds and the smack heads. God, we loved to party, just as long as we were home in bed by 11, possibly 12 if it wasn't a school night.

I got a bit of a crush on a girl in our gang. Pretty soon it was obvious my feelings were reciprocated. We went out together a few times, snogging each other's faces off when the urge took us. As our passions increased, so did our desire to tell each other about our virginal, or otherwise, status.

'I'm a virgin,' Melanie told me one night.

'So am I,' I lied, thinking that it might be imprudent to tell her that I had actually shagged someone, but, unfortunately, that someone was my surrogate mother. I thought it might get us off on the wrong footing. I had absolutely no intention of taking any relationship too far – at best I could be described as nervous around women.

The rest of our gang thought it was lovely that Melanie and I were going out together. It was all terribly ... nice.

One night though my whole college world was turned upside down.

I went round to Melanie's place, as usual, to chat and snog. All very fine well-behaved studenty kind of stuff. Unusually, Melanie revealed that she had purchased the biggest fuck-off bottle of white wine that money could buy. Her intentions were clear – she wanted to get shitfaced.

We ate something – it could have been anything from a cuppa-soup to a donner kebab (we were students after all) – and we downed the whole bottle of wine. Our snogging became a little more heated and we ended up doing that reciprocal oral sex thing that the whole world has come to know and love as the 69.

I know what you're thinking – how ungallant it is to kiss and tell. Not so, dear reader. Read on …

She asked me if I had any protection. I told her that I had borrowed a friend's air pistol when I was younger, but other than that, no. So, apart from the oral stuff, nothing much happened. We woke up the following day in each other's arms.

'That was fun,' I smiled as I remembered the night before.

'What was?' Suddenly she was terribly hostile.

'You know.' She fucking did know – she'd been present and correct all throughout the previous night's shenanigans.

'No I don't!' she spat. She suddenly sounded terribly childlike, like she was stamping her foot.

I slowly and falteringly recounted, blow by blow (pun not intended) the events of the previous night.

'You took away my innocence,' she said quietly. I was gobsmacked. No I hadn't. Well, I mean, if I had it had been reciprocal, consensual. What the fuck was she implying?

We got dressed and got the bus to college – comedically, ironically, outrageously – the 69. We went to classes as normal, bantered with folk as normal. Everything as normal.

That night, I went round to Steve's house. Everyone from the gang would gather there to decide what entertainment was in store. I knocked on the door as usual. Steve came to the door, as usual.

Unusually, though, he put his arm across the door to block the entrance. I looked at him quizzically.

'Melanie's here,' he said by way of explanation.

'So?' This couldn't be happening.

'She told us all what happened … '

'What exactly did she say?' I couldn't help myself – I could feel the anger welling up inside me.

'She told us that you'd got her drunk and … ' he shrugged in that 'you know' kind of way.

'And you believe her?'

'Well, she's really upset, Chris.' Steve started to close the door on me.

I gently put my hand on the door, yielding as it closed in my face. I stood for a while. What the hell was I going to do now?

I went back to my ridiculously small room in my ridiculously small flat, sat on the floor underneath the window and cried. I cried for hours. My head was spinning. Should I leave college? But I haven't done anything wrong … I'll go across and confront them … But no, their minds were clearly made up. I felt incredibly lonely. It was unbearable. How could I show my face in class?

Round and round it all went, until Mum walked in the room.

No, no, no stifle the urge to flick back to Chapter 3 – yes she was dead and no, it was absolutely nothing like *Dawn of the Dead* or *An American Werewolf in London*. This wasn't Mum circa 1986, this was Mum circa 1976, wearing a large, leafy patterned knee length dress with brown clompy wedge-style shoes, a perm and horn-rimmed glasses.

This was hypnogogic big style.

We talked for about an hour. We talked about me growing up. She told me she was so sorry and sad when she thought about it. She was really proud of me though. She sat near me but we didn't touch. I really wish we had – just a brush of the leg, a finger even. Anything. But we didn't.

She told me everything was going to be all right. I shouldn't worry about these so-called friends, they'd all come back round when they realised the truth of the story.

She asked about Jim and Dad and Stuart and Louise. I wanted to ask her if she had known about Louise's abuse.

I just bathed in the comfort and love of her being there. She looked at me with sad yet happy eyes. I so wanted her to stay. I think she wanted to stay there with me, but she couldn't. The hour she was with me seemed to last forever, but it could never be long enough. All too soon she was walking out the door, looking back at me and telling me not to follow her.

Although I felt incredibly sad at her leaving, I felt stronger and happier for seeing her.

Of course, the following day I reflected on the previous evening's visitation and concluded, unequivocally, that I was completely crackers. Any previous doubts as to the validity of this belief were confidently chucked out of the window.

Over the next few weeks I gradually inveigled my way into another group from my course. It was horribly raw for so long – I felt so alienated and ostracised and then, very slowly, over the next year or so, different members of the original gang came back to me. Gail, Lyndsay, and Steve all told me that they never really believed what Melanie had said.

Well that's all right then. Yeah, welcome back. Sure, everything's back the way it was.

Or not.

Back at the hospital I was doing some of the best client-centred work I'd ever done.

Tony was a tall, lithe black guy who had been on the ward for roughly a year. He was affectionately known by the ward staff as the karate kid, given his unfortunate habit of occasionally striking the male members of staff in a martial arts style. His attacks would almost invariably cause a rib or a nose to be broken. Much to the anger of many of the staff, once he'd assaulted someone he would completely relax and allow himself to be removed from the situation and placed in the Time Out room or in the 'off-privileges' room which was furnished with nothing more than a big soft chair. Many of the staff wanted him to resist or put up a fight when he was taken away – this would allow them to 'restrain' him in a boisterous manner.

But no – Tony would quietly hold out his hands, effectively surrendering to the ward staff. He wasn't terribly popular – especially among those who wanted revenge.

'Just remind me again what the purpose of this hospital is?' A couple of the guys had been ranting about how they wanted to mete out their particular brand of justice on Tony. I just felt that their memories would benefit from a bit of a shake. They grumbled and mumbled that, if Tony had done this in the street, he'd have received a good kicking.

'But we're not on the street, are we?' Tony was in hospital with what was believed to be cannabis-induced psychosis. 'It's really not going to help his cause if we batter the shit out of him.'

Wankers.

The fact that I was able to philosophise about the finer points of Tony's care and support in the hospital didn't detract from the horrible truth that I was actually shit-scared of him. I was the only male member of staff on the ward who hadn't had a bone broken by him. Add to this, he had recently developed the somewhat undesirable habit of sneaking up behind me and quietly whispering in my ear, 'Here I am, Chris.'

This, as you can imagine, did more for me than a lorry load of All-Bran.

Whether I was standing talking to another patient or a member of staff really didn't matter to Tony. He loved to appear next to me and make his presence known. 'Okay Tony, that's enough!' I blurted out one day. 'How do you think this makes me feel? It's like I've got my very own stalker.'

He smiled gently and kind of quizzically at me. My mind was racing – I liked Tony. When he wasn't breaking bones or inflicting double incontinence on me he was friendly, affable and funny. 'What do you want, Tony?' It was a bit of a wide reaching, ridiculously open question, I know, but it caused him to think.

After a long pause, where our eye contact never broke, he said, 'I like football.'

That, dear reader, was good enough for me. 'Well, let's play football, then,' I grinned like a, er, you know, loon.

I knew this would be acceptable to everyone concerned. The management – who were clearly concerned that their staff were regularly taking time off work because bits of them were falling off; the staff – because they weren't terribly keen on having bits of themselves broken; the other patients – because, as a rule, they found the violence very distressing; me – because I was beginning to have dreams about Tony sneaking up on me, and Tony – because someone would be giving him their undivided attention. It was a win, win, win, win, win situation.

Tony and I were given the nod from the powers that be to play football for several hours each day. My prayers had been answered. I was a professional footballer – kind of ...

We played together in the concreted exercise area just next to the main ward. In between remarks such as, 'Nice control,' and, 'Neat,' and 'My Granny could've stopped that,' Tony and I spoke about everything.

We talked about his hopes and aspirations – he's always wanted to be a professional footballer. He'd played professionally for one of the lower league teams before his life took a bit of a turn for the worse. He wanted a flat of his own, with as little social work and health input as possible. He realised that things weren't going to change terribly quickly if he kept on battering people to a pulp.

The problem was that, in a psychiatric institution, your average punter feels little or no sense of power. He gets up when he's told to, he eats when he's told to, he leaves the ward when he's told he can and so on. Tony had found a way to exert power over the very people who he felt wanted to control him.

His violence was nothing to do with psychosis – it was to do with a desire to flex his physical and psychological power. On that ward, among his peers, Tony was king. The problem for him was that this was the very thing that was keeping him from realising his real goals and dreams.

In playing football with me day after day, Tony demonstrated that he had control over his aggressive outbursts. He became the model patient. In between our soccer sessions he participated fully in all the groups and sessions that were put before him. The aura of fear that he'd generated around him vanished in just a month.

I accompanied Tony to his review meeting where he was interviewed by a number of health professionals and a couple of members of the public. I wasn't allowed to speak – I was there purely for moral support.

Again and again they asked him if he was going to leave cannabis alone and again and again he politely, but firmly, told them that he saw no harm in it. They stressed that they wanted him to move to his own flat in the community, but only if he agreed to having substantial support from social services and the health. He managed to knock them down to one supervisory visit per week.

I left the ward a few weeks before he did. I returned to North East London Poly safe in the knowledge that this was one square peg who would be returning back into his local community, exerting as much appropriate power to allow him to live the life he wanted.

Yes it was scary. Yes, he had challenges ahead of him. For me though, it felt great.

*

Following the Melanie debacle, college life was really beginning to pick up. I'd met up with an attractive and feisty Scottish woman to whom I'd be married five years later. Poppy was a hard-working art student who, for me, was refreshingly normal. I thought I'd never get a proper girlfriend, never mind a wife.

Two thoughts kept going through my mind. 'Don't fuck this up,' and 'Just fit in.'

Not the most challenging rules for a relationship, you'd think. That's what I'd hoped.

To keep things going nicely I made the decision to tell her as little about my childhood as possible – especially the Louise and sticking the comb handle through my arms kind of stuff. Why would she need to know any of that? It would only serve to push my status from 'eccentric' into that of a far less acceptable and much more scary 'nutcase'.

In retrospect ...

To the outside world I'm a happy-go-lucky, extroverted kind of a fellow. Nothing bothers me and nothing is too much trouble. When too many social demands are put on me, though, the cracks begin to show.

I think it was all pretty normal stuff to begin with. I seemed to enjoy my own space more than most, which, on reflection, seemed to challenge the extrovert label somewhat. Then there were a couple of incidences that made me think that all was not well. What the hell they meant is anyone's guess – they just felt odd.

First of all, Poppy and I had been out shopping. We'd got separated and so we did our own thing for a while. I was perusing the frozen food when suddenly she snuck up behind me and put a bag of frozen peas over each ear. Hilariously funny.

The problem was that I was unable to calm down from the initial fright. I felt incredibly angry well into the next day. Even the mention of it makes me clench my fists. I wanted to hurt her – the feeling of which didn't sit terribly happily with me.

The second situation / event was equally as innocuous. We'd been having a minor disagreement about little or nothing when I stood up to go out of the room. I wasn't running away from the conflict, I was going to make a cup of tea or go to the loo or something of that ilk.

Poppy took my arm to stop me leaving, feeling that that part of the conversation had yet to be concluded. My first reaction had been red-hot anger. I had an incredible urge to punch her hard in the face.

Thankfully I didn't. Instead, through gritted teeth I was able to snarl, 'Don't ever do that again.' She looked shocked and scared. I would have looked shocked and scared had I been on the end of such a radical change of mood.

I apologised for each a few days after they'd happened. Although it felt like I was being sincere, there was also an acknowledgement that it was probably best that Poppy avoided sneaking up behind me and / or blocking my way – at least for the time being. The 'time being' as it goes, has spilled over into about 20 years.

I buried both of these 0-to-100 moments in the dark cupboard under the stairs. That wasn't me. I'm nice, friendly – happy-go-fucking-lucky. Best not to think too much about them. They were two minor aberrations – nothing to worry about.

Anger aside, I was developing a few other foibles that proved to be far more destructive to our relationship. I think these foibles can be rooted in one simple desire. That is, the desire to be the centre of people's attention. Not like an actor performing on stage. No, that would be transient and meaningless. I wanted to be at the centre of folks' lives.

I wanted men to admire me and I wanted women not just to find me attractive, but to love me.

Things started to unravel fast over the Christmas of 1989. I was sharing a house in the East End of London with Poppy and her friend and fellow artist, Ellie. They had both gone home for the festive period. I was working in London and, for whatever reason, had chosen to go back to Corby for Christmas later that year.

They had a friend on their course, Liz, who was also delaying her return home. Poppy thought that, since Liz and I appeared to get on well, it would be nice for us to keep each other company before we went to our respective homes.

Liz clearly liked me more than the earlier, 'appeared to get on well' statement would have you believe. In no time at all she was spilling her innermost thoughts and secrets to me. She talked about her friends and family and the loves she'd won and lost. As we talked, I found myself wanting to be everything to her – *for* her. I imagined a life with her, having children with her – two tortured souls against the rest of the world.

We had a couple of drinks in the local pub and then we went back to my place and shagged. Then we talked some more and then we shagged some more. I relished being the centre of her life. I *needed* to be needed.

The first morning when we woke up together I said something that, I believe, would make most women run a very long way. I said, 'Liz, I've got an incredibly strong urge to cut off my left arm.' It was true, the short mental film of me hacking my arm off with a meat cleaver played over and over again.

She said nothing. Maybe she thought I was joking, or she was hearing things or … who knows?

When we all got back from the Christmas frivolities things had changed within me, and between Poppy and me. Liz started ignoring her at college or being downright rude. Then she started telling Poppy how she didn't understand me and that only Liz really did.

Poppy would come home and recount these tales of woe. I felt incredibly torn. I had my fantasy life with Liz and I had my real life with Poppy. I wanted to protect them both at the same time as being with them both. In reality I had *no* life with Liz. In total, I'd been with her for about three days. I knew *nothing* about her. That really wasn't a problem for me – where reality left gaps, fantasy was more than happy to step in.

After about a month of this strange backwards and forwarding where I wasn't seeing Liz, just hearing about her newly found strange behaviour at college, I decided to confront her. 'You can't keep being horrible to Poppy,' I told her flatly.

She was incredibly angry and upset as I explained to her that I would be staying with Poppy. I told her, in no uncertain terms, that it was over between me and her. No wonder she was fucking angry – with the intensity of our pre-Christmas relationship, she was well within her rights to believe that we'd be picking curtains together in the new year.

'Did you fuck Liz?' Poppy asked me outright after most of the dust had settled.

'No.' I denied it as flatly as I could. I didn't want to protest too much because I felt that would simply add to her suspicion. She took me at my word and life continued as before. Liz continued to be shitty towards her for the rest of the course – but said nothing about our fleeting relationship.

For the next four years – a time that included our marriage and the birth of our son – I became a serial adulterer. To be fair on me, I became more of a serial fantasist. I had six further relationships that were exactly the same as I'd had with Liz, each of them rooted in my desire to be the centre of that person's world. Each with the bizarre made up future attached to it. Each with the confused 'what the fuck was that about, Chris?' woman attached to it.

Add to this the feeling that came with having sex with Louise. The belief that really, there was no sin that could equate to that – which gave me free rein to do anything.

Poppy isn't stupid. Call it women's intuition, call it patently dodgy behaviour, but she knew that this was going on. True, she didn't know to what extent it was going on – but in her heart, she knew it. So many times she would ask me if I'd been with someone else and so many times I'd deny it.

We became more and more distant. She began to withdraw because she just didn't want to feel the full force of the pain when the truth finally poured out. I began to withdraw from her because the pain of the guilt that I was experiencing was becoming intolerable. The guilt was everywhere. I was angry, distant and introspective. I got myself to the point where I was convinced that I could never tell her about anything – the self-harm, Louise, or the affairs. I had to leave.

This would be best for her, for me and for our son. We'd all start all over again and we'd all live happily ever after.

Unfortunately this too was intolerable. Work was awful. My home life was awful. I was awful. This was the point where I went into hospital. Instead of killing myself, I slept for hours and was given the offer of psychiatrists and psychotherapists.

Still, I told Poppy nothing. Still, I continued to have relationships outside my marriage.

I was having a relationship with a woman that I'd met on my course at college. I'd told her everything about me – including the self-harm and Louise – and she still appeared to want to be around me. I fantasised a future for us. *She* fantasised a similar future – she phoned her fiancé while I was with her and told him she'd met someone else. It was a very short phone call, I thought, to end a very long relationship.

I had told a couple of other students on my course about Louise and all of my head stuff. They'd made all the appropriate student social-workery noises but for me, they did nothing to change my own mental judgement of me.

I ran away from home. I packed all my belongings into the back of my work-provided burgundy Ford Fiesta and drove off into the sunset, never to return.

Well, in reality, I never got as far as the sunset. I stopped at the fantasy woman's house and decanted all my stuff into her living room. Poppy went looking for me – speaking to a couple of the people off my course who were able to point her in the direction of my new home.

Poppy arrived at fantasy woman's house and pressed the buzzer. She and I spoke briefly through the intercom and I went down into the street to talk to her. She had her mum's car and our two-year-old boy was sitting in the baby seat on the passenger side.

I was crying uncontrollably. I found speaking very difficult as I felt I had to fight and contort my mouth around every word. 'Why are you crying, Daddy?' my son asked, genuinely interested in why his father appeared to be out of control.

Through all the tears and snot, I was able to say, 'Because I've been really bad.'

Poppy told me that she just wanted to know that I was okay and that she was happy that I hadn't done anything to myself. I went back upstairs to fantasy woman's flat. A flat that she'd just bought with a shed-load of inheritance money she'd just received. The same inheritance money, I believed, that was going to allow me to start anew. I'd found that social work, the job that I'd always wanted to do, was shite – and this woman, along with her new-found wealth, would allow me to pursue my first love – writing. It was all sewn up.

I stayed awake most of the night thinking about what I was doing. I'd made a decision on behalf of Poppy – I had decided that she would hate me and kick me out if she heard about all the terrible evil things I had done. That just wasn't fair. She really deserved to know what had happened and what was going on in my head.

I drove back home the following day and told her everything. A friend of mine had told her about Louise already. I didn't feel angry about this breach of trust; they were only doing something I should have done years ago. As I told her, I realised I was putting my future in her hands. Any choices about where I'd live and who I'd be with were hers to make.

She'd obviously been waiting for this moment for some time. I didn't receive a frying pan around the head as some people may have expected. Instead she told me she was relieved that I'd come clean, and that she wasn't mad for suspecting that this had all been going on. She told me that she still wanted to be with me and that we could work on our future together.

I didn't feel the fireworks of happiness and relief go off in my mind. Instead, I felt a quiet determination that said 'Don't fuck this up.'

Where had we heard that before?

I went back to fantasy woman's flat and told her that I was no longer going to be living with her to love her and carve out a career in writing. No, I would be going back to Poppy and my child. She was angry for a short time, and then resigned herself to the fact that it had all been a bit of a strange fantasy. She phoned her fiancé to tell him it was back on. They ultimately got married and had a clutch of children.

As for me? Well, I had a lot of work to do in my personal, recreational and professional life. Was I up to the task?

*

Social work continued to be a bitter disappointment to me. Following my sudden departure to the loony bin, my manager agreed to revise the structure of the hospital social work team to look at an equitable share of the work.

I worked on a variety of wards with a variety of clients, carers' groups and professionals in an attempt to find my niche. I worked on the oncology wards, the care of the elderly wards, and the neurological wards. I was rubbing shoulders with all kinds of wonderful, inspiring people, people who were getting on with their lives despite their often terrible situations.

I worked on the rheumatology ward where I ran a weekly group telling clients, carers and professionals what they should expect from the social work department. People were amazed to find that we didn't just ensure that folk got the benefits to which they were entitled.

It was here that I met a wonderful young woman called Tanya. She had most rheumatological conditions known to humankind. The most amazing thing about her was, she wasn't dead. The second most amazing thing about her was that, instead of lying down on her back, waiting for that inevitable day, she ran a group called Young Arthritis Care (YAC). That name still makes me smile.

She realised that there was a huge amount of arthritis sufferers who didn't go into hospital and, as such, just weren't getting access to my deluxe social work spiel. She decided that I would become a regular speaker at her YAC meetings. Her enthusiasm and charisma was such that it was impossible to refuse.

'We can't pay you money,' she told me as she made her proposal.

'That's fine, because I don't want to be paid,' I smiled back at this tiny, yet larger than life 19-year-old.

'We have to pay you something, though.' She was quite insistent. 'You can't do this for nothing.'

'Well, I'd be in breach of my social work contract if you paid me anything,' I insisted. 'Can't we just call me a do-gooder and have done with it?'

'What do you like to eat?' she grinned, clearly refusing to take 'no' for an answer.

The meeting with YAC was at 7.30 in the evening – attending the group meant that I was missing out on my tea. 'Fish and chips,' I finally conceded.

And so it was – Tanya paid me in fish and chips to talk to YAC.

Everyone who came in touch with Tanya loved her. Her consultant, me, her family, her personal care assistant – everyone loved this young woman who clattered into their lives brandishing her Zimmer frame, or whizzing around in her electric wheelchair or, for a time, racing around in her purple Renault Clio.

Sadly though, Tanya and I had to go our separate ways. I left my job in the hospital to work in a social work team in the community.

Before I left though, I used the strength that she had bestowed upon me in all of my professional life. I would challenge my employers strongly when they suggested that they wouldn't fund a certain care package or other. I would fight for the rights of the unheard client groups.

Even in the politically correct world of social work, clients can be split into 'worthies' and 'unworthies'. Folk who have developed MS, cancer, or rheumatoid arthritis were considered to be worthy of hours of social work time. These poor people had been struck down by terrible conditions that had nothing to do with them.

Alcoholics and drug abusers on the other hand – well that was an altogether different story. These people had brought their problems on themselves. These folk who lived chaotic lifestyles, who were gradually killing themselves, didn't really live up to the "worthy" label. Even the part of the social work department that was designed to support these people was self-serving and self-congratulatory. They ran a "two strikes and you're out" policy. This meant if your person-with-an-addiction punter failed to attend two meetings with the specialist worker, the support they received would be withdrawn.

The result? The people who were already halfway out of their addictive lifestyle would get all the support they needed. The poor sods who were really struggling to make any sense of anything were merrily abandoned.

I made it my own personal policy to mop up this flotsam and jetsam of the social work department. These people, I believed, were the very reason why the social work department existed. Sure, it was nice to work with folk who were already some way to helping themselves – but for me, the real work was with those people who were completely on their arses.

Talking of which, I was becoming a complete pain in the arses of social work management. I made it my business to know social work legislation inside out and would happily tell any manager when they were breaking the law.

I was angry. I was angry that the social work department allowed its funding to be cut back and cut back while the need for social work, because of the ever-expanding older population, was increasing.

At the time, the Director of Social Work and the Head of Social Work on the council were well known for their intense dislike of each other. Their petty politics meant a worse deal for the social workers and, ultimately the punters. They must have realised one day that the masses were aware of their relationship.

They decided to get the wheels of the council propaganda machine in motion to combat these terrible rumours. They made a video where they did a little double act. Each would tell us the wonderful work that had been done by the other – with lots of smiling and back-slapping throughout. Clearly they were unable to keep this sycophancy going long enough to do it live in front of the masses – so they sent the video out to be enjoyed by all. We could feedback to the middle managers who watched with us.

There were about 40 of us at this particular screening of Isn't Everything Lovely in the Council? (I might have made this title up for comedic effect). We sat through the hour-long presentation which climaxed in them shaking hands vigorously to show just how sincere and meaningful it had all been.

A middle manager stood up at the front of the room and asked if anyone had any questions. I looked around at my colleagues who were just staring blankly at the screen in a stunned silence. I put my hand up.

'Yes, Chris?' the middle manager enthused at the prospect of anyone saying anything to keep the propaganda ball rolling.

'D'you think he,' I said pointing at a picture of our director, 'could have got his tongue any further up his,' now pointing at the picture of the Head of Social Work on the council, 'arse?'

That brought them back to life!

'Well, I don't think that was very useful,' spat the middle manager venomously.

To be fair, it wasn't very useful. It also wasn't really the sort of thing that social workers say. The reaction from my colleagues came in three forms – the snorting laugh, the quiet comments of support, and the derisory, 'Oh my god!'

For me it was symbolic of the fact that I was beginning to feel that I just didn't fit in with these people. This career I'd chosen – was it all just a big mistake? Should I have just been doing something altogether different?

After seven years of hospital work, I decided it was time to go forth into the community. Things were beginning to get in the way of my career progression there anyway. Primarily, my mouth was getting in the way. I found myself in a state of almost permanent anger on behalf of the punters. Paradoxically, this was an anger I was unable to use on behalf of myself. So, as long as I was able to fight the corners of other people I could be as assertive as I liked.

At times I was the best social worker in the world. I would empower and enable folk wherever I went. The problem was that there were long periods where I wasn't able to support anyone. Starting off with my admission to hospital, I had three long periods off work, diagnosed with depression. Each time I would return to work and gradually build up a head of steam where I was, once again, the people's champion – in my mind at least.

Each time I applied for senior posts or specific training I knew I was going to be turned down. My manager and I just saw things a little differently. Like so many people in the department she felt that I wasn't the right kind of person for these jobs. They needed someone who was very organised and consistent. Someone they could rely on to be the same person day after day. Someone who didn't rock the boat.

Roughly, the opposite of me.

So I moved to the community team in the belief that I could restart my whole career. I could keep my head down and progress through the ranks – just as I deserved. My new manager, Karen, was great. She gave me just the sufficient amount of rope to hang myself. Figuratively, you understand.

I was given all the slightly offbeat clients. People with mental health problems, people with alcohol problems and people with drug problems. This was the stuff I'd been craving. I could change the world of social work once and for all.

I was given the opportunity to train folk. I was seen by some of my colleagues as being somewhat academic – so training seemed to fit in well with me. And then I found my Achilles' heel. As far as political correctness was concerned, I felt that I was God. I would work with anyone regardless of any differences they may have. No matter their colour or their illness or what they'd done – I was their man.

I was allocated the case of a man roughly the same age as me, who had been diagnosed with borderline personality disorder. When I had studied psychology approximately ten years earlier, our clinical psychology lecturer had been particularly scathing about this condition. She had felt that this was the diagnosis given to crazy folk when the psychiatrist had no other label to slap on them. It was a meaningless diagnosis, having so many diagnostic criteria jammed under one heading as to render it redundant.

On top of this, we were told that it was completely untreatable.

So when Callum's case landed on my desk, all the prejudices that I held against this diagnosis – the professionals who had given it, and the clients themselves – all rushed into my mind. 'This is just a case where the psychiatrist couldn't be arsed to come up with a proper diagnosis,' I ranted to anyone who was willing to listen in the large, open plan office I worked in.

Somewhere at the back of my mind a small, quiet alarm bell had gone off. I chose to ignore it.

Having listened to my vitriolic rantings for a few days, Mike, a fellow social worker, handed me a fistful of printed notes that he'd downloaded from the internet. 'See, Chris,' he said as he went through the papers in front of me. 'It's a condition that's different from anything else. This isn't a psychiatrist copping out, it's a proper diagnosis ... '

Mike was right. There before me lay the headings and sub-headings that health professionals would use to assess and diagnose people with this, somewhat bizarre, condition.

According to the notes it was still untreatable. The best hope for any professionals working with these people was to manage them – not to hope for change or improvement, but to set up services that could contain them. This wasn't a view particular to me – not many professionals relished the idea of working with someone with borderline personality disorder. Some GPs would only have one person with this condition in their practice, while some psychologists would state that the best place for someone with BPD was far away, preferably in another country.

The word 'manipulative' screamed out at me from any text that I cared to read. It was with this in mind that I first met up with Callum.

Callum had a long history of complaining against and 'sacking' a variety of social workers and health workers that he'd become tired of. In true Chris Young social work tradition, I thought it would be best if I started my work "where the client was at". If we could start in a similar place together then it was more likely that he and I would move forward together. Sounds lovely, doesn't it?

The other part of my plan was to build a good relationship with Callum – this would mean he would have trust in all that we did together and, as such, have ownership of the tasks and goals we set.

Okay, that's quite enough bollocks for just now.

My big mistake here was that, apart from scanning the paperwork Mike had given me – thinking to myself, 'Oh, that's nice, there is a clear definition of BPD,' – I didn't read up on the condition at all. Callum tore me apart.

I'm sure it wasn't his intention from the outset, but by the end of my so-called intervention I was run ragged. Had I bothered my arse to read around the subject, I would have at least discovered that BPD sufferers are renowned for their difficulties with relationships. Callum immediately experienced difficulties with ours – he told me he felt that I was his first true friend …

I explained that our relationship was professional and that it was my job to assess his needs and provide the services he required. I explained that, given the apparent complexity of his condition, I would be involved in a number of day-to-day activities with him.

As the weeks and months went by, this meant accompanying him to everything from DIY stores to his art exhibition with our local art therapy providers. Very rapidly our relationship boundaries became completely blurred. He carried on taking from me as long as I was willing to give. My usual philosophy of empowering someone to the point that they realised they could do a lot for themselves, by themselves, had died in the water.

I didn't have a fucking clue what I was doing or what I was supposed to be doing. Any boundaries that I tried to create – for example, you can only see me / phone me between certain times – were simply ignored.

Nowhere in my social work toolbox or vocabulary was there the ability to say, 'Callum, will you just fuck off and leave me alone? I've got 30 other clients for fuck's sake.'

No – I carried on with the impossible task of trying to be all things to this man, trying to come up with a definitive answer as to what he needed. But each time I appeared to be getting close to a solution, the goalposts would shift again and I'd be as clueless as I had been before.

One week, his main issue would be housing, then benefits, then employment, then education, then bereavement, then self-esteem, then his relationship with health professionals, or his relationship with the police. Then back to DIY.

He phoned me at all times during my workday. If I didn't pick up the phone, he'd come to the office – refusing to leave until he saw me. My client-centred approach that served me so well when I worked with other punters was failing me badly now.

Finally, after about ten months of this I had to concede defeat. There was no answer to his problems. His problems were the answer to his problems. Without his problems, he had nothing. All I was doing was keeping it all going. He felt that as long as he had a problem, then he'd have my undivided attention.

I was devastated. Never before in the world of social work had I failed so spectacularly. I agreed for the case to be passed on to one of my colleagues.

'I was going to sack you anyway,' Callum told me when I explained that I was no longer going to working with him. Great, my first experience of working with someone with BPD and it had been an unmitigated disaster. Like Callum, I saw him as the poor innocent victim in all this. I took the vast majority of the responsibility for the breakdown in our relationship – any residual blame I passed on to psychiatric services. Nice one, Chris.

I came away with the belief that I'd certainly have to think long and hard before I worked with someone with this condition again.

*

The perception of failure didn't have a great effect on my mental health. Again my mood took a downward turn, and again I took six months off while I took a variety of antidepressants to fend off the effects of situational factors. My behaviour became erratic and unpredictable.

'Chris, what have you bought now?' Poppy sighed in dismay as she walked into the living room after a hard day at work.

'A disco!' I declared – partly over-exuberantly and partly angrily. How could she not understand that £3,000 worth of disco equipment would be the answer to all my problems? The stress of my day-to-day social work life would be soothed as I sped across the country to a variety of village halls with the sole intention of making the ears of the younger generation bleed.

I'd bought the works – I had the lights, the mixing desk, the great big, fuck-off speakers and, of course, the smoke machine. Poppy's nostrils were flared in anger for quite some time following this particular adventure.

Yes, it was fun. Yes, it allowed me to express my more inventive and creative side. But an answer to my problems? No, not really.

I hadn't thought about the difficulties I would experience when my mood was low. At the very best I sounded disingenuous. At worst, I sounded like a psychotic version of Victor Meldrew, telling people to fuck off and saying 'No, I'm not going to play that coz it's shite.'

Well, *you* try acting happy when you're depressed.

I was desperately looking for something – anything – that wasn't social work.

The next stop on my journey of discovery was hospital radio. Before I continue I'd like to take this chance to encourage anyone and everyone to try out being a presenter on hospital radio at least once in your life. It's truly the most fun you can have – it's also the most cringeworthy experience you can ever have as you forget how to work the machinery, or you forget what you're talking about.

It kept me off the streets. But only for a short while. Even though I loved it, I lacked the emotional energy required to keep it going. I had a family that required my input with swimming clubs and galas and any number of other sporting activities you care to mention. I went back to social work.

In the meantime, Poppy tried to stay true to her words. She clearly wanted everything to be fine between me and her but, to be frank, she lacked conviction. The more she thought about my strange behaviour and my sexual indiscretions, the further she moved away from me. She put more and more time into her sport. Well why wouldn't she? With sport there's a direct relationship between what you put in and what you get out.

With me, that relationship was far less predictable. Over the years we became more and more distant while, in her sport, she was becoming more and more successful. She found herself competing at Scottish, then British, then European levels.

I tried to push my case. I told her that if we didn't do something to nurture it, then our relationship would die on its arse. 'I just want to go out with you once a month.' I was almost pleading. Not a pretty sight – but I thought that if we gave each other time, then perhaps we could make a go of it. But I guess I'd made my bed. Whenever we locked horns over one thing or another, the spectre of my numerous affairs raised its ugly head. I felt completely defenceless.

She was always too busy. Whether it was with her stuff, or the kids' stuff – my stuff invariably took last place. I couldn't help but indulge in a bit of self-pity. For someone who'd been deprived of love for all those years I needed *more* affection, not less.

Back at work, I'd been putting a lot of work in with my clients and it was going pretty well. Unfortunately, though, I was beginning to spin out again and took yet more time off. I had the same old symptoms, the same old inability to focus on anything. This time it felt particularly bad for me because I'd been taking a drug called Venlafaxine, which I believed had solved all my mental health worries.

Once again it took months before I found myself rising out of the dark mist. My GP was giving me the largest dose of Venlafaxine that he was authorised to give me. It dulled my symptoms. Fuck, it dulled reality.

I went back to work, still not feeling quite right. I had a return to work meeting with my manager, Karen. The first thing she said to me was, 'Chris, Steve's dead.'

Steve was one of my clients who had had severe alcohol problems. Any money he'd ever had had gone towards buying cheap vodka and his house was barely habitable. But together we'd managed to turn his life around: or so I'd thought. We'd applied for funding through a local furniture initiative and he'd joined Alcoholics Anonymous. Things had really looked as though they were improving.

I closed my eyes tight shut. Somewhere in the distance I imagined the sound of a hammer striking another nail into the coffin of my social work career.

My first reaction was to get up and walk out. In my mind's eye, I kept seeing his smiling face. I kept thinking about how he and I had really connected and that he wasn't just 'another alcoholic' as some of my colleagues had the habit of calling this client group. 'How?' I could take a good guess – he might have been drinking the gloss paint we'd got for his skirting boards.

'He went to casualty complaining of headaches – they think it was some kind of stroke.'

Fuck, fuck, FUCK.

Karen talked about my other cases and what they'd been up to, but all I really heard was a distant mumble. I needed out of this. I needed out of this fast.

Management could be the answer I was looking for, I decided. To be frank anything could be the answer I was looking for – I sure as hell couldn't take much more of this.

The next year was a bit of a blur as I realised my cunning escape plan. I took the Practice Teaching qualification that allowed me to teach social workers in training. It also gave the powers that be the evidence they required that I was committed to social work.

With this experience and my new qualification neatly tucked under my arm, I got myself a job as a senior with a different local authority. At first, I thought it would be ideal because it was roughly divided into two. One part of me was purely a senior social worker with responsibilities for running duty. This was the system whereby all the new referrals were processed and triaged. The role also involved supervising social workers and some unqualified staff. In the other half of the job I dealt with complex cases. That usually meant cases where folk had complained or where the client as seen as particularly challenging.

In reality, for me, it turned out to be two jobs that should have been done by two people. There seemed to be some cultural acceptance within all of this that the job was un-doable. As long as you came into work every morning with that premise at the forefront of your mind, then you'd be fine.

I could do busy. Busy is my middle name. It felt different from my previous job. In that local authority the set up meant there were a lot of social workers to do the job – but few resources to give to the punters once they'd been processed. Here they had few workers and loads of resources. This meant the onus was on the workers to get folk through the system as quickly as possible.

I found this hard. My own particular brand of social work involved getting to know the client so that I could get a clear picture of what was going on for them. In social work language, I liked to get past the presenting problem to what lay beneath.

Not here though. We never got past the presenting problem. It was all terribly unsatisfactory for me.

I managed to work for a full year there before the dreaded illness washed over me again. I was really fucked off. I didn't want my new employers knowing my business. But I couldn't hide it. I was beginning to fuck up at work – making simple mistakes which meant folk weren't being seen in time, or they were getting the wrong kind of service or, in some cases, they were getting no service at all.

This just wasn't working. Something had to change. But what? I couldn't give up my job and retrain– it would throw us all into penury. I felt cornered, trapped.

'Take a look at this,' Poppy said one day, handing me an article from the Observer. It was all about life coaching. I'd always slotted this under pseudo-scientific, self-help for the middle-class bollocks. However, I read the piece in the magazine and it looked structured and solid. More to the point, it looked like the way I worked with my social work clients.

It's always been my policy to enable folk to do things for themselves. If, as so many social workers do, you just do stuff for your punters, then you just set up a state of interdependency. They need you, and you need to be needed. I always felt that I'd done my job when the client told me they didn't need me any more.

I looked around on the internet to find a suitable life coaching qualification. I finally decided on a course that was based in England that was linked into the Open College. At least it had the pretence of being vaguely academic.

I really enjoyed it. Part of the course involved being coached over a six-month period by one of the organisation's own coaches. It was great – my coach supported me as I set up my website and got all the gubbins together that a fledgling coaching business required.

For about a year I was mild-mannered Chris the social worker during the day and dynamic, go-getting Chris-the-coach in the evening.

While my mental health was intact, this all went swimmingly. Poppy took a lot of the responsibility for looking after the offspring, ensuring that they got to all the places that they needed to, while I grew my empire.

In October 2007, everything fell to bits. Now that she and I were working in different towns, Poppy and I had been seeing even less of each other. Our relationship had deteriorated into a kind of administrative arrangement. We had always gone through good and bad periods, but for the previous two years things had just felt distant. Earlier, in May that year, I had confronted her with this. The physical side of things had long since bitten the dust.

I asked her what was going on. I asked her if I was wasting my time when I tried to hug or cuddle her – or show her any sign of affection.

She told me something that my small, sensitive mind couldn't really deal with. Poppy explained that she no longer found me attractive. I had put on some weight over the past few years and this just didn't sit well with the way she saw the world. She hung out with sports people – seeing any kind of excess weight as disgusting.

I was devastated. Anything we had at that point broke. I felt that we'd been hanging by a thread for a long time and, at that point, that thread snapped. Very quickly she realised what she'd said – but for me it was broken. I knew that she really meant what she had said. My mind kind of stopped feeling anything at that point.

We went for counselling, but that was hugely problematic in that she wanted to use it as a vehicle to get back together while I saw it as a way to separate amicably.

At work, things were beginning to affect me more and more. Situations where my professional distance would normally protect me were becoming overwhelming. I was called out on a duty visit. There was a man with schizophrenia who had left the local psychiatric ward without permission. He had been doing well in the community but had recently started to hear and see things that weren't there again. The ward had been reviewing his medication when he'd legged it.

I'd been working with his mother who had some problems of her own. I thought it might be a good idea to pay her a visit to see if she knew where he might have vanished to. As ever, she was wonderfully accommodating of me when I knocked on the door. She welcomed me in, sat me down on the sofa and had thrust a cup of tea into my hand before I had time to say, 'Do you know where your son is?'

'He's in the attic,' she said as if this was a perfectly normal state of affairs, 'He's terrified.' He was in the attic and he was indeed terrified. I managed to coax him down for a chat. He talked at great length about how 'they' were after him. He told me how they read his mind and passed strange and threatening messages to him through his mobile phone. After about an hour of this he vanished back into the attic.

I went back to the office and spoke to the duty doctor on the psychiatric ward. After a short discussion she confirmed 'they' would be coming to get him. She would arrange for the police to get him back onto the ward for treatment.

I had done this kind of thing on numerous occasions. This time, though, I found it horribly distressing. I couldn't get the image of this terrified man out of my head. I even felt kind of complicit in his terror because it was me who had arranged for 'them' to come and get him.

I wasn't cut out for this anymore.

Over the past year I had been working closely with another man with schizophrenia. Paul was great – only his family weren't quite up to looking after him any more. I had supported him to get a flat in the community where he had input from me and the local community psychiatric nurse (CPN).

Paul wrote great poetry. No, I'm not being patronising – if it had been shite I would have said, 'Paul, maybe you should try something else.' It flowed beautifully, dripping with metaphors and meaning.

He'd flunked out at school, mainly, it would appear, because he scared the shit out of the teachers. With his particular brand of schizophrenia, he would tell people that he could communicate telepathically and that the 'Evil Eye' was omnipresent and was out to get him.

He tried to persuade me that his view of the world was right and mine was wrong.

I sat down with him in his living room and, on a huge piece of white paper I drew a large circle.

'This, Paul,' I said, 'is my reality.' He watched closely as I drew another circle that partially overlapped the first. '... and this is your reality.' He nodded. 'The bit where they overlap is where we share realities. Do you see?' Paul liked this diagram a lot.

'I'm not going to tell you how to see the world, and at the same time you're not going to tell me how I should see the world. Okay?' I was quite pleased with it as well.

We agreed that any work we did together would be located in that small overlapping area. Thankfully Paul's hopes of going to college, and some of my more stupid jokes lived happily inside that area. 'Paul, I want to go about with two light bulbs in my pocket,' I said to him one day.

'Why?' He generously played along with so much of my inane drivel, bless him.

'Just in case someone comes up to me in the street and asks for a light – I can pull out one of the bulbs.'

Kindly, he asked the obvious question. 'What about the other bulb?'

'Ah, well,' I said grinning at my own comedic genius. 'That's for when they say, 'no, I meant do you have a match?' D'you geddit?'

He stayed with me mainly through pity and curiosity. The light bulb joke was our 'in-joke'. No matter what was going on, we could always manage to conjure a smile between us at the mention of this truly awful gag.

Paul had a small plastic dinosaur that he kept in a lampshade next to his door. Whenever I came to his flat, I always had some inkling of how he was feeling when I looked in on it. Sometimes he'd put a jolly little hat on it, with party poppers all around. Sometimes he'd have it lying down surrounded with little plastic bottles, to imply he'd got shitfaced the night before and that he may not be particularly good value for money that day.

It was kind of like *ET*, but I liked to think it was a bit more sophisticated.

There were times when Paul was reluctant to take his medication. Although being mentally unwell caused him some problems with the people in his local community, Paul loved the fantastic rush it gave him. Just when he was on the cusp between sanity and madness he would find himself at his most creative. The problem with that, though, was that he would rapidly get to a point where he found it difficult to differentiate between the world he'd made up and the real world outside his living room window.

As I watched our shared reality shrink, I tried to persuade Paul to get back to taking his medication regularly. I kept in close touch with his family, the CPN and the psychiatrist in an attempt to monitor his progress. It just wasn't working though. He stopped keeping appointments with me, his family and the health professionals.

After about a week of him slipping off the radar, I finally caught up with him on his mobile phone. He agreed to meet me at his flat the following morning.

The following day I arrived as arranged at his flat. I looked inside the lampshade to see what cryptic message Paul had left for me that day. There was no little plastic dinosaur inside. Instead there was a small, handmade wooden coffin surrounded with a variety of tablets.

Oh my fucking god, I thought. *He's killed himself.*

I knocked on the door for about 15 minutes, but there was no reply. I drove round to his parents to get the spare set of keys to the flat – but Paul had taken them away with him the previous week. He told his dad he was sick of him trying to control his life. There was nothing else for it – I contacted the mental health team who swiftly gained the permission of the court to gain access to Paul's flat.

The police knocked down the door to his flat. He hadn't killed himself. He was assessed by his GP as not being detainable under the Mental Health (Scotland) Act because he was not deemed to be a risk to himself and / or others.

Paul correctly concluded it was me that had informed the mental health team. We didn't have that discussion, though, until the following week, after he had been locked up following an incident where he'd been wandering the streets half-naked, screaming and shouting at unseen assailants. He was a bit pissed off at me for getting the police to destroy his front door.

'What would you have done in my position?' I asked him. After a lot of thought he agreed that I hadn't had a choice in the matter.

The whole Paul situation knocked me sideways. I felt that I just wasn't coping with the stress of all this stuff. I was completely over-identifying with him. Work was coming home with me and, to be honest, home was coming to work with me.

Back in my home life I was building up, once again, to a confrontation with Louise. I had decided to have it out with her once and for all. I had to get this abuse thing straight in my mind.

Before this mighty confrontation though, Poppy and I got invited to party by a sporting contact we both knew. For the first time in over a year we agreed to go to out together.

It was all very pleasant. We had a few drinks and socialised with our friend's new neighbours. They were from England. The woman, whose name escapes me, told me she had been an administrator in a psychiatric hospital quite close to the one where I'd been working all those years ago. She told me she thought people like me were amazing for being able to work with this client group. I took the compliment as it was intended, at the same time thinking, *If only she knew what was going on behind the scenes*.

'Wasn't it terrible about what happened to that guy, Tony?' she said out of the blue.

'What guy? What happened?' My mind was suddenly racing. No, surely not. There must have been hundreds of guys called Tony in the psychiatric hospital system.

'Oh, he was a lovely black guy on the ward next to where I worked,' she began, 'It was awful what happened to him.'

'What happened?' I began to feel light-headed.

She told me how this guy, Tony, had got into a fight on one of the wards. The belief at the time was that he had been racially abused by one of the other patients and had taken swift action by engaging him in a bit of a punch-up. She explained that Tony had been removed from the ward by a few of the nursing staff in an attempt to settle things down a bit. Tony, she told me, was more than a little pissed off at the fact that it was him being carted off to another ward and not the other guy who had started it all. As such, he put up a bit of physical resistance by punching one of the nurses.

He was restrained by a number of nursing staff, who held him down until he stopped moving. The reason he had stopped moving was because he was dead.

This couldn't be my Tony, I thought to myself. Sure, he had the same second name, but it was a common name.

I didn't research this for about a week. I was in a kind of denial. When I finally sat down and typed his name into Google it all became horribly clear. This was the same guy that I'd played football with all those years before. The same guy who'd shared all his hopes and dreams with me. He had died about ten years after I had last seen him. This simply couldn't be! This was one of the best pieces of work I'd ever done with anyone and now ... Fuck.

A governmental report was written about his case, blaming no one for his death. They did raise some training issues though. Fantastic.

My head was spinning. I was beginning to feel out of control. No one could understand the black hole of despair Tony's death had left.

I kept in touch with a few of the folk from my previous job. I liked to be kept up to date with all that was going on in my old patch. There was a woman, Susan, who I'd enjoyed sharing the odd story with, having gripes about management with, and generally having a bit of a hoot with.

We arranged to meet up a couple of times to catch up properly. On this occasion she bought me a pub lunch. She told me about a particular manager with whom she wasn't having a good time. Then she went on to flatter me remorselessly, telling me that the old place just wasn't the same since I'd left. It was all lovely stuff.

When we parted that day, Susan told me that she'd paid for the lunch so that I'd feel obliged to see her again to repay the favour. I promised that we'd see each other again really soon and we parted with a big old friendly hug.

Occasionally I'd see her driving around and I'd invariably make those exaggerated hand actions that stated, quite clearly I thought, that I'd give her a ring soon and that I'd buy her lunch.

It never happened. Several months after I'd had lunch with Susan, I got an email from Mike. In it he told me that Susan had killed herself.

No, no, no, fucking no.

I had no idea that such a thing had ever crossed her mind. I would never have thought she'd have reached such a state of despair where she could see no other way out.

I went to her funeral, meeting up with all the other folk from my old workplace that I'd promised to go and have lunch with. It was fucking miserable. As I watched her coffin being lowered into the ground, I was struck with a horrible thought. *That could be me.* It wasn't so much *Oh my god, I might have killed myself.* It was more of a, *killing myself is really a feasible option* thought.

Don't worry, the comedic angle of the suicidal life coach wasn't lost on me.

*

Even with all this going on in my mind, I was determined to go and see Louise to have it out with her. She was pretty pissed off that I was bringing the subject up *again*. This was the third time: once when it happened, once in 1993 when I was bonkers and now, here I was having another shot at it.

She saw us as two consenting people who had been going through a turbulent time in their lives seeking comfort from each other. Over the years I'd come to see it as something altogether different. I was 15 years old! This was abuse in the eyes of the law – so, in my opinion, it *was* abuse. I was vulnerable, emotionally immature, and I'd gone to her for help ... and she'd fucked me.

The thing is, I still really struggle with the rights and wrongs of it all. It's so easy to rationalise that, because I was 15, it was abuse. But that's where I get stuck. I participated in this terrible act – this awful thing. I felt – at times *feel* – as culpable as her.

It was all so confusing. While I was at her house we listened to all the sixties music that we'd listened to prior to the fuck up. I bathed in my memories of her bohemian lifestyle and ...

Well, and *nothing*. I couldn't feel anger, never mind express it. Once again, I'm left in a strange world of frustration where I can't show my feelings to her, to me, to *anyone*.

I came back home feeling frustrated and pathetic. We'd sort of agreed that if I still wanted a relationship with her then it was in my hands. I guess she was demanding some kind of closure on it all – she couldn't be doing with a relationship where every so often I'd explode and throw all kinds of accusations at her. I kind of went along with that.

Shortly after I got back I received another email from Mike. Jackie, a woman who I'd been the practice teacher for in her final year at university, was dying of cancer. Again, I was swamped with all the thoughts and feelings attached to my time with her. This young woman had hopes and dreams and now …

By the time she died a short time later, I was incapable of feeling.

*

Okay, it's time to be completely honest. Over the past 15 years, it has never been convenient to look at what was going on for me. I've suffered from a raft of bizarre symptoms for as long as I can remember. I've just chosen to put them to one side. Whenever someone asks, 'How are you?' I always say I'm fine, great, or at the peak of my game.

Ella, a good friend of mine at the time, asked me what *I* wanted. I thought about this over days and weeks. What did I want?

I hadn't a fucking clue. It has always suited me to look at the problems and needs of other people. Thinking about me has always left me feeling acutely uncomfortable.

When Susan died, I knew it was time to stop pissing around. I decided to sit down and really scrutinise what was going on in my head – no matter how uncomfortable it was.

I was ably assisted by a counsellor that was provided for me through work. She told me that nothing of what I said throughout our sessions would be fed back to my managers – unless I spoke about feelings or desires that may pose a direct risk to myself or others. 'So what's going on for you, Chris?' Marion asked me at the start of our second session.

After a pause where I thought to myself, *Here we go then*, I let her have both barrels of my mental turmoil right between the eyes. 'You know I've been signed off work?' I asked – just to make sure she knew where things were at.

'Yes, Chris.' The fact that she said my name a lot had a strangely soothing effect on me.

'Okay. Every day I have around 100–200 vivid thoughts of violent self-harm. They're absolutely compelling.' My images of self-harm were – are – horribly imaginative. They play over again and again, unsummoned and unwelcome. 'In one vision, I attack myself with a meat cleaver. I hack at my legs and body, cutting through flesh, bones and tendons.' Marion nodded. 'In others,' I could feel the cold sweat on my back as I recounted them, 'I hang myself with a rope. I can feel and smell the rope as it tightens around my neck.' She continued to listen quietly, maintaining eye contact throughout. 'These suicides can be spectacular,' I smiled humourlessly. 'I imagine that I've tied the rope to a fixed point on the wall of a block of flats. I see myself tying the rope around my neck and diving, crashing through a window, leaving myself hanging.'

I was concerned that this might be upsetting for her. If it was, she certainly gave no indication. I continued, 'In others, I use a knife. I can plunge the knife straight into my forehead, twisting it ... ' Accustomed as I was to seeing these images, it was still shocking for me to actually be recounting them to another person. 'I can use the same knife on my eyes.' I always thought this was particularly cruel – I love my eyes. 'I'd slice the blade horizontally across them.' This was beginning to feel gratuitous.

Marion began to look uncomfortable. 'I experience feelings of intense emotion, apropos of nothing. I can suddenly feel incredibly sad or incredibly angry without knowing why. The feelings just kind of bubble to the surface. They're completely beyond my control.'

She looked slightly more uncomfortable. 'I'm nearly done.' I didn't want to upset her, but at the same time I didn't want to stop – this was the first time I'd told anyone, so I wanted her to hear everything. 'The images that are most common involve me cutting my wrists vertically – then pulling out all the muscles, blood vessels and tendons ... '

When it had become clear that I'd stopped my regurgitation of self-mutilation Marion said, 'That doesn't *sound* like any depression I've come across before.'

'No,' I said quietly and thoughtfully. 'It doesn't, does it?' We sat in silence for a bit while we both thought about what might be going on for me.

'There's more.' Oh well, in for a penny ... 'I seem to have long lapses in time when I'm just not there.'

'What do you mean?'

'Okay, let's imagine me at work. Usually when one of my colleagues comes into my office and says, 'Chris, can you get this or that done,' they can guarantee that I'll get the work done, promptly and efficiently. On some days though, I fully *believe* I've been working, only to find I've done absolutely nothing, for hours.'

'What happens?'

'It's as if I'm not there. I float off into some inner world. Some days the punters and my colleagues get the deluxe Chris, where I bang out loads of work. But on other days, it's like – I don't know – like I never actually turned up that day.'

'Go on,' this was 'active listening' at its very best. I needed to pour out the whole lot and Marion just let me.

'It's like a third of the time I'm Chris the super-social worker, a third of the time I'm completely out of it, and a third of the time I'm apologising for not getting stuff done, or covering up my mistakes.'

I told her about the ridiculous series of events that preceded this particular absence from work.

'So, how does that make you feel?'

'That's the thing – I got to a point where it was like flicking a switch. I just don't feel anything. I don't care about anything or anyone.' Again, a brief, humourless laugh. 'Which isn't that useful if you're a social worker.'

'No.'

'We had some workers from the local hospice come into the office just before I went off on sick leave. They were talking about a wonderful service they'd set up where they supported the children of terminally ill folk. They got the kids to write stories, or show how the felt through art ... It was really a great resource.'

'You don't sound convinced.'

I wasn't convinced. 'They got the terminally ill folk to write letters, or make up boxes of memories so that their children could remember them when they'd gone.'

'How did it make you feel?'

That was the million-dollar question.

'I was furious. I hope my anger didn't show – but where the fuck were they when *my* mum was dying?'

We sat in silence for a bit. There was one symptom that I was particularly unhappy about. A symptom which I felt moved me along the continuum of madness to fucking loony – it's a scientific term; you wouldn't understand.

'There are days ... ' Oh well, here we go. 'Usually about three in a row, where I don't believe the world or anything in it is real.' I looked for a reaction from Marion, but there was none. She just kept her eyes on mine and continued to listen.

'I can rationalise with myself. I can tell myself not to be so fucking stupid, but in my heart of hearts *I just know that the world isn't real*.' We sat in silence again. I imagined tumbleweed being blown across the floor between us. What could she say to all this? 'I've, er, got an appointment to see a psychiatrist next week,' I said helpfully.

'Good,' she said absent-mindedly.

Marion was accustomed to working with stressed-out, occasionally burnt out, council workers. She agreed that what appeared to be going on for me was beyond her sphere of knowledge.

A week or so later, I met up with the aforementioned psychiatrist, Dr Brown. I had been referred to her because my GP had agreed that he wasn't terribly sure what was going on for me – although she thought it might be bipolar disorder. Over the next few sessions I told her everything, from what happened with Dad and Louise to everything I'd mentioned to Marion.

Dr Brown said a number of things, including, 'You are a very vulnerable man', 'I'm not really sure what we can do for you,' and 'I'm going to refer you for psychotherapy.'

She told me that there was a long waiting list. She told me that she wanted me to stop taking antidepressants. She didn't think they were doing anything for me.

'You are a very violent man,' she said. 'Don't worry, I don't feel in any danger while I'm with you – it's all inwardly pointing.'

As we talked, something else became apparent to her. When I was telling her about all my imagery and tales of woe about my childhood, I always threw in little one-liners – it was like I wanted to alleviate the situation by trying to make her laugh. She seemed more than a little pissed off when she realised that she'd been colluding with this.

When I was talking to her I never showed any anger or sadness. I was happy to laugh in places, but I never showed any negative emotions even when I was talking about the really miserable stuff. 'You're completely incongruent,' she observed at the end of one session. 'It's as if what's going inside is the opposite of what's going on outside.'

I thought about this for a moment. She was absolutely right.

'I want you to go away and think about this.' That made me smile. It was the sort of line that a teacher would come out with: 'I want you to sit in the corner and think about what you've done.'

Over the next few weeks I entered the world of self-diagnosis. I had a degree in psychology for fuck's sake, I might as well use it. Three weeks later I found myself sitting face to face with the lovely Dr Brown again. I was smiling – perhaps just a little smugly.

'I've got dissociative disorder,' I said with absolute conviction.

'Well, you certainly haven't got bipolar disorder,' she said with equal conviction.

We wandered off the diagnosis theme for a bit while we talked about what had been going on for me over the past three weeks.

I'd told her previously that I curl up in a ball under our cabin bed at home for about an hour each day, crying uncontrollably. I don't know why; I just feel intense and raw emotion that I just can't seem to control. At these times I feel suicidal. I had previously worked with a psychologist who used cognitive behavioural therapy techniques to help me through my darker times. Essentially what happens in my mind is that, the second I think of killing myself, the faces of my children appear. While I'm lying there – turgid with the stress of all the distressing images as they cascade through my head – I am also able to start chanting a quiet mantra to myself. 'This will pass.'

I subjectively measure my levels of suicidal-ness on a scale of 0–10, where 0 would be no thoughts of the deed and 10 would be actually doing it. Most days I float between 4 and 7.

Over the past three weeks, however, I'd discovered that I'd hit 9 ½. The intensity of feeling built up and built up horrifically, with images coming thick and fast. At one point I felt that it had subsided sufficiently for me to phone Poppy, just to check what time she and the kids would be back from work and school.

I was wrong. I started off quite calmly when the answer machine on her phone asked me to leave a message – but by the time I had finished I was crying hysterically. She phoned back. 'Chris, have you done anything stupid?'

I was aware that she was in the car and that our daughter was sitting next to her saying, 'Is Dad crying?' This made it worse for me – I'd managed to hide the most severe bouts of this from the kids in the past but now – fuck, all I had to do was speak ...

'No, I'm okay. ' I managed to blurt out.

'I'm going to get Maggie to come round.' Maggie was a friend of ours that lived just up the road.

'Okay,' I said. I put the phone down and found myself screaming. I don't scream. I'm not the sort of person who lets rip like that. But now, seemingly, I was.

So, back in the office with Dr Brown.

I had always thought that I'd self-harmed back in the day because of self-hatred or because I was so spaced out I needed to feel something – *anything*. But together we worked out that there was another reason why I'd stuck the handle of the comb through my arm all those years ago. To take away the pain in my head.

'You could try ice cubes,' Dr Brown suggested. 'Some people find it useful to hold onto ice cubes as an alternative to self-harming.'

'Thanks – I'll try that.' Could that really work, I wondered?

We talked a little more about psychological turmoil and the like, and I brought the conversation back to all things diagnostic. 'If I haven't got bipolar disorder, what do you think I've got?'

'I don't believe in labelling people.' Was she stalling?

'But if you were to label me?' I had to know.

'You've got the classic symptoms of borderline personality disorder.'

Oh my fucking god!

I'd so wanted to have something bizarre, something quirky and exotic. I knew it wasn't depression. I thought dissociative disorder would be just the thing. I didn't want a fucking condition that not even the professionals could see in a positive light.

She was right though. Dissociation is just part of it. Depression is just another part of it. *Oh my god*, I thought. *I'm doomed.*

CHAPTER 11

FINDING HOPE

Just to reiterate, I really believed I was doomed. I had just been diagnosed with an untreatable condition that was seen in a somewhat discriminatory way by many health and social care professionals.

As a social worker I was also aware of the recent implementation of The Mental Health (Care and Treatment) (Scotland) Act 2003. This was an act that had been developed partly with people with borderline personality disorder in mind. Even though it was recognised that, at the time of writing, there was no treatment for people with my condition, the act allowed for such people to be detained – to be 'cared for' if necessary.

I suddenly felt like I was skating on thin ice.

To be fair, in my experience anyway, the Act hasn't been used as a big nasty club to imprison anyone with more than a touch of lunacy. It just made me feel that little bit more vulnerable.

I briefly spoke to Louise about my diagnosis. I've no idea what I expected from her. *I hate her, I love her, I hate her, I love her ... Surely she's as much a victim in all this as me?* I just didn't know what to do with this stuff. I stopped calling her. The disparate feelings were just intolerable.

I felt isolated after years of being away from England, my family and friends. I felt desperately alone. Thank god for Derek. For whatever reason, I was able to talk to him and he listened. He's always been supportive.

*

Back at work, my social work career was gradually disintegrating before me. I got to the point where I felt that there wasn't a length of time long enough that would allow me to recuperate sufficiently to return to my job.

One of the department's middle managers suggested to my boss that I should be sacked due to incompetence. Ah, that'll be the sensitive social work approach to mental health problems. I explained to my boss that when I was well, there was nothing wrong with my work. Thankfully, he agreed.

When I got the diagnosis though, we agreed that the time for pissing about was over and that we – sorry, *I* – had to concentrate fully on my health. I had meetings with Human Resources and Occupational Health.

'Oh, we've got loads of people working for the council who've borderline personality disorder,' Fiona the HR woman said earnestly in one of our meetings.

'Really?' I said, with more incredulity than I'd intended.

'Loads,' she said, with great confidence.

'Do you know what BPD is?' I asked, just to be sure we were actually talking about the same thing.

She looked kind of sheepish and then said, 'Er ... no.'

To be fair to Fiona, it was her role to attend these meetings and, if I was deemed to be too loopy for my current job, she could stick me in any other council job that was available at the time.

I had a number of meetings with Alison, the lovely occupational health doctor, whose job it was to assess if I was fit for my job. If not, then any job and, if not, was this state of affairs unlikely to change in the foreseeable future?

Over several meetings it was becoming more and more clear that I was going to be disabled out of the job that I'd wanted to do since I was 12. Moreover, in my current state of mind, I was unable to do *any* council jobs that were available or even unavailable.

One day I was sitting in a car just outside the occupational health department waiting for, what turned out to be, my final meeting with Alison.

While I was waiting, I had taken the opportunity to phone the lovely Ella, to discuss everything that was going on for me. I was crying on and off, feeling pretty distressed at the imminent demise of my career. 'I just can't see a future for me in social work,' I blubbered down the phone.

Unfortunately, all Ella heard was, 'I just can't see a future for me ...' when my mobile phone stopped working. It was like a comedy sketch where the old pirate is lying on his deathbed and he utters his final words, 'The treasure's buried in the uuuurrrrggghhh ... '

I hadn't realised just how awful this had sounded. I just thought, *Fucking phone*, and promised myself that I would phone her back when I got home. I went into the meeting with Alison, crying. It didn't get any better from there. In between sobbing and biting my finger I managed to say, 'Sometimes it feels like I'm holding a gun to my head – it's like I'm holding myself hostage.'

Alison made me promise that, after our meeting, I would go straight to my GP. I told her about my phone not working, and I reassured her that I would phone him as soon as I got home.

In the meeting, Alison and I finally concluded that it was time for me to stop work. She agreed to complete the relevant paperwork that would free up my pension and allow me to leave the council quietly. I was relieved and absolutely gutted all at the same time. All I could see was a big black abyss where my job used to be. Oh bloody fucking shit.

I drove home – occasionally stopping to use windscreen wipers on my eyes as I cried all the way.

My 17-year-old son was at home. I was desperate to hold it together for him. I got in the door – ideally I should have been wearing dark glasses – and smuggled myself off to the bedroom.

I phoned Ella. 'I'm afraid I've got a bit of a confession to make,' she said, a little nervously.

'Go on – I'm sure it's nothing.' I was in a strangely buoyant mood now.

'I've, er ... phoned the police.' She had been so concerned when she'd heard my last words over the phone that she really thought I was in danger of doing something to myself. 'I asked them to make sure that you'd gone to your meeting,' she said by way of an apology.

I explained that, in her position, I would have done exactly the same. I went off and phoned the police. 'Hi, Mr Young, we'll send two police officers round to your house in a couple of minutes,' the operator began.

'No you won't,' I replied with great finality. 'I've got my son here and I don't want him to have any idea about what's been going on.'

The police were great. They met me at the local station once I'd been to see my GP. 'It's okay,' I said, 'he's given me some drugs.'

'Anything good?' smiled the young copper.

'I'll get back to you on that,' I grinned back.

My GP had given me Carbamazepine to stabilise my moods. Although it never quite lived up to that hope, it did accelerate my body's ability to metabolise alcohol – which made me a terribly cheap date. I inadvertently got shitfaced on just one bottle of my mate Jim's home brew.

This was strange for me because, as a rule, I was pretty obsessive about reading up on what drugs might do to me. I guess things had been so crazy in recent times that I would have taken anything just to feel a bit better – to hell with the side effects.

'I see you came off the pension scheme late last year,' the kindly man from the pensions department spoke gently over the phone. I can't remember his name, so we'll just call him 'Tactless Bastard' for now.

'Yes, I know – money was a little tight so I just came off the scheme for a bit while I got things together,' I explained.

'Because you'll know that if you'd stayed on the scheme you'd have got—'

'Don't tell me,' I was quite forceful. I didn't need to know.

'You'd have got—' he was clearly a little miffed that I'd interrupted him.

'Really, don't tell me. I don't *need* to know.'

'You'd have got *twice* the lump sum and pension that you're going to get now.' That obviously made him feel much better.

Does anyone out there want to buy a kidney? Just a thought.

I went to my final meeting with my old boss and Fiona. It was all nice and informal. I was a bit tearful. 'Why are you upset, Chris?' My boss clearly hadn't turned up to the sensitivity part of his training.

'Because he's being disabled out of the job he's done for 15 years!' Fiona jumped to my defence, astonished at his lack of empathy.

'It's just a bit sad,' I confirmed.

'Although you've been disabled out of the council,' Fiona explained, 'you haven't been struck off as a social worker.'

Is that a good thing? I thought to myself.

'Do you know, Chris,' my boss continued on his tactless course.

'I'm jealous of you – you know, getting out of social work at such a young age.'

Whoopy-fucking-do! How lucky was I?

*

I'm really sorry – I'd almost forgotten that this chapter bore the heading 'Finding Hope.'

So far, all I've done is whinge on about how I've lost my job, how the police came round because they thought I was going to kill myself, how I'm taking some tablets that get me pissed quicker, and I'm only getting half the pension I would have got had I not opted out of the scheme. Not quite brimming over with hope, is it?

The great thing about having time off work is that it gives one time to read – no matter what state my mind has been in, I've always managed to squeeze in a little bit here and there. It was with this in mind that I picked up Rachel Reiland's autobiography about how she overcame borderline personality disorder.

Cured? Of BPD? No, I thought, *that can't be right*. Everything I'd heard about this condition said, 'You've got it for life – put up with it.'

As I read her inspiring story, I found myself thinking, 'No, it can't be cured – maybe she just didn't really have it in the first place.'

But that just wasn't the case. Where my anger points mainly inwards, hers appeared to be projected mainly outwards – but that's where the differences between our symptoms began and ended. We have the same condition. Well, she *had* the same condition that I find myself floundering about with.

In her book she describes that she was fortunate enough to stumble across a psychotherapist who was a leader in the field. She talks about how her parents were able to supplement the cost of her three sessions a week as she slowly trod that road to recovery.

For almost a full week, I was high as a kite at the thought of this disorder not being a life sentence. I was angry at the thought of my profession and other professions that really matter seeing this as untreatable and incurable. And here – *here* was a book written by a Canadian woman who, around ten years ago, recovered from borderline personality disorder.

I was euphoric. That is, until I was gradually struck by the reality of it all.

She was fortunate in that she'd stumbled across someone who was at the head of the game. What would happen if I wasn't that lucky? What would happen if I underwent years of psychotherapy with someone who was just pretty good? What kind of psychotherapy did the NHS provide? Would it be once a week? Or would it be three times a week as Rachel enjoyed?

Suddenly this felt altogether worse. Great, there's a cure – but you can't have it because you're not in the same fortuitous circumstances that the author of this book found herself. Now I was looking at the world from an altogether more desolate standpoint.

What about me? Why couldn't I be lucky enough to get this treatment?

I had to do more research. This wasn't the end of me. If this Reiland woman could be cured, then so could I.

When I studied psychology at the good old North East London Poly, there was a kind of self-deprecating belief that was common among our lecturers that, by and large, the UK was always around ten years behind the United States in its thinking. There was always an argument that they were better funded or academically lucky. There was no way they were more advanced due to educational excellence. No way, no how.

We were *British* after all.

I wondered to myself if there had been any great advances in the treatment of BPD in the States, or anywhere for that matter, that didn't leave it down to luck or stupendous wealth.

You'll be delighted to know that the internet was fairly dripping with references – not least the great work done by Marsha Linehan. She developed a treatment for borderline personality disorder called Dialectical behavioural therapy – DBT.

One website I visited described it thus: 'Dialectical behaviour therapy (DBT) is a relatively new intervention that combines both cognitive and behavioural techniques in treating borderline personality disorder (BPD).'

Note the words 'relatively new intervention.' This was written in 1993 – 15 years ago! Why the hell were we in the UK still scrabbling around with the belief that this condition is permanent and untreatable?

Chapman and Gratz (2007) describe DBT in the following way:

DBT is a comprehensive treatment for BPD with five key goals, often referred to as the five 'functions' of BPD (Chapman and Linehan, 2005; Lieb, Zanarini, et al. 2004):

1. *Help clients to become more motivated to work towards a life worth living, and to stop engaging in life-threatening behaviours such as self-harm and suicide attempts*

2. *Help clients to learn important new skills needed to reach their goals*

3. *Create a treatment environment that promotes progress and improvement, and help the client structure his or her environment in a way that promotes progress*

4. *Help therapists stay motivated and skilful in helping their clients*

5. *Help clients transfer what they learn in therapy to their real lives outside of treatment*

In order to help clients accomplish these goals, DBT involves four primary components:

1. *Individual therapy*

2. *Telephone consultation*

3. *Group skills training*

4. *Therapist consultation team.*

Apparently Linehan and her followers were experiencing significant success with BPD sufferers using this treatment. I asked Dr Brown if this kind of malarkey could be made available to me.

Well bugger me backwards if it wasn't being practised here and now in darkest central Scotland!

For me, it was interesting to find, on one hand, that I had a psychiatrist who was keen for me to pursue this treatment to combat this nasty condition, at the same time as having a GP who made it clear that he wouldn't have told me about my label of BPD given the negative connotations.

As long as this 'untreatable' myth continues to be sold to the masses, the more the status quo will continue where the sufferers of this condition continue to miss out on the treatment they require.

And I thought *I* was crazy?

That's not all!

There's another treatment that has been developed in England that appeared to be having similar success to DBT. *Mentalisation-based treatment* (MBT) was recently developed by Bateman and Fonagy.

Chapman and Gratz (2007) described this treatment thus:

... MBT is a psychoanalytical treatment, not a cognitive behavioural treatment. What this means is that MBT is more of a 'talk therapy' than DBT. In MBT, most of your time is spent talking with your therapist and learning about yourself and your relationships with others, rather than learning new skills and doing lots of homework assignments, as you would in DBT. Although you might walk away from MBT having picked up some of the same new skills you would get in DBT, you would learn those in a more indirect way.

So, there we are – not one, but two potential treatments. And there was I, like so many of the social care and health worker population, floating along in a little bubble where I believed that the best we could hope for these people (including myself) was containment?

'Why do you believe that this treatment will help *you*?' my mother-in-law asked me one day.

'Because,' I said. I thought this was obvious. 'If I don't have some hope, I'm gonna find myself hanging from a fucking tree.'

That didn't quite come out the way I wanted it to – but it was kind of indicative of just how much I needed this.

*

While I sat on the ludicrously long waiting list for psychotherapy, Dr Brown and I dabbled a little in one of the areas of individual therapy that's provided in DBT.

It's a procedure called 'mindfulness', where the person concerned learns to become more aware of themselves and their environment. So instead of floating off into strange and sad worlds – ignoring the *sensation* of living – the mindful person learns to meditate and focus on the things that they want to focus on.

This type of meditation has its roots in Buddhism. Essentially it involves finding yourself somewhere dark and comfortable – usually seated upright. Then, while you're comfortable, you focus on your breathing. You don't change your breathing, you just keep it steady as your chest rises and falls, rises and falls.

Now the brain – being an inquisitive soul – soon catches on to the idea that you're trying your best to think about nothing. It'll start saying, 'What about this?' and 'What about that?' or 'What's for tea?' and so on.

To the inexperienced meditator, this is a complete pain in the arse. It's so easy to start thinking things like, 'Fuck, I can't even meditate properly. What hope is there for me?'

The guidance that I like is this:

Imagine each rogue thought is an old man with dementia. It's not his fault when he wanders out of his room – he's confused. Just take him gently by the arm and guide him back into his room without judging him. Sounds wonderfully simple, but it takes a lot of practice.

I found a guided meditation commentary on the internet. I found it very effective. So much so that I went straight on into what they called, 'meditation for forgiveness.'

I was guided to imagine myself in a darkened room. In that room, there were two chairs. Along one of the walls to the room there was a door. The door only opened from the inside – so only I had control over who came in.

I was told to imagine a long line of people waiting outside – each had a reason for me to forgive them. If I couldn't forgive them, then I could never move on. When I was ready, I was asked to open the door to let the first person in.

I imagined that it would be Louise at the front of the queue. I opened the door. It wasn't Louise – or my dad, who I thought would be a very close second. It was *me*.

I invited me into the room and sat me down opposite me. I said nothing. I just looked into my lovely blue eyes, reaching out my right hand to hold my left cheek. I leaned my face into my hand and a tear trickled down onto my palm. I never stopped looking into my eyes. I *so* wanted to be forgiven – but I just didn't know why.

All too soon I got up and walked out. It was time for someone else to be welcomed in.

I opened the door again. This time it was Dad. He didn't say anything, he just looked at me without any expression on his face. We sat and looked at each other for what felt like an eternity. I thought about all the things I had to forgive him for. I didn't know where to start. I didn't know *how* to begin to forgive him. He got up and left.

The voice from the internet told me to invite the next person in – only this time it was more directive. It told me to invite me in. Obviously the voice wasn't aware that I'd pre-empted it earlier. Obediently though, I welcomed myself back in. We smiled at each other, sharing the joke – a moment of humour in the sadness. And then it was over.

The whole thing took no longer than half an hour.

It all felt incredibly powerful. I didn't understand any of it. I was terrified. I felt that I couldn't do that again without somebody being present to look after me – to keep me safe. I was willing to wait. I knew I wanted to know more about me. I knew I want to feel more.

One day soon, perhaps. One day soon.

*

I started writing my book in an attempt to make sense of everything. It was my hope that while I was thinking about all the great and the good things that had happened to me I'd experience some kind of *catharsis* – a connection with the world and all its contents.

But no, no, sadly no. In writing it, I felt no connection. I couldn't even feel sad or happy as I remembered all the fine things that had gone on during my rich and varied life. At best, I felt like a concerned observer – a reporter writing about a series of events – some happy, some sad, some pleasantly ridiculous.

I *did* manage some tears at one point. I cried as I remembered what I did to my lovely cat, Ginger. It did, however, help me to realise that having a condition like this isn't about apportioning blame. Like so many mental health problems, BPD is rooted in the organic and the situational. It used to make me laugh when I was studying psychology – whenever we were asked a question about anything, the answer was always 'a bit of both'.

I can't blame Jim for not experiencing the world in the same way as me – nor can I blame Louise, because of extraneous circumstances out of her control, blurring the boundaries between love and sex. I can't blame Stuart for burying his head in the sand. I can't blame me for spinning out of control. We all deal with things, whether they be positive or negative, in different ways. Some people face up to their problems, while others pretend they never happened.

In my experience, both approaches work and both approaches don't. What about Dad, though? What sense can I make of that?

'Why are you writing, Chris?' Dr Brown asked me recently.

'To help me make some sense of all this, I guess,' I said. 'And, hopefully, to help others – whether they're punters or professionals – to realise that there might be some hope with this ridiculous condition.'

She nodded sagely.

'I want to show the normality of madness, how it's something that can happen to anyone – well, *almost* anyone – given the right circumstances. Or the *wrong* circumstances, if you see what I mean?'

She smiled.

'I want to document my passage through therapy too,' I smiled. 'To show folk that there is treatment available that actually works – that doesn't cost the earth and that isn't down to the vagaries of whether or not you've got a good psychotherapist.'

'Okay,' she said, 'okay.'

*

It was one thing to write about my journey into borderline personality disorder and a completely different thing to start dealing with it. Where did I begin? Did I just throw myself to the greater knowledge and experience of the professionals, or did I fight to preserve the essence of what I believed myself to be? After all, what part's me and what part's loon? Can they ever be separated? Do I have to be stripped down to the mental bone, to be built up again, phoenix-like, out of the ashes of my former self?

I've always had great pride in myself for being different. For being a square peg, for thinking differently from those around me, for daring to say the things others want to say but can't. It goes right back to my childhood after Mum died. No, that's not true – it goes back before then. It goes back to the time where my mum made me feel special, different from other people.

I was scared that if I looked back, exploring the development of my shonky self, I would find things I didn't want to uncover. What if it was the treatment I received at my mother's hands that made me the person I was today, and not the neglect and sexual abuse I experienced at the hands of my dad and Louise?

In the years following Mum's death, I hung onto the hopes and dreams that I'd created with her support. As she grew in godliness, so dad grew in evilness and uselessness. I polarised them completely. Good and evil, Yin and Yang, Godley and Creme ...

Was Dad ever that evil and, following the same line of thought, was Mum ever that good?

If Mum was everything that was angelic and beautiful in the world, where did that leave me – her favourite child? Perhaps the whole situation made me wonderful through my association with this wonderful person?

If she's that wonderful and I'm that wonderful – where the hell does that leave the rest of the world? How can anyone or anything ever live up to those expectations?

Maybe, just maybe I'm not a square peg. Maybe it's the rest of you. Nobody can fit in with my expectations – no one can fit this near impossible heaven on earth that I've created.

I went back to Corby to find myself. I went to the crab apple tree where me and Bruno had holed up while pelting Corby's walking dead. It was so nearly the same. It still had its two tiers – but it had no apples. Someone had torn out its heart. It was still alive, but someone had dug into its bark and set it on fire. Oh fuck, it's *ET* all over again.

The crab apple tree is a symbol of me. Only *Gardeners' Question Time* could help me now.

Inappropriate humour. That same humour that's shielded me from reality all my life. Thank god for inappropriate humour.

I'm not sure what I'd been expecting from my visit to that most sacred of trees. Perhaps I was hoping to see something of the spirit of me. I could still see us there, Bruno and I giggling and snottering at the misfortune of others – but these were ghosts. My youthful self had gone.

I took a walk up to the cemetery. Perhaps Mum and Dad would have some words of wisdom. Dad had been buried on top of Mum – we'd used the same gravestone to mark his departure. It has all the usual stuff hewn into it – 'loved … greatly missed mother.' The pretty standard cemetery phrases.

After my mum's blurb, the words 'and also' had been inscribed to introduce the reader to my dad's demise. Why did that bother me so much? I guess I thought, as far as an introduction to an epitaph goes, it's just a bit shit. I don't know, it feels a bit like, 'Featuring, for one night only …'

But that doesn't matter, does it? I was also irritated by the fact that some unknown mourner had seen fit to change the plot into some kind of theme park of sadness. There were artificial flowers, an unkempt lavender bush that was threatening to overrun all of the adjoining plots, some solar-powered lights at the bottom of the stone and, hanging from the tree, just at the foot of the plot, were some wooden wind chimes – clonking gently in the breeze. They could stay, I decided, but as for the rest – for fuck's sake …

I cut back the lavender bush and removed some of the less tasteful decorations from the grave. I gently placed a bunch of sunflowers on the grass in front of the stone. There, that's better. I stood and stared down at the ground. The chimes gently caressing my ears as I hoped and dreamed for some kind of answer. I cried as I imagined the tangled mess of wood and bone and earth and sinew that lay under the neatly mown grass.

Standing at the graveside, a single thought bubbled to the surface. *How did it get to this?*

I'd lost my job, I'd caused my wife so much emotional upset that she didn't know whether to love me or shoot me, I'd destroyed our relationship with infidelity and erratic behaviour. I'd pushed my family away and I didn't know what to do with them. I loved them and hated them all at the same time. My children had an uncertain future, their home and lives like sand slipping through my fingers – all because of me.

I screamed. The mourners quietly attending to the graves of their loved ones looked up in shock as my terror and anguish echoed around the cemetery.

This has to stop, I thought. *I cannot and will not continue like this.*

*

As a social worker and a life coach, I was bestowed with an empathy that allowed me to see the discomfort and suffering of other people – even at times when they thought they were hiding it well. This may well be a function of my BPD – where I have become stress-intolerant, driven by a desire to identify and sooth psychological discomfort in others. I've been accused of being telepathic on more than one occasion.

That all felt like a distant memory now. I saw anything and everything that happened around me not as an event in itself, but in the impact that it had on me. The effect that Susan's suicide, the death of my student and my clients had on me was all that had come to matter. I was unable to think of these things in terms of the impact it must have had on them, their friends and their families. It had all become about me. I measured the world through the amount of suicidal thoughts and images of self-harm it generated at any given time. My thoughts and concerns for others had all but vanished.

I needed to get out of my head. I needed to see things as others do – feel things that others feel.

There were nights where I would lay awake thinking about my lovely children, who I knew I adored. But while this happened I was alarmed at my lack of feelings for them. I taunted myself with vivid, awful thoughts of them suffering terrible injuries, but there was no emotion there. It was almost like I'd forgotten how to love. And then – for a week, a month, a day, or even an afternoon, that ability would come back to me and I would bathe in its warmth.

This inconsistency is so difficult for me to deal with. It must be nearly impossible for others.

This had to stop. I could not and would not continue like this.

*

Recently I read a book called *Against Therapy* by Jeffrey Masson. After taking it, as prescribed (by me), three times a day I concluded that therapy was clearly for folk who had no friends.

I've always been amazed at how the tendrils of self-doubt surround and caress me gently – duping me into thinking, 'Here's an old friend to look after me. I don't need these other people – there's no one who wants me around anyway' and so on into a self-destructive miasma.

I had friends. For fuck's sake – I had so many friends I was beating them off with a stick. It's just that they couldn't understand this nonsense that was going on for me. Sometimes they'd even collude with me. They couldn't work in a systematic way that challenged my faulty thoughts and reinforced the good ones.

No, I needed help. I can see now that the simple act of reading that book was helping me to sabotage the help that was potentially available to me. I needed to be able to treat my friends as friends, and professionals as professionals.

Most of all, more than anything, I wanted to be able to function in society, in the workplace, and with my friends in a consistent way.

I wanted to show that this bastard condition is treatable and that there's a whole world out there – where I, and other folk with this illness, can love and be loved.

One of the central beliefs of coaching draws on an analogy of a plane depressurising in flight. During the pre-flight pep talk, the passengers are told that, in such an event, they must look after themselves first. Only then will they be able to look after others.

And that, dear reader, was me. Until I sorted out what was going on in my head, I would continue to clatter around, causing psychological destruction and mayhem wherever I went.

I was due to start a course of psychotherapy at the beginning of November 2008, and god, I was ready for it.

CHAPTER 12

THE WAIT FOR THERAPY

The wait for therapy was terrible. I felt like a punch-drunk boxer whose corner should have thrown the towel in three rounds ago. Instead, I continued slugging, head down. *Keep on going. Keep ... on ... going.* Like so many folk in the mental health system, I'd been left languishing on a year-long waiting list. I'd left the family home with the belief that my behaviour had become so erratic that it was harming the children.

I also felt that my non-relationship with Poppy was causing me irreparable damage. Her bland, 'shit happens' responses to my devastation at the death of another person I'd worked with, calling me a drama queen when I told her I felt I was on a precipice, the physical rejection – it was all taking its toll. I was too scared to live, but terrified of dying. The years of psychiatric drugs were having a negative effect on me. Weight gain is one of the most common side effects for many. Which would you rather be – fat or mad? Tough choice ...

I can't say I blame Poppy. On and off I'd given her a tricky life. Looking back though, I think I did my best, which may or may not have been good enough. But it was really all I had.

I have to laugh now when I think back to how furious she was with my family that they hadn't told her the extent of my madness when she first started seeing me – as if I'd come with some kind of guarantee where I could be returned to the shop to have my factory settings restored. But back then it sickened me. We were utterly done.

I presented myself as homeless to the housing department in Edinburgh, at the same time as trying to present myself with a semblance of pride, self-esteem … self-worth? I'm not sure which, but I'm pretty sure I failed.

I left my home with the lingering image of Poppy cuddling the kids in my mind, all of them with their backs to me. I felt defeated and I loathed myself. I was isolated and wallowing in a deep pit of despair.

I popped back the following day in the car, because I just couldn't stand the feeling of being away from my kids. I'd hoped that just being near them, in the car park next to the house, would somehow bring me some solace. I've no idea how long I sat there for. Poppy's brother came out to the car to speak to me. He was kind but firm, telling me that my very presence was freaking everyone out.

I drove back to the homeless accommodation – that oxymoronic place – that I'd been provided with. Staying there the first night, I reflected on the fact that perhaps I hadn't stressed the suicidal ideation I'd been experiencing sufficiently, since the windows of the flat opened wide enough for me to throw a cow through.

It was big, awful and empty. I was self-harming as if it was going out of fashion. I broke one of the knuckles of my right hand after one particularly unsuccessful fight with the kitchen wall. I cut myself with anything that was readily available. I had bruises all over my face from where I'd punched myself. These behaviours that had been previously been so secretive were now emerging wherever I went. I was punching myself in public – an almost Tourette's-like compulsion – while screaming and shouting at some unseen assailant, traumatic memories cascading, unbidden, through my mind.

One such episode happened while I was sitting with Poppy in the car. Almost casually, she explained that the children had asked why I hadn't left earlier. I'd felt – hoped – that leaving was the one thing I'd got right, and now here I was being told my children didn't want me in their lives. No amount of face punching could make that better.

*

One of the things that comes with losing your job is uncontrollable debt. We live in a world where shiny things are made immediately accessible to us by the truckload, through why-wait-when-you-can-have-it-yesterday credit. But these fine purveyors of instant finance are less friendly when one approaches them uttering the words, 'I haven't got a job anymore so I can't pay you ... er ... *anything* just now.'

Combine that with a benefits system that sees claimants as shirkers, as malingerers – claiming money fraudulently because they can't be arsed to work, and you get a perfect storm.

As an ex-social worker I had a perfect record of supporting folk with their claims for disability living allowance (DLA) or Personal Independence Payment (PIP) as it is now – money to which they were entitled. But when it came to claiming it for myself – well, that was an entirely different story. Even though I knew that the claims process was particularly treacherous for people with mental health problems, I was gobsmacked when I received the letter back explaining I was entitled to nothing.

I knew all about the review process – even though I had never needed it in the past – and very soon I found myself in a horrible situation, wearing my Ted Baker suit, crying and wailing at that small group of folk who were destined to award me the smallest amount of DLA possible.

I wore that suit to the meeting to give me confidence – to make me feel happy about myself. As the meeting went on, it became clear that it wasn't quite working.

I'd failed to realise that the mere fact I'd been able to get into a suit – even though I'd put it on to make this process somehow manageable – would be used against me in the assessment process.

Well, I could hear them thinking. *If he's able to attend an interview smartly dressed, then he's obviously able to look after himself.*

I was crying uncontrollably – contorting my face to get even the simplest words out. The panel of a doctor, a lawyer, a disability expert, and an official recorder, all women, all looked incredibly uncomfortable at my internal angst. I didn't care though. These bastards – these representatives of a benefits system that just isn't fit for purpose – were going to endure just a flavour of my mental turmoil.

I felt ridiculous, pilloried. I imagined myself in the stocks with people laughing and mocking and jeering, throwing whatever shite they had to hand. I felt like my mum had dressed me that morning, and now I was gradually sinking – a little boy in a man's suit.

I knew the system. I reluctantly accepted that my word, and those of my GP and my psychiatrist, were insufficient for the Department of Work and Pensions to award me anything other than a pittance. And so I bit the bullet, swallowed my pride, and accepted that the application would have more validity if I got a social worker to support me through the process.

This was uncomfortable to say the least. I'd been a social worker in Edinburgh and, as such, I was reasonably well known among my colleagues across the city. The thought of sharing my crumbling world with someone I knew was intolerable.

Thankfully there was a system within the department to seal my records, so that they could only be read by the people who worked with me directly, or their managers. In no time at all I was back at the good old Royal Edinburgh Hospital, chatting with a mental health officer (a social worker who was long experienced in working with people with mental health problems) in a brightly lit, sparsely furnished interview room.

I remember pressing my mouth to my right forearm – a precursor to biting it – as this bright, middle-aged woman guided me once again through the form I knew so well. Looking back, I can't help but wonder how difficult it must be for people who are stepping into this shadowy world of benefit claiming without any knowledge or experience.

'It's okay for you to bite your arm if you want,' said the MHO. With that one statement, I felt somehow accepted – that I wasn't being judged for all my whacky behaviours. Throughout that interview I bit by arm with different levels of severity, although I never drew any blood. The pain somehow made the process more tolerable. That single act of empathy helped me more than I can put into words.

Needless to say, within a few months I was getting the benefits to which I was entitled – something that made the rest of the process a bit more bearable.

The guy who was employed by the City of Edinburgh Council to support people who got into difficulties with debt was, in my case, out of his depth and overworked. He reminded me of me when I was a social worker. He would promise the earth, then he'd offer significantly less, each time coming up short.

My creditors were getting more and more arsey, and I just didn't have an answer for them. Eventually, against my misplaced loyalty for a council service, I turned to the Dark Side and went to the Citizen's Advice Bureau. And I never looked back. The guy who helped me ensured I kept all my creditors plates spinning in a way that was manageable for me and acceptable for them.

The whole process, though, had been exhausting and demoralising – queuing up for hours on end with other social work clients, all of us unable to acknowledge each other, avoiding eye contact because of the horrible, churning, internalised feeling of abject failure in the pits of our stomachs.

There must be a better way.

*

With my financial ducks in a row, I was able to reflect on how I'd ended up where I was. It was a process that provided the tiniest chink of light, a process that asked the question, 'What now?'

Dr Brown, my psychiatrist, told me the drugs I'd been taking for depression were less than useless, and, as such, I should stop taking them immediately. With all my knowledge, life and professional experience, I can be a bit of an arse at times. This was one of those times. Taking her at her word, I instantly stopped taking my Venlafaxine.

There was no tapering off for me – oh no. I'd be fine, I told myself. The sooner I was off the pills, the sooner I'd be able to take ... *Good god!*

I'd like to state here and now, that if anyone reading this wants to come off Venlafaxine – otherwise known as Effexor – you must do it slowly. You must gradually reduce the dose over weeks, if not months. Otherwise ... well, otherwise you might enter into the bizarre world of pain I experienced for nearly a month.

I'm sure antidepressants have wide ranging effects – and side effects – for millions of people. As mentioned earlier, my libido (specifically my ability to er, reach fruition) had been hugely subdued. The sudden removal of the chemical castration meant that ... er ... how can I put this? It was like I was suddenly a teenager again, and that I was having to deal with the head of steam that had built up over the years. In short, my parts worked.

Alongside that, there was the weird pain / pleasure thing that seems to be known across the internet as 'brain zaps'. They're like little bolts of lightning that start in the middle of the brain and feel like they fly out the end of one's nose. They aren't entirely unpleasant. They hurt – I'm not entirely sure if this was to do with my attraction to pain – but I rather looked forward to them. Initially they were frequent (they occurred 10 –15 times a day) but over the months they gradually ebbed away to nothing.

I would have benefitted from knowing about both of these symptoms before I started experiencing them.

With the isolation and time on my hands, my headspace returned to a place it had been in my teens. When I closed my eyes – though often I didn't need to close my eyes – I was met with the images of people I'd known well who'd died. They were all being thrown onto a huge heap by some unseen giant using a massive pitchfork, their bodies lifeless, my vision of their faces vivid. Mum, Dad, my cats, my goldfish, my tortoise, my nana, Paul, a friend from school who'd died in a car accident – they were all on the pile. There was another athlete who'd died in his early twenties from sudden death syndrome, my friend who'd taken her own life, my student who'd died of cancer … countless clients in an endless, unforgiving cascade.

Mark Speight, the children's TV presenter, hanged himself on the 7th April 2007. I became obsessed with the events surrounding it. I wanted – *needed* – to know everything there was to know about it. Again, it felt like the door had been left slightly ajar for me.

I'm not entirely sure of the circumstances that brought me there, but I found myself in the horses' field next to where I'd once lived. It was a fairly sunny day, with white fluffy clouds bobbing about. The children were elsewhere. I'm not entirely sure where they were, but they don't feature at all in this memory.

I zoned out, dissociated. I have no recollection of where I went or what I did in that short period of time. Maybe it was 20 minutes, maybe an hour. When the world came back, I was lying on the ground near a holiday chalet that had been put up in the field – and I was eating mud. My mouth was full of it and both hands were covered.

A man from the chalet shouted, 'Are you okay, mate?'

Perhaps this was all it took to get me out of the dissociative fugue, or maybe I'd already come out of it. At any rate, I jumped to my feet, shouted back something like, 'Yeah, I'm fine' and wandered off towards the stables.

Just like all those years before in the hospital, I was relaxed, calm and disconnected. I walked into one of the stables and closed over the lower door so I could still see out. I took one of the horse's lead ropes, threw it over a beam in the roof and fashioned a functioning noose. I stood on one of the horse's buckets – a pink one – while I checked that the beam was strong enough to take my weight. I swung on it without even a creak. I put the noose around my neck, looking at the lovely sky and listening to the wind as it gently washed through the trees.

It was a perfect day to die. The air felt clean in my nose as I put the noose over my head, feeling the rope against my neck. Possibly the same sabotaging voice as before spoke out – again, quietly ...

I wonder if this is what's meant by 'kicking the bucket'?

With that, the spell was broken. I was suddenly shocked, exposed to the terror that such a close encounter with death can bring. I took the noose down from the beam – and stepped off the bucket. I left the stable, looking back incredulously at what had so nearly happened.

*

'Well, they seemed really laid back ... '

This was one of the key comments that made me fall in love with Ella. She is irreverent, hilarious, lovely, and beautiful. It was 2008 and we'd originally met online, where she'd openly mocked the photos on my life coaching website. To be fair, I thought they were pretty good, having been taken by a guy who was a self-proclaimed member of the paparazzi. Ella, however, had been a bit more scathing.

She'd expressed an interest in life coaching and how it was done, what was meant by it, and the like. She told me that in exchange for some words of wisdom on this hybrid of counselling, mentoring, cognitive behavioural therapy and management skills, she, being a photographer and all, would take some altogether more impressive pictures for my website.

This all turned out to be so much stuff and fluff. An easy friendship gradually moved into so much more. In among all my mental chaos, Ella went out of her way to take her time to understand me, listen to me, and work out that I was so much more than my illness. She went out of her way to learn more and more about this crazy condition I'd been lumbered with. She did her research and found a variety of books, from memoirs to academic tomes, that helped both me and her to understand what might be going on for me.

She was there when I started writing again – something I'd stopped doing, except in a professional capacity, for years. Living hundreds of miles away, she patiently listened to me on the phone as I took my faltering, Bambi-like steps back into the world of storytelling. I'd always loved writing science fiction and making up stories I felt hadn't been told yet. I liked crafting the kind of swashbuckling tales that I'd like to read myself.

There was a problem though. After so much time, whenever I tried to write fiction, it kept on coming out as an autobiography. The main character wasn't just like me, he was me. I know it's important to write about what you know, but this was taking it to the extreme. She gently coaxed me to write that autobiography – to clear the way for future fiction. Gentle hands.

In a world where I'd failed spectacularly, here was someone telling me I had some worth – that I was valued and, after some time, something to be cherished. I was open and honest with her. This wasn't going to be an easy ride. I was fucking crazy. Unpredictable. Suicidal.

Using a diary, she helped me to chart the course of my dissociation, something that I was only just beginning to get some kind of handle on. Together we looked for the triggers and patterns, anything that would help us get an idea of what this was about.

I fell for her, hook line and sinker. I was constantly questioning the validity of my feelings and that made it astonishingly hard for her – but she held on tight. One minute I'd love her dearly – hugging her as if my life depended on it – the next, I was unable to feel anything. The very act of touching her was so alien to me, to the extent that it felt that I was handling a piece of meat. I'm reliably informed that women don't like that type of disconnection.

She took the time to monitor me as I dipped in and out of reality. My periods of dissociation would last for anything between three days and three weeks. Each time I'd reliably emerge, still loving her, still ready for that life-depends-upon-it hug.

Which takes us to that day in a Corby cemetery, where I'd finally decided she should meet my parents. Mum had been gone for 31 years, Dad for nearly 18. Ella stood with me in silence – I thought introductions would have been, at best, weird – respectfully absorbing the atmosphere.

She waited until we were walking away to hit me with what I still believe is one of the greatest one-liners ever: 'Well, they seemed really laid back ... '

That's my Ella, that is.

Ella's point of view:

When Chris dissociates it feels like he has gone away and I know he will be home at some point. It is like a very thick block of ice between us. I can just about see him, but he is distorted. Every now and again he seems clearer for just a few seconds, and then he is gone again.

My instinct is to hug and love Chris, but it is just not what he needs when he can hardly recognise me. When he dissociates he suddenly goes white in the face and looks like he might throw up. I used to take it all personally, thinking I'd done or said something to trigger this. We diarised his moods and it does, unfortunately, seem quite random. I carry on with my world while he is gone; as long as he is safe and warm and fed it is very simple. I just wait it out and it is always lovely to have him back. He is either fun, intelligent, with a massive thirst for life, or he is absent, distant, unwell. It is like living with two different people.

Luckily when Chris is back in the world we have a deep love for each other and we make each other laugh every day. I feel blessed to have such a wonderful relationship with him and the difficult times are far outweighed by the loving times.

'The Second Rule of Fight Club Is That You Do Not Talk About Fight Club'

I was still mad. My emotions were still swinging out of my control. I still found it difficult to see any kind of a future. Although I loved it – love it – I still saw writing as a hobby, not something I'd ever make any kind of living out of. After being sent on my way in social work, I struggled to see anywhere where my particular skillset could nestle down and make itself at home.

I had a discussion with my psychiatrist that went something a little like this ...

'I've found a group of people with borderline personality disorder who meet up regularly in Edinburgh. I was thinking about—'

'No! You mustn't meet up with them – these are really sick people!'

'Hey, I resemble that remark!'

Bugger that, I thought – *these are MY PEOPLE!*

It'll come as a surprise to nobody that the people who attended this group – which met up in a variety of funky cafes around Edinburgh while calling themselves 'The Meadows Book Group' – were fabulous. They weren't 'borderlines', they weren't aggressive or manipulative, they were people like me who were trying to make some sense of this bizarre condition. Membership of this group was incredibly validating. Surely if these people, with the same condition as me, were lovely, then that might mean that, at a push, I might have the potential to be ...

Naomi, who ran the group (at the same time insisting she didn't – although we all knew it would all fall to bits without her), worked for a collective advocacy organisation in Edinburgh called CAPS.

Their aim was to bring people together so their voices were louder and their impact was stronger. She was – still is – wonderful. She helped me to see skills and talents that I thought had died with my career in social work. She liked the way I was able to talk clearly about what it's like to live with BPD and what the practicalities are around it. In no time at all she had me speaking at conferences, helping with projects, and helping her speak openly and candidly with other folk with the condition, social and health care professionals and friends and families.

I found myself playing a voice part in a short film about dissociation, called *Submerged*. Johanna, the filmmaker, enjoyed my input so much that she later asked me to be the subject of a full-length documentary.

*

'What's the worst thing you've ever done?' Ella asked, pretty much out of the blue one day.

Quick as a flash, I replied I'd shagged Louise, a woman 17 years my elder, so close that she was like a mother to me, a woman who had welcomed me into her home – fed me, watered me, nurtured me, provided me with a surrogate family. And I'd repaid them by having a sordid affair.

'How old were you?' Ella asked, not unkindly, almost blandly.

'I … er … I was 15.' I was remembering the conversation I'd had with Jim all those years ago. I'd been so keen for him not to think of what had happened between me and Louise as abuse. On top of that, I hadn't wanted to appear a victim in his eyes.

Ella changed tack ever so slightly. 'If you'd had a social work client who'd approached you with this story, what would you think?'

Cognitively I knew the answer to this. It was really that clear cut, that black and white. I wanted to be honest and open but emotionally it was far more complicated. I loved Louise. She'd been such a massive part of my life. Yes, she'd been a mother to me. And it had all turned upside down.

'It's abuse,' I eventually conceded. The words felt almost hollow. I thought again of a conversation I'd had with Jim. If you were personally responsible for your behaviour at 18, what was so different about 17, 16, or 15? I was stuck. I remembered my son when he was 15. He seemed so young, so naïve. Perhaps it would have been different for him. He'd been exposed to less. Well no, maybe not less. But he'd been exposed to a *different* world, perhaps one where he'd not been asked to grow up so quickly.

Had I grown up quickly? Sure, I could hoover and make mince soup and put up Christmas decorations from an early age, but somewhere my development had halted.

But how could it be abuse when I was more than big enough to look after myself, when I was able to physically push her away?

The shame and guilt I'd been carrying around all these years engulfed me like an old, familiar blanket. Male childhood sexual abuse was something that was so rarely talked about. Culturally there were undercurrents of, 'You lucky bastard – getting your end away to an older woman.' It was a physical act, after all.

Women just didn't fit the template, the stereotype of what an abuser looked like: the Child Catcher out of Chitty Chitty Bang Bang, the slimy stranger that calls over to little girls with a promise of sweeties if she gets in his car. Think of Stranger Danger! Think of gangs of marauding paedophiles congregating on the internet, preying on our innocent children ...

I felt sick. I'd been brought up in that culture, that world where a woman in her thirties with a husband and a family just didn't fit ...

And anyway, she'd been abused herself. She'd told me. We know that, statistically, people who have been abused are more likely to go on and abuse themselves. Louise herself had told me that it had been difficult for her to separate physical and emotional love. So she was a victim in all this too. And yet I knew that those statistics still represented a tiny minority of people who'd been abused.

Somehow, I was able to see myself as different from my social work clients, the people who present as vulnerable in situations such as these. Vulnerable and innocent victims of abuse. If that stood for them, why not me? What was so different about me?

Ella chummed me down to visit Louise and her family. She had no idea what to expect, so she came armed with a casserole. The best form of defence, and all that.

She'd been surprised that on meeting Louise she'd found her to be friendly, hospitable, intelligent, witty, well-read and kind – all the things I remembered. We had the casserole and spent some time chatting about the old days, carefully navigating around those nasty abuse rocks. At one point, it felt that Louise was interviewing Ella as my future partner – much in the way a mother would. Did she love me? Was she kind? What about her own family? What about Chris's mental health?

Finally, Louise and I were left alone in a small room. After some light chit chat around the loveliness of Ella, I raised the question of abuse once again.

'I've told you I'm sorry,' she said. 'What more do you want?'

Fair point. What did I want? What could she do to make everything better? I was stumped. I guess in retrospect it would have been great if she hadn't told everyone her version of what had happened – that I'd been in my mid-twenties and, as such, had been a consenting adult knowingly entering into a relationship. It had been our secret, after all. Seemingly, there was no answer. It was clear she couldn't give me what I needed, whatever it was.

We played some sixties music, returning to that same old comfortable relationship we'd had, on and off, for years. Ella must have been thinking something along the lines of, *What the fuck just happened there?*

Jim came to visit me. For years I'd wanted his approval. I so wanted him to be proud of me and to approve of me. And yet here I was, crazy, having lost my job and left my family, now having a long-distance relationship with a photographer who lived 300 miles away. I felt sick with shame. I was prepared to say anything to Jim to make this all better ... to make him feel better about me.

As part of this plan, I explained at length how I was a lying, duplicitous bastard who couldn't be trusted. It was like I couldn't tell the difference between fact and fiction – that my whole life had been a façade. Looking back, I was presenting him with one of those eternal puzzles – if a liar tells you that they're a liar, then, by the simple fact that they've told you, they must be telling the truth ... there lies infinity.

I don't remember too much about his visit. I recall he had an angry outburst when I explained that I'd told his ex-girlfriend about me and Louise.

'Why the fuck would you do that?' paraphrases him well I think.

He also delivered a shiny new X-Box, complete with Halo – a mindless shoot 'em up kind of a game – I could argue that playing computer games is not entirely unlike embarking on guided mindfulness, but I think that would be a little frivolous.

But mostly, the fact that he'd come up to see me, was what I valued most.

*

During one particularly bad episode, I was screaming, biting and punching myself. Ella told me she had Derek on the other line, and that he was going to talk to me. I was devastated. I couldn't not talk to him though – it was Derek! Even through my madness I heard myself apologising again and again as I paused to scream and bite and punch ... all the while he was gently telling me it was okay. It would be okay.

Derek came up. It was so great to see him. In the maelstrom of what had been going on he was, probably completely unintentionally, a guiding light. He knew I had the craziness about me, but over the years I'd somehow hidden some of the more unsavoury parts from him.

He'd always been my best friend – we'd been through so much together. Even after huge gaps in seeing each other – of which there were more than I'd have liked – we somehow always manage to pick up as if we were half way through a sentence. Over the past few years, though, the distance between get-togethers had grown; I'd become so absorbed in all things family and work that I'd only see him once every one or two years.

So there he was. It was like we'd never been apart. Before I knew it, he was off buying me a sound system so that I could get more X-Box bangs for my bucks and to ensure I could annoy the neighbours with my poor taste in music.

I'd bought a projector to do presentations when I was a life coach. This fine piece of technology came in very handy for showing films and playing Halo. The new sound system made the whole experience immersive. We set it up in the spare bedroom, a room that had weird hooks attached to two of the walls, with no real windows to mention. We tactfully christened it the 'Gimp Room' as we imagined the horrors and weird perversions that may have gone on in there. It turns out the large hooks on the wall, that wouldn't look out of place in a slaughterhouse, were for putting up a washing line ... That said, it remains the Gimp Room to this day.

We spent hours watching *The Deer Hunter* and shooting aliens over the few days of his visit.

I don't think I'd fully registered it, but Derek had timed his visit around my birthday. We've always made a point of trying to talk to each other on our birthdays – and only very rarely would we exchange gifts or cards. That's just the way we'd kind of evolved.

Imagine my gobsmacked joy then, when I watched him, this manly fireman sort of a guy, walking down the stairs of my apartment, carrying a Thornton's chocolate fudge cake with a lit candle sticking out the top, singing, 'Happy birthday ... '

I was so happy, I very nearly exploded.

Only Derek could deliver a 'Jesus loves you, but I think you're a cunt!' card to compliment this most sensitive of moments.

*

Naomi had told me about some research into borderline personality disorder that she felt I might be interested in taking part in. Given the apparent paucity of clinical knowledge in the area, I was keen to help in any way I could.

In no time at all I was meeting up with the consultant psychiatrist who was heading up the study. We'd chosen a fine café, supplier of all things cakey and sweet next to the Royal Edinburgh Hospital that had the wonderful name Loopy Lorna's!

After some friendly chit chat and banter, I felt that it was time to get to the root of this clinician's experience, skills and knowledge – and perhaps find out a little about his motivations. 'What training have you had in the area of BPD?' I asked.

'What, including my basic medical training?'

'Yes.'

'And my psychiatry training?'

'Well, yes.'

'And any training I've had as a consultant?'

'Yes.'

'... er ... it's about half a day in total.'

He went on to tell me that this was essentially why he was doing this research. It was his attempt to further the clinical knowledge – of which I think we'd established there was very little – around borderline personality disorder, or emotionally unstable personality disorder as many clinicians in the UK were beginning to call it. (That was how it was described in the NICE guidelines.)

'And you're a specialist?' I smiled.

'Yes,' he grinned back.

There were a number of different parts to the study: questionnaires, open interviews and the like. The two parts that stood out most for me were the following.

1) I sat in front of a computer screen with a switch that I would click one way for 'Yes' and the other way for 'No'. I was told that I was going to be shown the faces of a hundred different folk, of different ages and genders. I had to decide whether or not I'd trust that person given the limited information of what their face looked like.

   Simple.

   I took my participation in this study very seriously, so I wanted to answer as authentically as I could to expand the world's knowledge of my stinky condition. I had a preconceived notion that I, being a carey-sharey social-workery type, would have a very positive outlook on my fellow folk and, as such, I'd trust everyone.

   Imagine my surprise, then, when I scrutinised face after face, that I trusted nobody. Not one. I might have fudged the results a little when my internal dialogue finally persuaded me to respond positively to the face of an older lady … I didn't want to appear to be a complete crackpot.

2) Another part of the study involved a functional MRI scan – my head was read by the big clunking machine while I completed a number of simple tasks. I explained to the consultant that I'd been "bottled" in my youth and that I was intrigued to find out if there had been any permanent damage caused by this enthusiastic beating.

After the readings, we popped into the little side room where the MRI dudes sat and pored over the resulting images.

The first shock for me – and this was as huge as it was unexpected – was that the inside of my head, by and large, looked pretty much like the inside of anyone else's head. To this day I've no idea what I thought I was going to see – possibly some confirmation that, although I walk among you, I'm not quite like you? Who knows?

As the image passed by on the screen though, there it was, for all the world to see, a dent on my skull with ancient scar tissue to match. Confirmation that my skull had been fractured all those years ago. The consultant shouted, 'Look, right there is where your skull was fractured,' or something very similar.

Hard evidence that I could take back to my own psychiatrist to enable her to utter that now famous line regarding the effect of the fracture on my future mental health, 'Well, it wouldn't have helped ... '

*

Ella and I were in Nottingham to see Mumford and Sons. I was driving around the intriguing one-way system they have there when I started to become agitated. I rapidly pulled the car over into a lay-by and, with that (from Ella's perspective anyway), I was gone.

From what she could see, I'd changed from being a forty-something-year-old man to a young child – possibly around four. Apparently, I was very obedient, which, on reflection, doesn't really sound like me. This was a fine thing, since I can't imagine what would have happened had I continued to drive. This was alarming. She knew my mental health problem was multifaceted, but this was something new entirely.

She phoned around a number of friends (she knows a psychiatrist, a psychologist and a social worker). It was like she was having a multidisciplinary meeting in the car. What should she do? Where should she take me?

Thankfully, the consensus was, since I appeared relatively quiet and calm, that I should go back to hers, which was about a two-hour drive away. At one point she had to go to the loo. She pulled in next to a pub and then thought, 'What on earth do I do?' It was like leaving a child in a car in an unfamiliar area, only this child was the size of a man and, for all she knew, was liable to wander off. She locked me in the car, rushed off and rushed back, and was delighted to find I was still there.

I seemed to be lost in an inner world until we arrived at the gate to her garden. I re-emerged momentarily. 'Oh, hello ...' I think I smiled, before vanishing off again.

While she was watching this child in a man's body, I was enjoying the experience of feeling like a boy in a boy's body. I was lost in the world of my childhood, at the square round the back of my house where me and my friends used to play a variety of games like hide and seek, kick the can, kerby, and football. In my mind we were catching butterflies in jam jars near Calum McKay's house, and all my friends were there – Michael Murray, George Taylor, Paul Rigby and his sister Cheryl, Calum ...

The sky was a vibrant blue and the bricks of the garages that had served as goals for our football matches were a crisp yellow. All the while I was playing I knew my mum was there, looking after me, looking out for me. I never saw her throughout this entire episode, but she was just there, and all was well in the world. My world.

I loved it. I bathed in it. The whole wonderful experience began to break down, though, when memories of the real world began encroaching. The clincher was when I remembered I had an eighteen-year-old son. There was absolutely no coming back from that – no matter how much my mind twisted and turned to hang onto my childhood world, I was completely unable to consolidate parenthood with being a 4-year-old child.

In total, this episode, this period of dissociation, lasted for about 3 weeks. Ella put me in a darkened room with loud American cop shows blaring in the background, feeding me crisps and high carb food.

We often joke that with the TV shows I'm getting two for the price of one. Although I seem to be absorbed in the dramas in my dissociative state, there's very little I can remember about them when I resurface.

Frivolity aside though, we were both on a steep learning curve and Ella, bless her cotton socks, was demonstrating loud and clear that she was in it for the long haul.

*

I'd waited over a year for the confirmation that therapy was to start on such and such a date. The letter, when it came, was disappointing. I hadn't been invited to start therapy – this was a letter telling me that, after a year, I was going to be assessed for my suitability for psychotherapy. After all this time – after raising all my hopes – I was struck by the stark realisation I could come away with nothing. And then what? To say I was desperate was putting it mildly.

The assessment took place at the psychotherapy department at the Royal Edinburgh Hospital. Already I was replaying my last failed exposure to the sacred art almost 20 years ago. The guy who'd told me that my dreams about my teeth breaking and falling out of my mouth had been a reflection of my fear of dealing with what was going on inside my head – the same guy who tried to flog me an extra session a week at whatever price … What if it was the same guy all these years later? Would he recognise me? Would I recognise him? Would it be the same old sitting-in-silence-until-I-started-to-babble experience? Was I up for that?

With my mind still spinning, I was escorted into a large, comfortable office to meet a guy who was the spitting image of Benny from ABBA.

It felt like an interview. He stopped short of asking me what I would be bringing to psychotherapy, but it didn't feel far off. I wanted to be open and honest, at the same time hoping against hope that my answers would be the right ones to get me that golden ticket. I knew from people I'd spoken to before that I had to be just the right level of crazy. Too mad, and they couldn't deal with me – too sane and I didn't need them.

I told him about my self-harming and was completely knocked off my stride when he said, 'Well, that's not very intelligent, is it?'

I stifled my urge to break my chair across his teeth, and answered meekly, 'No, no … I suppose it isn't.'

I would have said anything at this stage to get in the door. I would have dressed in a chicken suit and danced down the Royal Mile if he'd told me that was the way in. I'm not sure he knew the level of the power he was wielding.

He told me he thought I'd be suitable for group psychotherapy. *No! Fuck no!* I wanted a psychotherapist of my very own! Someone who would be mine, someone who would cure me of this fucking bastard, whatever it was, condition …

I gave him a greatly diluted version of my concerns, to which he replied, 'In one-to-one psychotherapy, you have one mirror reflecting back at you. In group psychotherapy you have a number of mirrors.'

I was sold. It actually sounded like exactly what I needed. Only I had to meet his colleague who ran the group, just to ensure I was right for the group and the group was right for me. Another assessment, just what I fucking needed.

Over the next week or so, I tried to persuade myself that that this would be the final hurdle. Surely he wouldn't waste everyone's time with this unless he thought it would work out.

Really I had no idea. Time and time again, I'd torture myself with his 'well that's not very intelligent' statement. Over and over again

I wondered if I shouldn't have told him about my self-harming. But what *should* I have said? I was such a fucking idiot!

I had an altogether gentler interview with his colleague. Very early on she told me I'd be starting soon – it would be for an hour and a half, twice a week, in the same room with up to eight people. The therapy would be open ended – I would leave when I felt it was time to leave – and no, there wouldn't be individual psychotherapy sessions where we would assess my progress.

The rules were simple: attend the meetings and do your best to be on time – but remember that hour and a half is your time, so some lateness, as long as it wasn't disruptive for the others, is perfectly acceptable.

The next rule was fresh out of Fight Club. 'The second rule of Fight Club is you do not *talk* about Fight Club.'

We were strongly advised not to discuss what goes on in the sessions with anyone outside the four walls of the group – whether they were members of the group, friends or family. That way everything that happened within the group was directly observable.

The open-ended nature of the therapy beautifully reflected the amount of time it had taken for my messed-up head to get to where it was today. So obviously it was going to take significant time for me to get it to a … er … better place. And no, we never talked in terms of me being cured.

And that's all I can tell you, specifically, about what went on in psychotherapy. Sorry. What the fuck did you expect? Haven't you seen – better still, *read* Fight Club? Well, don't judge me until you do … Seriously though, I felt that group psychotherapy was – still is – sacred. It's that trust that, for me, makes it so incredibly powerful.

No, of course I'm not going to leave you hanging like that … I can still tell you how I feel this wonderful experience went some way to changing me – and how that change enabled me to take my next faltering steps in life. The following chapter describes how therapy has helped me change certain behaviours typical of my BPD.

CHAPTER 13

HOW THERAPY HELPED ME

The Narrative

Over the years, I'd got into the habit of neatly packaging up bits of my life into self-contained stories – each with a beginning, middle and end. Although each tale would be delivered in a friendly, often humorous way, very often there would be no way in for the listener. The humour – again, at first glance, a friendly, come-on-in-and-have-a-cup-of-tea kind of behaviour – acted like an insurmountable wall, a learned defence just in case there was a danger that someone could reach the soft flesh within.

I'd thought that writing the first part of this book would prepare me for the process of psychotherapy, and to an extent, it did. Memories of stuff would generate more memories, re-establishing old neurological pathways like an explorer hacking back the undergrowth with a machete. For much of it, it felt like I was a ghost writer for someone close to me, like I was telling someone else's story – often with little or no emotional connection.

This was reflected in my desire to tell Mark Algacs that my mum was dead, but it was okay, we'd be getting free school dinners now. It's the reason that, throughout my formative years, I'd protect people when they made the heinous faux pas of asking what my mum did for a living, only for me to say, 'She's dead, but don't feel bad. It's all okay. I'm over that now.' I did exactly the same when Dad died. 'No, really, don't feel bad ... it's fine ... IT'S FINE!'

Maybe it started after Mum's funeral, when I was met with a long queue of folk telling me that I had to be strong for my dad? Or perhaps it started long before then, when I was born into a country that had a 'Keep Calm and Carry on' attitude towards everything?

The thing was, just like trying to squash an unburstable balloon with your hands, the emotions never went away. The more I'd try to suppress my feelings, the more likely they were to pop up unexpectedly between my fingers. They would then manifest themselves in the shape of violence against my loved ones – Derek, my cat Ginger, my brother, and whole mixture of sundry folk at school and beyond. That then spilled over into violence against myself, physically and internally through depression, vivid thoughts of self-harm and suicidal ideation, and those long periods of dissociation.

The process of change probably started with a conversation with my psychiatrist, when she told me (somewhat tetchily because I'd pulled her into my world) that I was incongruous. What was going on inside didn't match my outside. Yes, what happened was awful, but look at me – I'm hilarious!

Connecting my emotions to those events – and to new events – was, and still is, a long and gradual process. I now take time to look at things, not just as a story, but as something I was, and am, immersed in. Often, I have to retrace my steps and look at things again and again. Have I storified something? Or have I experienced it more fully? Often, it's a bit of both, but I'm getting there.

Anger is an Act of Violence

Well, no, obviously it isn't. But for me, this is a core belief that I developed over many years, that has had a profound effect on how I interact with the world.

Prior to therapy, I despised any form of anger in myself. Anger in other people is fine, but often I'd find myself bending into all kinds of contortions to make it stop. I'd do anything to find that common ground – occasionally finding myself in the bizarre position of completely agreeing with two people's standpoints when they were arguing with each other.

This, I believe, was born out of the horror of beating my brother up while dissociating when I was seventeen or eighteen. Somehow though, I'd bundled up violence in the same package as anger, shouting and any kind of disagreement – severe or mild.

I remember Ella seeing a manifestation of this early on in our relationship. We were going out for a meal, and she asked me if I would like to go for Indian or Chinese. I shocked her by going into some form of mental paralysis as I tried to come up with what I perceived to be the right answer. I was unable to tolerate the thought of getting it wrong. My BPD superpowers were on overdrive as I searched for some facial cue, intonation in her voice, or any kind of clue as to what she preferred, just so I could make everything emotionally quiet and okay.

Somewhat weirdly, as a social worker, I was usually able to short circuit those feelings in order to be appropriately assertive on behalf of my clients.

This hasn't gone away overnight. I still frequently wrestle with making my needs completely known, even to myself, let alone the people who don't live inside my head. For me, this was one of those key issues where it was / still is essential to dovetail what was happening in psychotherapy with the real, outside world. For me, having people around me who love me and who are keen to support me – especially Ella – helps so much.

I still self-harm, although I do it more rarely now. My main issue is dissociation. I still lose roughly a third of my life to being in that out-of-body / fugue state. It's still almost impossible to find any obvious triggers to it – the mind is an astonishingly complex thing. And some of the roots of a dissociative episode are so convoluted, most of the time we can't fathom what they are. I know if I'm very busy I'm more likely to zone out – but other than that, I'm pretty clueless.

Pants on Fire

One of the symptoms of my particular brand of BPD, was the propensity to tell lies. These lies were, by and large, spur of the moment and ill-thought through. I think, if we were to label them, we could call them really shit lies. This, for me, wasn't born out of a desire to be duplicitous, to lure people into my dark world of deceit. It was an almost reflexive response for me, used in order to avoid any manner of conflict – including any potential discomfort I'd anticipate in others. This has included anything from 'Of course I love you,' right down to, 'Yes, I did the dishes' and everything in between.

It was chaotic. I believe that this is why some professionals still hang on to that belief that people with BPD are manipulative. To me, manipulation implies a complex web of skilled behaviours that lead to a desired outcome – world domination and the like. My experience – and I'm only speaking about myself here – is that I'm dazzlingly shit at using lies to get what I want out of another person. All my lies ever did (and I'm not suggesting that chaos didn't ensue around them) was allow me to avoid emotional pain. Not exactly your arch Bond villain.

This was one hell of a battle. When I say 'almost reflexive' I mean, at times, reflexive. For a long time with Ella I found myself backtracking on things I'd said. 'Er ... what I really meant was ...'

It was incredibly difficult – but over the years and especially through my therapy, I gradually learned that nothing devastating would happen when I allowed disagreements to take their natural course.

'All the World's a Stage ...'

I was the youngest in our nuclear family when Mum died. When Dad was unable to fulfil the parental role, and I was unable to step into his shoes, it was Jim who stepped up to that mark. Jim, a boy who'd just turned 13 and was exactly one year, one month and one day older than me. He became his version – a version I accepted at the time – of a Mum and Dad combo.

He did his best in the chaos of our lives – but he was 13! Any anger and vitriol I spilled out earlier in this story must be taken in the context of this elaborate roleplay. A roleplay where I remained 'the youngest' with all the lack of responsibility that goes with it.

As I grew up, I was always amazed at my friends who rebelled against their parents during their teenage years and early adulthood. It was a rite of passage to take the first faltering steps at assertiveness, essential for leaving home or becoming independent. Not having any parents to speak of, I had nothing to rebel against. Or so I thought.

But I *had* rebelled against Jim, who I'd seen as this strange Mum / Dad hybrid for all these years – even up until my mid-forties. I was astonished when I made this realisation in psychotherapy. I'd rebelled against Jim, got angry with him, blamed him, loved him and kept on pining for his respect. I had a gut-wrenching desire for him to be proud of me. I always knew if things turned to shit, he'd rescue me. Even when he didn't, I still believed he would. I was his youngest child after all.

One of the regrets I have is never knowing my parents as real people – and not just some fantasy characters fulfilling the role of what a perfect mum or dad should be.

Psychotherapy allowed me to begin to change that mindset. It allowed me to explore what it must have been like for my dad – the oldest brother of 12 kids, a boxer, a Glasgow hard man, a soldier who saw the most bloody and horrible battles of the second world war – to get everything he ever wanted and then have his dream life torn from his grasp when the woman he loved died so young from bastard cancer. He'd been in love, with children, a job, a lovely house, and frequent holidays in Butlins, and it had been taken away from him. It kept me mindful of how he lost his way, self-medicating with whisky, setting himself the task of being around me and Jim until we finally flew the coop. He wasn't just a dad. He was a man, with all that entails.

In my mind, I'd made Stuart into a generic adult. He was a grown-up. For years I never considered the fact that he'd lost his mum at a ridiculously early age, and that he'd somehow managed to beg, steal, and borrow the money to come back from South Africa to see her for one last time. On the flight back, he'd known he'd never see Mum alive again, and that he wouldn't be able to afford to come back for her funeral.

As the youngest, I'd expected him to *do something* to rescue the family, simply because he was an adult. And I never really lost that way of looking at the world. I had an egotism that ignored the fact that Stuart had this own family, a job, a life, and was suffering from the pain of losing his mum in his mid-twenties.

He'd certainly had a shot at coming to my rescue as I've discussed, when he took me in as a 17-year-old. But to be fair on him and his family, I must admit it was already too late at that point. The craziness was upon me.

Over the years, I'd made Mum into some bizarre caricature of what a mother should be. Never wavering from my 12-year-old perspective, I was unable to see her as anything other than perfect, loving, caring and nurturing; a perfect mix of *Little House on the Prairie* and *The Waltons*. In later years, as we were separating, Poppy made the suggestion that no woman ever stood a chance with me because I had this fantasy figure as a backdrop. I think she may have had a point, – but I don't think she was entirely right. By this time she'd fallen into the trap of blaming me for every difficulty in our marriage, right down to global warming. I did have a label, after all …

Me, bitter? Maybe a little.

What Was Love?

Although my relationship with Ella was developing beautifully, there were times where I'd steer into mental cul-de-sacs, dead ends that declared that this relationship was flawed.

I imagined my head was made of Lego – that psychotherapy had taken it apart, piece by piece, only to throw all the bits up in the air. I knew my mind would come down in some form or other, with all the pieces still there – but I had no idea how that was going to turn out.

It was with this in mind that I wasn't entirely sure what love was. What kind of love was valid in a relationship? Was I allowed to experience motherly love, sisterly love, friendly love, all bundled up in my new relationship with Ella? Louise had once told me that, long ago, she'd mixed up physical love with emotional love. I questioned the validity of my love with Ella. Was it a function of my madness that I saw all these different types of love in our relationship? What did it all mean?

It was in the midst of all this that I placed a big question mark over my sexuality. I didn't know if I was straight, gay or anything in between. I was struck by a short mental video I played over and over again in my minds' eye. I was around 13, and a friend of mine (we'll call him Drian) was standing in front of me. We were chatting about some youthful something or other, and he was undoing and retying my school tie. I remember being mesmerised, watching as I developed a year-long, never-to-be-spoken-about, crush on him.

Psychotherapy took me back there. Once again, my mind began swimming with these thoughts, these doubts, these speculative meanderings. What if I was gay and I was just taking Ella up some garden path, only to abandon her later, dragging yet another person into my bizarre life?

At the same time, I was pulled into a religious whirlwind. I was taken back to a conversation the young Christopher had had with a young girlfriend at infant school. I would have been about seven when I told her that God was my friend. And he was! I knew exactly what he looked like – huge black oval eyes, a short, skinny frame with long, elegant fingers.

I remembered the conversations I'd had with a locum GP. They told me I should turn to God, and Poppy had suggested that a lot of my mental health problems were due to my lack of faith. Even my GP told me he'd pray for me.

Had I turned my back on God when mum died? I remember laughing at Gradscope, an all-new singing and dancing piece of software that I'd found when I graduated. It was meant to point you in the right career direction. I'd eagerly punched all my data in, with the hope that it would tell me to apply to become an astronaut or something equally exciting. But no, each time I punched my details in – and I did this three times in the hope that it would offer up something else – 'Church of England Minister' came out at the top of the list. This had me intrigued since not once did it ask me if I believed in a god. Maybe it was time for me to re-establish my faith?

I found myself walking past trees, dogs and cats – anything living – and feeling the rage of envy as I looked at them. A tree knows how to tree, a dog knows how to dog, and yet I had no idea how to human. With my lies I could be whatever I thought people wanted – perhaps needed me to be – with my thoughts of love, sexuality, relationships, I found myself paralysed when I tried to even consider what it was like to be Chris. I had no idea who I was ... and yet ... gradually, almost imperceptibly, those Lego pieces started cascading down ...

I Fucking Hate You!

Forgiveness doesn't feel like a powerful weapon in the battle against – well, anything really. Imagine if we went around forgiving folk all over the world for the pain they, or the groups they affiliate with, have caused you in the past?

I've both loved and hated Louise, on and off, over the past 30 or so years. I've felt a hate so pervasive that it would leap to the front of my mind, seemingly apropos of nothing. There were times where I'd have killed her for this thing she'd done to me. But weirdly there were other times where I'd hear a piece of sixties music that would light up some lovely memories with her, motivating me to phone her with a cheery, 'Do you remember that time when we … '

I'm not entirely sure what guided me to it, but one day I found myself reading *The Forgiveness Project*, a book where a number of individuals explore the notion of forgiveness in the context of something horrible that had happened to them. Its wonderfully unpreachy words guide the reader to consider what forgiveness might mean for them. At no point does it say, 'You must forgive!' Clearly, forgiveness works for some, and not for others.

I decided I'd try this mindset on for size, to see if it would fit with Louise. Someone had commented that if you let yourself hate someone, you are effectively allowing them to live, rent-free, in your mind forever.

Almost immediately, I felt a huge pressure on my shoulders lift. This was a radically different way of looking at things for me and, somehow, the world felt a little clearer. I decided I would give myself some time for this way of thinking to bed down, so I could fully explore what it meant for me.

Before I'd really discussed this with anyone, I got a phone call from Louise. I was walking across the Meadows in Edinburgh, on my way to psychotherapy. We chatted a bit before she told me she was very ill and that we needed to talk. I listened and told her that I'd come down to visit her as soon as I could, to talk about the things that I'd been trying to work through. I didn't mention forgiveness …

The next few days raced by alarmingly quickly. I received a phone call from Louise's daughter telling me that she had widespread cancer leading to kidney failure, and that she was slipping in and out of a coma. I immediately sent a card to the hospital, to tell Louise how I'd forgiven her. I asked her daughter to read it to her when it arrived.

I contacted Ella and explained everything. I told her I had to get down to the south of England to see Louise as soon as possible. Ella arrived in what seemed like no time, ensuring that her boys were looked after and all things work-related were catered for. I drove down from Edinburgh as fast as I could. Arriving at the hospital, I got to the ward and found a roomful of folk sitting around Louise's bed. The atmosphere was upbeat and friendly, but Louise was in a coma from which she never recovered.

The naively hoped for happy ending was never realised. Her daughter told me she'd read the card to her, but it was unclear whether she'd heard or understood.

Had I forgiven her?

Well, yes and no. For me, forgiveness isn't a tangible thing, nor is it an absolute, black or white, on or off thing. It's a process, a journey ... with a whole bunch of pitfalls and detours along the path.

That's a journey I'm still on today.

I'm Cured ... CURED, I Tell You ...

Over the two years or so of psychotherapy, my Lego bricks gradually fell into a Chris-shaped form. One that was the same but radically different from the guy who'd met Benny from ABBA that short time ago.

I was well on my way to being me, but at the same time I recognised that I wasn't cured, whatever that meant. I was still dissociating roughly a third of the time, although my self-harming had reduced significantly.

I'd figured out who I was as a person through looking back, further and further, to a time where things hadn't turned to shit, where I still had the wide-eyed optimism of childhood. I was going to be a writer, a public speaker, or maybe even a stand-up comedian. I'd recognised that going back to social work – even if they'd have me – would be destructive for me at this stage. My unrealistic desire to save the world – to save the younger me – through this most noble of professions, would never be realised.

I'd learned to accept myself – I knew a cure was a fantasy, but management was infinitely possible. I could, and would, live a rich and fulfilling life because of the point psychotherapy had delivered me to.

This hadn't happened in isolation though. The microworld of therapy – where I was learning to be a different version of myself – dovetailed with the changes in my 'real', wider world.

I knew I had value. I knew that, despite all the stuff that had gone on before, I wasn't inherently bad or poisonous. Neither was I all things good. I'm simply a man, with all that entails.

I knew I had skills, such as those that had delivered me to a career in social work and, fleetingly, in life coaching. I had skills and values that had been galvanised through training. I hoped that one day soon I'd be able to re-enter society in a way that was both meaningful to me and it. Naomi had assured me I could.

Most of all, though, I'd learned that me, Chris, was both able to love and be worthy of love. The Chris that I'd tried to hide all these years *could* be adored by others. This charge was led by my darling Ella, like Joan of Arc galloping on a magnificent horse, sword held aloft, armour glinting in the summer sun, screaming, 'This man is loveable. I adore him. I dare you to challenge me!'

And Derek. Always, always Derek ...

CHAPTER 14

WALK A MILE IN MY SHOES

' ... when you have eliminated the impossible, whatever remains, however improbable, must be the truth.'

Sherlock Holmes

'Do you really have to do this?' Ella and I had already been on quite some journey when I finally put together my plans for Walk a Mile in My Shoes.

It was 2011 and psychotherapy had helped me reach a much healthier place. But I was still haunted by the hundred people from the BPD experiment whose faces I hadn't trusted. I wanted to – scratch that, *needed* to – demonstrate to myself and others that people were both trusting and trustworthy. I wanted to prove to myself that my new-found belief – that everyone was basically fabulous – was true. I needed to do something to show the world that people weren't as unkind and dangerous as the mainstream media would have us believe.

I wanted to hear from older people, people with physical disabilities, people with mental health problems, people with learning disabilities, people from minority ethnic groups, people who choose a different god and people who choose to live their lives in different ways.

But not just them. I wanted to hear the voice of the middle classes – the tax payers – the majority who feel they are unheard.

And so, starting this initiative really was a no-brainer, considering the prejudice that many people with mental health problems experience, and my love for our lovely country and its fabulous people.

The thought process went something like this …

Penumbra is a mental health organisation in Scotland. The word is an interesting one. A shadow is split into two parts: the umbra, the dark bit in the middle, and the penumbra, the lighter bit around the edge. The suggestion here – for me at least – was that people with mental health problems feel they are on the edge of society. But Penumbra kick back against that dark shadow rhetoric, and I wanted people to move away from their ignorance of mental ill health and into the light.

I'd heard reports on the radio that a huge percentage of folk wouldn't knowingly welcome someone with a mental health problem into their home. The exact statistics and reasons have been lost in the mists of time.

With these thoughts in place, I decided to walk around the edge of the UK to highlight the experience of people with mental health problems. I wanted to meet people and talk to them, encouraging understanding and tackling stigma against mental illness.

Yes, I appreciate this was a bit of a grandiose metaphor. But to me, it was perfect. I would start the walk on April 6th 2011, exactly 34 years after my mum's death.

I explained what I was going to do to my friends Maggie and Jim. They guided me to read *No Destination* by Satish Kumar, a Jain monk who, in the sixties, went on a peace march. I read the book and it was fabulous. Paraphrasing wildly, his journey started something like this …

Young Satish decided that nuclear arms were a ridiculous idea, so he'd go on a march to highlight what a bad idea he thought they were. He told his guru, who asked if he'd be taking lots of money with him and if he'd have lots of nice hotels to stay in on his journey.

Satish explained that everything was organised and that his guru had absolutely nothing to worry about.

But his guru explained that if Satish took money with him, he'd have no motivation to talk to people at the end of each day and the only people he'd meet would be hoteliers. And so Satish made the journey from India to America with no money.

I thought if Satish Kumar could walk from India into Pakistan when the two countries were at war and expect and receive hospitality from the people he met, then there was no reason for things to be any different for me as I walked around our lovely country.

As such, I planned to make my Walk a Mile journey with no money, relying solely on the kindness of other people for food, water, shelter and compassion. There would be some stops and starts along the way – I knew that having BPD meant I would have to return home for periodic rests or recuperation. I would be encouraging people to donate and sponsor me, and the proceeds would be split equally between two charities: Mind and Child Bereavement UK. I would go only with a backpack full of supplies, a head full of 'what if', and a belief that people would be fabulous.

What follows are some tales from different parts of my journey as a wandering loon making his way around the UK, challenging mental health stigma one conversation at a time. One book would not be enough to tell the full story, and the entries below don't give a full account of everything that happened, but I'm sure this will give you lovely readers more than a flavour of my Walk a Mile adventures. Enjoy.

THE PREAMBLE AND
THE FIRST FEW DAYS

Beast of Burden

So, I've packed my bag a whole two months early. It contains water, clothing, a sleeping bag, a tent, rolly-down mat thing, a stove and bits, a flask and first aid stuff. It weighs roughly the same as me.

When I start my journey north from Edinburgh on April 6th, will I have the strength to get to the outskirts of Auld Reekie (that's another name for Edinburgh to the uninitiated), or will I just topple backwards, to be found like an upturned tortoise on the road to South Queensferry – or, more optimistically, North Queensferry?

Already it feels like I'm mistrusting the very folk I expect to trust. The fine people of the UK will feed, water and shelter me. They will.

Do I chuck the tent, sleeping bag and all these symbols of mistrust, or do I bring them just in case? Far be it to compare myself to Gandhi, but when he died, he was found with a mere ten items in his possession.

I, on the other hand, will be carting about a whole ton of 'what if'. I have two months to prevaricate.

Definitive proof that construction workers aren't sexist

Yesterday I took it upon myself to have a dummy run at my walk to North Queensferry. This involves walking across the Forth Road Bridge – roughly a mile and a half long suspension bridge that crosses the Firth of Forth – from South Queensferry.

I'd had a bit of a panic when I found that Google Maps – *and* the handy-dandy map thing that comes with the iPhone – both said that I couldn't walk across the bridge, and that I'd have to walk an extra 40 miles to get across the river.

Even though I'd seen many people walk across the bridge, the spectre of doubt began to haunt me. But I was soon to find a number of happy walking stories on the interweb that involved said crossing.

So anyway, I began my journey meandering through the streets of Edinburgh, regretting the third cup of tea I'd had that morning. *No matter*, I thought, *I know of a public lavatorium in Corstorphine* (not a drug – actually an area of Edinburgh). I found the pressure rising as the expectation of the er ... *release* came closer.

Imagine my dismay when I found that the convenience had inconveniently been removed. It had been replaced by an off-licence (insert your own 'piss-up and brewery' joke here).

I could have popped into any number of supermarkets / burger restaurants sporting golden arches – but, somewhat inexplicably in retrospect, I decided that this would constitute as cheating.

It's okay – I'm mental.

The first few miles out of Edinburgh were slightly unpleasant, as I waddled in the hope of finding some secluded tree – you'd think the countryside would be full of them ...

Suffice it to say, the countryside is full of them. I followed the instructions of a jolly chap nearby. 'Walk along the road until you see some steps,' he said. 'When you get to the top of these, you'll see a cycle path that leads you up to bridge level.'

I went up the steps and straight into a building site, where I was wolf-whistled by a chap as he dangled off the underside of the bridge. I obliged by raising my kilt somewhat provocatively, to which he and his mates responded by demanding more.

Definitely not sexist: they would clearly sexually harass anyone.

I was given directions around the construction encampment by one of their colleagues and went on my way with the whistles ringing in my ears.

I've driven across the Forth Road Bridge approximately 12 billion times (give or take) but never had I set foot on it. One is immediately put at one's ease by a sign saying 'Distressed? Phone the Samaritans on ...'

I was struck that I could feel the movement of the traffic through my feet, even larger traffic through my knees, and those really big lorries through my ...

There are also gaps in the bridge! Sure, they're only about a centimetre wide (apparently they allow for the bridge to expand and contract) and that's all well and good – but you can see the sea (about 100 feet down) through them. Which is terrifying.

The other thing that didn't put me at my ease was the fence along the side. It's about five feet high. I felt it could benefit from being at least another 18 feet taller, just in case my slight frame was lifted by an errant gust of wind, I was bounced by a jogger, or I ricocheted off a cyclist.

And while I'm having a moan: they have 'person' hatches that are rectangular. So what? You don't care, do you? Well I wouldn't have either, had I not seen a children's programme that explained the reason why manhole covers were round. They are round so that it's impossible for them to fall through the hole they're covering. You haven't got the same certainty with your rectangle cover. I chose not to walk on them.

I walked past a number of folk on the bridge. None of us were going slower than one and a half times the fastest walk I'd ever done. We all had fixed grins that said, 'Isn't this a jolly thing we're doing? Aren't the views just ... aaaarrrgghh!'

I was in such a state of anxiety by the time I'd almost crossed the bridge that, when I heard a compressed air pipe that had come unstuck from something, I convinced myself the bridge was deflating.

I'm glad I'm brave and that I've agreed to comfort some friends as we walk across the bridge for real on 6th April.

Fall a mile on my arse

On a recent ramble around the mighty Arthur's Seat, having negotiated the slippy mud and the odd dodgy rock, my balance finally succumbed to the most massive of challenges. I fell over on a flat pavement.

Isn't adrenaline wonderful? You trip, you start to fall, your body reacts and suddenly you're in the Matrix.

Years of evolution ensure that, at this sudden exposure to danger, my senses are heightened and my reactions are faster. I'm better, stronger, faster (a line from the Bionic Man – ask your parents).

How did I use my new-found superpowers? I slipped gracefully onto my arse, carrying my full backpack, at the same time as thinking *I hope that woman 200 metres away didn't see that*.

She had. 'I saw you fall there.'

'The falling was easy. The hard part was getting up.' I'm dead funny, I am.

'Are you hurt?'

'No, there's loads of padding in the backpack,' I smiled as I thought about my laptop being bent in half.

She took my snappy one-liners not as an indication that I was well, but as an announcement for all to hear that I was embarrassed and I wanted her to go away. So much for evolution.

So much for the overall purpose of this particular escapade. I'm walking around the UK. I will be vulnerable and in need of help, food and shelter. So why, oh why, have I adopted this wonderfully British trait where help is seen as a four-letter word? (Yes, I know it is ... don't get smart, okay?)

I guess I need to evolve.

It's all well and good until someone loses an eye

It's tomorrow!

And yet … no, don't check your watch, calendar, or other timekeeping device. It cannot be tomorrow since, as in the words of the song, it's always a day away!

But therein lies insanity.

Which brings me neatly round to the big event. Tomorrow at 12 noon I meet up with a few folk at the Cramond Brig Inn for a small departure do. Then I, along with a few other eager people, will wander off in a northerly direction towards the aptly named North Queensferry.

This is it. Today I have no great words of political wisdom or anything desperately witty. For me it feels a little like a cross between Christmas Eve and the day before sitting your finals.

I've done all I can at this stage. I have spoken to lots of people to ask for their support. I have been in touch with a variety of media organisations. I have a backpack full of stuff that I'm sure will be useful at some point. I have had trial runs and I've stomped my way around Arthur's Seat.

As for you lot? Thanks for just being there. Hopefully you'll grow in number as I go.

I don't have anywhere to stay in North Queensferry. That's okay though – that's just how it'll be at times. Obviously ten packets of Supernoodles and three bags of M&M's will only take me so far, but this will be fine. This is going to work. We will find that big society.

'Love is never having to say you're sorry' – absolute twaddle. Love is holding your hands up and saying, 'Yes, I'm an arse' when the situation demands it.

Love is having a bunch of your mates sitting around you saying 'You're an idiot!' when I explained I had no alternative sources of energy for my fancy phone other than the kindness of other folk. I now have solar energy at my fingertips.

Enough now. I'll be off then.

Walk a mile, people.

CHAPTER 15

TALES OF A WANDERING LOON

Are we there yet? I can see the sea...

Neighbours, everybody needs good ...

In North Queensferry I was told, in no uncertain terms by some friendly locals, that security is tight and I'd best not try to camp in the village. And so I'm currently comfy in a tent on the Fife coastal path.

The kindness of people is very much alive and well. I had a great send off by a great bunch of chums including Ella, Ellie, Jim, Maggie, Ben, Susan and Lou. Naomi and Ellie, my lovely friends, joined me on the first part of my walk to kick things off.

Big thanks to Catie of STV for her glowing report on my adventure.

I met a friendly woman on the way into North Queensferry. So impressed was she by the tale that she slipped me a tenner for my cause. I then popped into the local pub and met Linda the social worker, who got me steak pie and chips and a pint of lager. She shared tales of physical abuse in her childhood and adult life – at the hands of her father and her partners. Only now, in her mid-fifties, has she got a real sense of self-worth. It was a pleasure to meet her.

Fought a bit with my tent in the rain and the dark – but all is well and lovely. Didn't I tell you people were lovely?

I guess we can say Walk a Mile in My Shoes is officially underway.

I don't want your charity

So there I was, walking along the coastal path – and I lost it. Wandering confused into the small town of Inverkeithing, I happened across some other weary travellers.

'Hello, Big Man.' This was Lou, who we'll get to know soon.

I'm not big. I have large bones – especially the big flabby one at the front, which I'll rely upon for sustenance when things get lean.

Lou, her brother-in-law, and their friend Helen were walking the coastal path for the MS society. I told her my story and said that I might have a contact in Dalgety Bay church just up the road.

'If that falls through, give us a call and you can come back to mine for scran and a roof over your head,' Lou responded.

But we'd only just …

'That would be great!'

We exchanged numbers and, compared to me, they sped off very quickly. Lou came back and thrust some change into my hand. 'Stick that in your sporran!'

My contact at the church in Dalgety Bay turned out to be the offer of a toilet stop and a cup of coffee, so I decided to take Lou up on her offer. We agreed to meet in Burntisland (neither burnt nor an island – the mystery continues).

I was half dead by the time I arrived. The heat was feisty (in Scotland?) and my feet had grown two sizes and were about to explode. I was picked up in their car and right then I knew they were going to be interesting. Lou is married to Louise and they have a lovely three-year-old boy called Nathan.

Lou, who did long walks for the MS society, has MS herself. I had to ask the question, 'What makes you trust a big bald guy in a kilt in your home with your family?'

'I trust my first impressions of people,' Lou responded. Really simple when you put it like that. Although her mates did ask her, 'Are you nuts?'

I was given spaghetti bolognaise and garlic bread and a beer. I was given a shower, and a big sofa to sleep on. They gave me a roll and sausage for breakfast, two rolls for lunch and chicken and potatoes for my tea. They also treated me to a map of the coastal path and the offer of two other beds for the night further on in my journey.

I was just accepted by this lovely bunch of folk – I was treated like an old mate. Even now I'm getting texts from Lou to make sure I don't wander off the track.

And it all started when I met them and laughed at the irony of someone collecting money for charity giving *me* money for charity.

It was better than I could ever have hoped for.

A big dog stole my homework

Okay, I'll be brief. I parked up on the side of the path for the night, having devoured a ton of free food from the Anstruther fish bar – the best fish and chips, bar none.

The urge came upon me for a number two this morning – so, turn away if you're squeamish. Realising I was on a public thoroughfare, I decided to do said business in the tent – on some wet wipes. I packaged this all up in said wet wipes and put it next to the tent for later burial.

'Hey! No! Put that down!' shouted a man a few minutes later, whose dog had just made off with the aforementioned jobby. Hmm. From nowhere in my previous experience could I come up with anything remotely useful to say in this situation.

'Hey you! Your dog just stole my ...' was just one of the things I didn't say. I later retrieved my savaged poo and buried it in true camper style.

I just hope he's not one of those jumpy-up-licky dogs.

Walk a mile away from dogs such as these.

100 miles gone (or thereabouts) several to go

Blown away. Not in your Quentin Tarrantino style – oh no. I'm just so happy that the kindness of others seems to be boundless.

The two Lous invited me along to see Lou sing in a bar in Dundee. She sings beautifully – not unlike Adele. Lou introduced me to the pub owner, telling him briefly about my little caper, and he instantly donated £20 to the cause and gave me a free bar tab. Needless to say, I went mental and had three pints.

I stayed with Lou's parents last night. They fed, watered and sheltered me. They washed my kilt and Lou ironed it. There is nothing more boring than ironing a kilt.

As I sat pondering the day, showing young Nathan my William-Tell-overture-on-my-teeth-with-a-pen trick, singer Lou came down to me. She ignored my request for a sausage sandwich and furnished me with the full Scottish and the mother and father of all packed lunches.

It was fantastic. Lou said, 'At the end of the day it's just food and shelter.'

Yeah, right.

As I walked out of Dundee with a skip in my step, safe in the knowledge that I have somewhere to stay tonight – Lou's brothers' place – I got a text from my friend Jan to say my story was in the Dundee chronicle. She'd sent my tale of happy wandering to them.

Sun shining, I walk into a small town called Monifeith and was met by three guys on bikes. They're getting away from it all by cycling from Aberdeen to southwest Scotland. I briefly told them my tale and they dipped into their pockets to give me donations.

'Whoa – I only need a bit of cash for juice and the like,' I said. 'Any donations should go to my virgin donation website.'

'Buy yourself something! Get yourself a beer!' said Paul, Lee and Mark as they thrust cash into my hands.

Life is good. The people of the UK – as I thought – are amazing and kind and generous.

I know I'm beginning to go on a bit, but I need to talk a bit about the whole mental health thing. Even though it's my aim to highlight the experiences of people with mental health problems, I still find it all a bit tricky.

The other night, when we were all at Jan's, we were talking a bit about our maladies. Jan spoke a little about her ME and Kittie's MS. Lou talked about her experience and fears around her own MS.

My turn. 'Go on, Chris, tell them about your borderline personality disorder!' So I did, to a certain extent. I gave a list of symptoms, from unwelcome imagery of self-harm flowing through my mind, to dissociation where I can zone out for minutes, hours, days, or even weeks occasionally.

Whereas I could happily listen to their problems (even smiling at the thought of Lou's disobedient legs), a quiet voice of judgement was sounding at the back of my mind. *They've got real problems. If you could just pull yourself together!*

Which is the very message I'm fighting to combat. It's just a little hard at times to swim upstream. But with the help of these people, with the help of you guys, that swim's becoming easier.

100 miles in? Bring it on.

This is my mental health problem.
Please do no read this if you're likely to be upset.

So, here it is. The very thing that I've been singing and dancing about. The very thing that I've been trying to shout about – and yet keeping to myself.

Today I can hardly move. It normally takes me 20 minutes to pack away my tent and stuff. Today I've taken two hours so far and I'm nowhere near finishing. I haven't even taken the tent down.

Walking helps. Putting one foot in front of the other keeps the bad thoughts in the background, murmuring angrily away. The thing is, denial is not the answer. These thoughts and feelings have been ready to pounce in my vulnerable moments and now here they are.

Get walking … get walking … a simple mantra, but it feels so far away today.

Today the images have me in their grip: images of violent self-harm, of a dagger plunging again and again into my face and my legs. Images of removing my lips, cutting out my eyes with a sharp blade – they're there whether or not my eyes are open.

I also have a ludicrous urge to take my own life. I will *never* succumb to this – never – but the paralysis I feel this morning is astonishing.

Today I have failed. Though I was affected by the death of my mum when I was 12, my father's alcoholism, and the sexual abuse I experienced, somehow today I am responsible for it all.

The failure at work – my inability to do my job, my inability to appear to be a father to my two beautiful children – is all my fault. I can see myself off sick from work again, sitting on the end of the sofa, looking into the middle distance. Inaccessible.

I think of self-harm – what kind of lunatic punches his own face, cuts himself and screams?

This happens so seldom in the presence of others. I keep my social façade going so well so much of the time because this – whatever the fuck this is, it's ridiculous – *this* is the stuff that the general public are afraid of. It's what people don't want to hear about. This is the unmitigated terror if it.

Welcome me into your house? Yeah, sure.

Walk a Mile in My Shoes?

So sorry. I will be fine.

This will pass – it always has.

Oh Chris, you've got to have a knife...

Racing at great pace – or waddling erratically as anyone observing may remember – towards Aberdeen, I met a most interesting man.

I'd spent most of the morning meeting the folk who passed me with a jolly, 'How are you?' or a truly banterous 'Beautiful day, isn't it?' If I was a fisher of men, then I wasn't catching m(any).

Charlie, for that's his name, was out for a run, and initially passed me like so many others had done. He went ahead a bit and then screeched to a halt in a Roadrunner-in-*Loony-Tunes* stylie. 'What in the name of all that is holy are you doing?' is what I think he meant to say. Instead, I heard, 'What are you up to?'

I told him my tale of wandering, adventure and swashbuckling derring-do.

We synchronised his watch and agreed to meet up near a local-ish hostelry, where he kindly offered to furnish me with lunch.

What a story! I asked him what he did for a living. Instead of coming back with what I expected, something about working in Aberdeen with oil and whatnot, young Charlie took in a deep breath and said, 'I'm a polar explorer,' in much the same way as someone might say 'I'm a milkman.'

Pause. Process. 'That's just knocked my coolest job in the world off its top spot.' I said. I didn't have one in reality. I do now though. Charlie takes scientists and similarly minded folk to the North Pole to do stuff and he was impressed with what I was doing.

I might have made up a bit about me wrestling crocodiles, but he's a polar explorer. I had to keep up.

He'd left school and ended up in the marines, doing the usual tours of duty. Now he was out, he missed the camaraderie – the close and very trusting relationships forged when you rely on others to watch your back. I think he was glad to be out though. He felt that our forces were being spread too thinly and weren't being given time to gather their thoughts.

Polar exploration, on the other hand ... he takes a dry suit so he can swim in arctic waters. He takes a shotgun to frighten off polar bears. People have asked me if I'm 'wild camping', but in this context, I'd have to say not. The thing I loved about this man was that he still didn't know what he was going to be when he grew up. His next goal is to be the first man to walk unassisted from Canada to Russia.

As with so many people I meet, Charlie has a direct link with mental health problems. Around two years ago his brother took his own life. Charlie proudly told me what a great chef his brother had been, and then, with a big smile, he told me that his brother was gay and had invariably been surrounded by beautiful women.

This same brother, he tells me, suffered prolonged periods of paranoid psychosis, believing that people were after him. He wasn't protected by the psychiatric professions. Charlie was frustrated that the folk looking after his brother never spoke to the family about his situation. His voice, I guess, joins that of the many families, friends and carers up and down the country. 'If only they'd asked us.'

His parents found him inside a cupboard where he'd hanged himself. He could have put his feet down to save himself, but he chose not to. The thing was, Charlie told me, his brother couldn't stand pain. Tragic.

That said, Charlie felt that his brother was at least away from the torture that his inner turmoil had caused for so much of his life.

Charlie is an astonishing man. And a generous one. He kept on gazing over my kit, asking if I needed boots (he was worried that if I kept my feet in the ones I had I'd end up with trench foot). He asked if I had a tent, a backpack, waterproofs and so on.

'You haven't got a knife?' he said with not a little incredulity, 'You've got to have a knife.'

I explained why I shouldn't have a knife. He agreed I was better off without one.

That said, his generosity was not going to be thwarted. By the time I walked away from this man and his van, which looked like something belonging to the A-Team, I was laden with his good will. He'd got me juice and sweets, and genuine polar explorer freeze-dried just-add-hot-water food. He pressed £50 into my hand, hoping that I wouldn't take offence. I'm smiling as I remember it.

Finally, ladies and gentlemen, I am now the proud owner of a spoon that's been to the North Pole. I love that spoon.

He also got in touch with the local Aberdeen newspaper on my behalf who got in touch with me and ran a story on Walk a Mile.

An amazing man. Another wonderful person.

The intriguing story of the man with the broken heart and the woman from the stars

My walk was now taking me to Fraserburgh and beyond. The most notable thing about this leg of the journey was that, quite suddenly, people were offering me lifts in their cars. Maybe I looked more fatigued than usual – or maybe they're just that sort of folk.

The offers of lifts continued and the thought of jumping in a car was mighty tempting – but that's not what this little escapade is all about. One guy stopped and said he'd give me a lift to a place called Crimmond, about another six miles up the road. I politely declined his offer, explaining what I was doing and that I'd get there soon enough.

'It's a long walk!' he beamed as he drove off.

It was, indeed, a long six miles. I arrived in Crimmond a while later, a bit sore and weary, looking around for somewhere to pitch my tent.

There was the guy who'd offered me the lift. He was taking a timid Rottweiler for a walk. 'I bet you're tired now?' he smiled at me. I conceded that I was and that I needed somewhere to stick my tent. 'You can put it up in my back garden,' said Kenny as he walked me round.

A cup of tea and fish fingers and chips later, we were getting on famously. He has what must be the second best job in the world. He drives high performance and luxury cars backwards and forwards between Peterhead and London. He loves it.

Kenny showed me pictures of himself a couple of years ago, when he weighed 28 stone. He now weighs 14.

'How the? What the?' I asked coherently.

He'd had a heart attack while he was driving. Apparently it had been touch and go, but they got him to hospital and put two metal tubes in his heart. That was his motivation to lose weight. 'I eat less fat and brown bread, and I take dogs for ten-mile walks in the evenings.'

No need for that pile of books that make you feel guilty and tell you that colonic coffee is the only way!

There is something about Kenny. He's kind and generous and very matter of fact. He likes to help people. I also think he might have a bit of a learning disability or have a touch of Asperger's. It was really lovely when he showed me his birth certificate. 'It's the original,' he told me proudly. 'Not like my brothers and sisters – they've only got copies.'

I thought of my tattered old replica and then we watched shit TV for a while. I thanked him for his hospitality and kindness and then escaped and went to my tent. I didn't expect to see him in the morning as I was knackered and he had an early start.

'Tea and toast, Chris?' came the voice through the tent at 7.30am. This was above and beyond. I started to thank Kenny but my gaze was met by his neighbour.

I suddenly realised it wasn't just his back garden that I'd camped in. It was a communal drying area.

I started to babble. 'Kenny said it would be okay if I camped here.'

'Oh, I don't care about that,' said the Liverpudlian woman in her early sixties. 'I've run you a bath. Would you like bubbles or no bubbles?'

'Er ... bubbles would be nice!'

I necked the tea and toast and jumped in the bath. Fantastic!

Bera – short for Beranice – explained that if she'd been camping, a bath would be just what she'd want. She thought I'd be no different. She was right. We talked and she explained that she'd been caring for her friend over the last six years, and she'd attended her funeral yesterday. She told me she'd received carers' allowance for her support.

How much did she receive, considering that she'd had to prove she cared her for her at least 40 hours a week to get it? Hundreds? A Bentley? A huge house?

Ninety-odd pounds is what she received.

'I'm all cared out now,' she told me. 'I want a job in Tesco or Asda.'

'Given up caring?' I couldn't help but laugh. 'You just ran a bath for a complete stranger.'

We talked about her younger years in the sixties. She felt the world was more optimistic then, especially with space travel.

She smiled and told me her name, Beranice, came from an old Greek story. A girl called Beranice grew her long, beautiful hair. When it looked like her father might not come back from the war, she told the gods she'd cut off her hair and give it to them if they would guarantee his safe return. There is a star constellation called Beranice's Locks. Wonderful.

We hugged and I went on my way. She went off on the bus to find her job filling shelves.

The woman who gave continues to give so much.

Walking a Mile Soon

Hi folks

Sorry for my recent absence. Yes, rest has been enjoyed. I have a broken rib from a fall and it hasn't been overly keen to improve. And, to be fair, my head hasn't been rushing back to a level place with any great speed either.

That said, today Ella and I will be going to stay at a bed and breakfast she'd booked prior to my spinout. I'll be back on the road on Thursday 26th May.

I've tried to acknowledge some of the things that got me into the pickle of only a few days ago.

First of all, this isn't a race. I've had a number of conversations with folk where I've felt apologetic for what I might see as low mileage each day. I recently had a chat with a guy who was walking about five miles a day more than me. He was carrying about half the weight I was, he was only walking 80 miles in all (I never thought I'd see myself writing the words 'only' and '80 miles' in the same sentence) and his journey was only going to last a few days. Mine, however, was different.

And yet I compared and contrasted. I felt I should be going faster. I have places to stay in Nairn, Inverness and probably the Black Isle. I'd decided I had to be at each of these by an arbitrarily set date. Set by me. It was becoming a race.

To this end I found myself walking on the main roads to places and feeling agitated when I was taking a longer route or becoming tired.

I should have spotted a problem in myself when I recently became inwardly narked because I'd followed a path alongside the beautiful meandering river Spey – walking through woodland accompanied by butterflies and the sounds of countless birds echoing through the trees – instead of walking along a main road, which would have been quicker.

I was struggling because the solar energy thingies attached to my backpack weren't providing sufficient energy to talk and use GPS and blog. I was struggling because my boots, which I felt should have lasted a few hundred miles more, had developed a hole in both soles and water was coming in.

This was never a race. This was always going to be a journey where I observed things happening without getting stressed. If people were to offer me support, that was great. If they didn't, that was fine too.

Somehow I'd managed to put all the support I'd received, the obvious kindness and charitable nature of those around me, to one side. For the first time I experienced doubt. Not in the project, or the people of the UK – but in myself and my mental health.

But again, that's surely what this is all about. It's about raising awareness of my own and other folks' mental health issues. Mine will ebb and flow as it has done for the past 30-odd years. There really is no reason why I should be miraculously cured because I'm storming out for a just cause.

I can be a big silly sometimes.

Fizzy head and aching rib aside, I'm going to revert to the gentler me. On top of that, I've now got some widgets that allow for longer periods away from the recharge points in people's homes. I have also ordered some boots.

They're all pretty obvious things, but when I allowed my head to become a little screwy, they were far from that.

Gentle hands, Chris, gentle hands.

A brush with Donald Sutherland

Today I was striding out towards Cullen, a small coastal town just off the Moray Firth. It was quite a walk, but I was rewarded by a beautiful scene over Cullen Bay and the picturesque village.

For my sins, I'd been craving a lager shandy for the past couple of miles. Having sighted the golf club that was to be my hostelry, I started off down the path. I was intercepted by a delightful older couple who listened to my story with great interest.

As I departed, Mrs Older Person said 'Give him some money' and her husband thrust ten pounds into my hand.

'Get yourself a drink,' he said. What a pair of mind readers.

I frolicked down to the golf club and ordered my eagerly awaited fizzy pop. I was greeted with the remnants of the senior golf day out. They were fascinated by my tour and soon made it impossible for me to spend any money. Kate, the barmaid, charged my phone and surreptitiously thrust some sandwiches in my hand. The seniors, although somewhat bladdered, advised me on how to deal with midges while agreeing that there really was no solution when I get to the west coast of Scotland. I'm doomed.

They tried to advise me where to stick my tent – politely – but were entertainingly incoherent. 'I'll just camp on one of the greens,' I japed, and was met by a joint steely glare that could melt granite.

Kate came to the rescue and showed me a path up to the clifftop where I camped ... nervously. I bravely left first thing in the morning, thankful that there was no wind and, as such, no need to be dragged off the cliff, clutching my tent, screaming.

Buckie was my destination. I wandered into the local supermarket seeking Irn Bru and artery-hardening pies. I met a woman who was filling shelves and she asked about my ridiculous backpack. I told my tale.

She told me how her husband had suffered from recurring depression until he became a carer. That has given him meaning.

'Can I buy your pies and juice for you?' she smiled at me.

'Sure, that would be lovely. Thanks.' I hoped to get her name and story, but she bought my provisions and buggered off.

Hit-and-run kindness, if you like.

I got to the far side of Buckie, and there he was – Donald "Call Me Donny" Sutherland.

He was instantly interested in me, my backpack, and my story. 'Do you want to come in for a drink?' he smiled.

Even at this late stage of the game, my pseudo-politeness still kicks in. 'No thanks, I don't want to be a bother.' But he was insistent, so I went in. I smiled as his wife gave me that, 'good god, he's brought another one home' kind of look.

That said, Clarinda was a lovely hostess. After serving tea she asked, 'Do you want a roll?'

'Yes, he does,' Donny answered for me. And when Clarinda asked if I wanted another one, he told her I did before I could even think about answering.

Now seemingly a collector of interesting jobs, I've placed Donny's job as third on the list of best jobs ever.

No, he's not that Donald Sutherland. But he is *the* Donny Sutherland.

His job, ladies and gentlemen, was a lighthouse keeper on a ridiculously remote rock of a place out in the North Sea. He showed me a photo of his beloved ex-workplace, showing me where he'd alight from his boat to go to work. It seemed impossible – an inaccessible rock.

He told me the tale of the three lighthouse men who went missing from a similar rock. Apparently, tea had been laid out, the meals and drinks were out on the table, but the men had gone. An absolute boys' own mystery.

As I left he shook my hand like an old friend. Again, I'd been made so welcome and I felt so cared for. He doesn't have the interweb so I promised to send him my blogs by post. I don't want to lose him.

The real Donald Sutherland – accept no imitations.

But you don't look like one

Striding out manfully towards Fort George (no, not a shopping centre – it's actually a real, honest-to-goodness fort on the Moray Firth) I met a man on a bike.

He said with some confidence, looking at the ominous sky, 'We're going to get wet.'

I said, with equal conviction, 'No, it's passing us by.'

Weather man, I am not. I found him down the road a bit, sheltering from the storm under a tree. 'I told you it would pass us by,' I smiled as I stood there dripping.

He was going nowhere. I had a captive audience, so I told him about my journey. 'Walking round the UK?' he laughed. 'You'd better watch out, some people might think you're as mad as the people you're collecting money for.'

'Actually ...' I told him about my own mental wiring.

He looked at me closely. 'But you don't look like one.'

A compliment? What on earth does *one* look like?

I thought back to the time when I was working in social services, with the chap who'd been diagnosed with schizophrenia. The chap in whom I'd seen no behaviours that fit in with the label of this mental malady. The chap about whom the psychiatrist had said, 'Well, he looks like a schizophrenic.'

Holy and, indeed, guacamole.

The other day I was walking into Inverness. I met a couple of boys, maybe 11 or 12 years old, who saw my backpack and enthusiastically asked if I'd been camping. I told them an abridged version of my tale.

'I don't mean to be rude,' started boy number one politely. 'But has anyone ever called you mad?'

Join the queue.

It's not an exact science, is it?

Maybe I do look like one. Do you?

The Ferguson Effect

I'd never met them before, and yet the Fergusons had been on board with Walk a Mile from very early on.

I'd walked from Elgin to Lossiemouth, from Forres to Nairn, and I was still over 20 miles from Inverness – my next official food and shelter point – when I received a message with a very important offer. It said:

'If ya need a bed tonight let me know John n I will come and find you. Karen.'

Following the redonkulous horizontal rain, where I felt a level of wetness normally reserved for lying in the bath or bobbing about in the swimming pool, I decided to accept this fabulous offer. We texted backwards and forwards until we agreed on a pick-up point. I plonked myself on the side of the (now dry) road and waited with anticipation.

The best way to imagine this scenario is to think about the meeting of pen friends.

'Helloooooo!' I found myself yelling when I saw her, with a manner ordinarily reserved for long-standing friends. They stopped. We hugged, we shook hands, and I was made to feel at home instantly.

Over the next few days John and Karen dropped me off and picked me up. They gave me packed lunches and their spare room. John took me to Tiso, a purveyor of fine hiking equipment, when my backpack Darth suffered a fatal wound. While I was blagging a huge discount from the chap in the shop I introduced John to him. 'This is John. I've known him, er ...'

I'd known him three days and yet it felt like I'd known him all my life.

Far more important than all the practical stuff was the warmth with which I was welcomed into their family home, the absolute friendship and trust I felt as I was introduced to their daughter, their grandchildren and Karen's parents.

John and I rapidly developed that childish relationship that only men can. In no time we were blaming each other for eating all the biscuits. For the record, Karen, it was me...

John took time out of his life to take me to places in and around Inverness that he loved. Incredible. He had something that was very dear to his heart and he wanted to share it with me. He took me along to Loch Ness and up a hill that gave a spectacular outlook over Inverness, the Black Isle and the Moray Firth. He showed me the cathedral and the castle – which looks not unlike the wooden castles we played with in our youth – which is now used as the local courthouse.

Days of wine and roses? John informs me that the courthouse is more likely to smell of Buckfast tonic wine and urine. Lovely.

Leaving was hard. It felt ... well, difficult. We hugged, shook hands and promised to meet again in the not-too-distant future.

Camping on the west coast? Don't mind if I do.

On my final day of walking into Inverness on the cycle path I was surprised to find myself completely ignored.

I said hello to roughly 20 folk – pedestrians and slow-moving cyclists – and discovered that I must be made of antimatter, as they all looked straight through me with absolutely no response.

Perhaps they were creating the equilibrium. The Fergusons had been so friendly, so kind, so generous and supportive that something had to give elsewhere in the social fabric.

The Ferguson effect.

In all seriousness, John and Karen's kindness made this ignorance all the more surprising. What did these people stand to lose merely by acknowledging my existence? Were they afraid? Shocked that someone they didn't know has said hello? Did they think that I'd recently been created at CERN? That if they interacted with me in any way we'd both cease to exist?

Probably not.

Yesterday I saw a tall young guy chatting to an older woman he'd just met in the post office queue. He was larger than life, interested and interesting – slightly disinhibited, but lovely to see. Some may say there was something wrong with him. Something wrong, – but plenty right.

Remember though, being too kind and friendly may cause others to be borderline antagonistic. That's the Ferguson effect.

Walk a mile with mediocrity.

The Black Isle

The first thing that struck me as I wandered onto the Black Isle was that it is neither black nor an isle. With this in mind, I've decided to call myself 'Tall Slim Hairyhead'. Well, if they can do it...

After crossing the somewhat windy Kessock Bridge, I wound my way down to a village – North Kessock. It was here that I encountered 'The braw wee road' that Ieen, one of my lovely hosts for the next couple of days, had described.

It's a single-track road that hugs the edge of the Beauly Firth. If you ever get the chance ... no, scratch that – stop what you're doing NOW and get there as quickly as you can. It is a stunning bit of Scotland.

Having experienced my virtual non-existence as I passed some of the good people of Inverness only a couple of days ago, I was unsure as to what to expect from the people of the isle. But it would appear that I'm everyone's long lost friend. Everyone I met – from the lady outside the shop, to the young woman taking her collies for a walk, to the man observing the wildlife – had time for a chat that allowed us to exchange just a flake of our lives.

Raymond Bell was the bird spotter, a Yorkshireman to his bones. He listened to my story. As I got to the bit where I said, 'I've been a social worker for nearly twenty years' he interjected with, 'and it did your bloody head in' in his broad accent.

Yep, that just about covered it. I'm thinking about using him to edit all my future sentences. Concise and to the point.

As I walked along the road, the weather swung from hot, to colder, to wet, to … I got a voicemail and a Facebook message from Teen. The message showed a picture of her house. The voicemail told me that she wouldn't be in when I arrived and that I should let myself in round the back, make myself tea and toast, and watch out for the dog (she doesn't like tall men, so I made a name change to Short Fat Hairylegs).

I appreciate this sort of thing goes on in London and other big cities all the time, but up here people are much warier of strangers. It put a smile on my face.

Trust. Does being trusted make someone trustworthy? (No more than 500 words, on my desk by Monday please).

But Teen is a friend of a friend. We were sorted really.

I was met by Skye the collie / spaniel crossbreed, who growled momentarily (I think she felt obliged), realised I was human once I took the backpack off, and then savagely went to sleep.

Two days of hope, optimism, dreams, righteous indignation, and a great sense of friendship ensued. Teen has bipolar disorder that casts a dark cloud over her from time to time. Her most recent depressive period was around Christmas, and shortly after that time, her mum died. In a world where many of us would have battened down the hatches and waited for it all to subside, she welcomed a nosey stranger into her home. She's taking a sabbatical from journalism at present, but was more than able to share some of her life and a good number of her contacts with me with an infectious enthusiasm.

Stewart, her partner, spent many hours into the evening telling me about his previous life and jobs and travels. His knowledge is best described as encyclopaedic. When I describe situations from my past, the edges are blurry – 'I went to a town called ... er ... and I met thingy ... who works with ... you know?' But his stories have a vivid vibrancy to them as he recounts exact names, faces, and places.

He told me a lovely story about when he was younger. He and his brother would get Waddingtons' Jigmaps (they are as they sound). On one particular map of the world was Lake Titicaca, a lake situated at great altitude between Bolivia and Peru. Being boys, they thought this name was hilarious, but he promised himself at that time that he would one day visit this crazily named place. And he did – he and Teen visited during their year-long tour of South America. I'm smiling as I think of his excitement in telling the story.

Teen filled me with hope. There are times when I read the news or hear something on the radio and it completely takes the wind out of my sails. It would be easy to feel a little hopeless as I think of Cameron telling us how multiculturalism has failed, how Vince Cable has fired off a less-than-subtle warning to the unions telling them that the laws may be changed to their detriment if they think about striking, and how they both talk about the importance of buoying up that huge labouring beast, the economy, putting it before people and communities.

'We're in this together. Some of us are more in it than others.' Stewart Buchan, June 2011.

There's so much to tell. This has been a wonderful experience. Teen and Stewart are no longer friends of friends, they're friends. And they've reached out to more of their friends so I can experience more of this rich tapestry.

Suddenly I have real and potential contacts all over Scotland, from the North of the Black Isle to the Isle of Eigg. More to the point, I feel mentally recharged and ready to set out once more on my walk.

It's stopped raining so I'm going to be 'Dry Walking Man'. That's how I got my name, but the mystery of the Black Isle continues.

Zip-a-Dee-Doo-Daa

Today, for whatever reason, the happyometer had cranked up a couple of levels, from 'Huckleberry Finn' to 'Zip-a-Dee-Doo-Daa'.

I'd lived at a castle for one night and I felt well rested, even though some sheep had tried to visit me in the night. But it's not all rock and roll.

I got up, packed, and was on my way. I scrutinised my map. It didn't look like there were many hills today – there were hardly any of those decorative contour lines. It was true. This was a rolling hills day as opposed to a 'you'll just have to go on without me' day.

I came to a sign in the road that filled my heart with joy. 'Elphin Tea Rooms – two and a half miles.' It was about half past three – so, if I cracked on I could get there before closing.

That said, this is all happening in the middle of nowhere – you can forgive people for shutting up shop early. With this in mind, I sped off like a cheetah (well, okay, an enthusiastic arthritic snail). It wasn't really the food I was motivated by. It was the company and the fluids, in that order.

Finally I saw the café nestling on the side of the valley. There were people still standing outside, so it must have been open. I was now motivated by food, fluid and then people.

'Sorry mate, they've just closed,' Ed, a citizen's advice worker, and his partner grinned at me.

Joining in with the joke, I quietly said, 'Oh, okay then,' and pretending to turn around and start walking off. Weren't we just a bunch of jokers?

We got chatting and Ed told me it was one of his pet hates that folk failed to acknowledge people with mental health problems.

'I mean, if you wander in with a big stookie' (a brilliant Scots word for plaster cast) 'on your leg, then people make way for you. If they can't see there's something wrong with you then they don't believe it.'

He handed me £10. 'Get yourself something nice,' he said as he nodded towards the tearoom.

Inside I started to babble. It was like all the previous days of perceived isolation had come to a head. I talked about food, water, Walk a Mile ...

David, one of the owners, explained why they'd all been standing outside, 'I was showing that couple one of the golden eagles that flies around here.' I was excited and gutted all at once. All along my walk I'd hoped to see this magnificent bird, and now, because I'd been fixated on food, I'd missed it.

David and Jenny, his partner, were really friendly, interested, and funny. 'He scared the eagle away with that kilt,' he explained in his fine Yorkshire accent to a couple sitting near me.

After cheese and corned beef toasties, a great big scone and jam, gallons of water, and gallons of tea, they asked me if I'd like a couple of rolls to take with me on my way. They were about to close and they wouldn't be using the rest of the corned beef.

As I bent over to put the goodies in my bag, the German woman behind me said, 'Make sure you get a photo.' I assumed she was referring to what I was wearing under my kilt, so I showed her it was okay, I was wearing boxers.

'No, of the eagle,' she laughed. 'I was talking about the eagle!'

Whoops!

I went to pay, only to be told 'No charge' as they handed me a bottle of water and a can of Irn Bru. We talked a little about David and Jenny's experience of being up here. They had come up from

Yorkshire seven years ago, for no other reason than they'd fallen in love with the place.

I was surprised to hear that this lovely couple had experienced prejudice from travelling Scots. 'Not more bloody English,' had been heard more than once.

Even though that had been an absolute rarity – they'd stressed that the vast majority of the time they'd been made to feel most welcome – the impact of this extreme reaction had been hard for them to deal with.

As I walked away I quietly cursed myself for missing the golden eagle. David had taken some time to describe what they looked like. And then to simplify it further, he said 'You know it's not a buzzard or a kite. Eagles are huge. You'll know ...'

About a mile up the road a huge thing banked round in the field next to me – followed closely by another. Two golden eagles! I nearly fell over with excitement.

He was right. They're huge, like flying ostriches. I'm David Attenborough, I am.

A few miles further there was another one. This one was surfing on the thermals as they came up the side of the hill next to me. He hovered stationary in the sky. Magnificent. Just beautiful. I could understand how they'd been bestowed with power and wisdom in any folklore you care to mention.

It suddenly struck me – I could take a photo of it. I rushed for my phone, and held it up just as the eagle dropped and banked around the hill. The photo I got was not dissimilar to the 'UFO flying over Corby' type pictures you can find on the internet.

It looked like dirt on the camera lens.

If you want to see a golden eagle, look at pictures of them. Better still, go to the Elphin Tea Rooms. The food's great and the people are lovely.

Okay, I'm a fraud

Today I wrote the 'Zip-a-Dee-Doo-Daa' blog. In actual fact, it was really easy to write. I felt I was writing about someone else. I probably was writing about someone else.

He was the happy-go-lucky extrovert. I'm the guy who hasn't got the capacity, the courage, the momentum to get out of the tent.

I could feel the fog descending yesterday afternoon. I chose to ignore it, to put it to one side. *It's not convenient*, I thought. *I don't want to cause any trouble. Folk are awaiting their exam results. People have other priorities*.

Today, the inside of the tent is all I can take. My air-filled mat, sleeping bag, kilt, sporran, headlight, first aid kit, coats, money gifted to me, bread and blister plasters, wet wipes and nappy sacks are all around me in the inner lining. In the outer bit lies my sack and my DAB radio.

What does this look like? To the external world, I guess I appear sluggish, almost other-worldly. Everything feels like a huge effort. The idea of putting all my bits and pieces together into a backpack feels unimaginable today. Walking, likewise.

It's all so far away. I've just noticed my breathing's laboured, like it's reluctant. I don't know.

In my head is a sticky mist. It's like I'm suddenly linked to all my previous episodes, crawling on the floor, my face in mud. It's like I'm hiding or just inert or maybe both.

I know it comes back – it always does – but each time I feel horribly defeated, flattened by this thing I feel I should have control of. I feel mildly irritated by myself. *Pull yourself together, it will pass*. And yet any sounds – cars and lorries and motorbikes passing on the road next to me – are intolerable.

'I won't do anything to myself!' is what I'll shout to anyone who asks. But the urge to batter my head in to just stop this fucking noise is astonishing. I want to say 'I'm a bit mad' in a frivolous way, a way that makes it more comfortable for others. I wouldn't wish this on anyone. I know the world is real, it's just that it's refusing to be just that. I'm doing my best to write down what's going on, but I feel so detached, so inhuman.

The urge to cut off my limbs, especially my left hand, is incredibly strong. I've no idea why. Thankfully all I have is my North Pole spoon.

I want it to stop, that's all. I want these recordings of my past playing simultaneously all around me – little vignettes each calling for my absolute attention – to go away. I want the pain, the guilt, the self-loathing to go away. My teeth are clenched, my hands tightening in fists of rage. My heart is thumping.

It will pass. It always does.

I promised myself I'd write about it. I can't face committing it to video though.

My other great urge is to apologise for the inconvenience caused. My promise is that normal service will be resumed shortly – in a day – a week – an hour – who knows?

Walk a Mile Max

When I was five my teacher, Miss Jones, called the whole class 'my children.'

One day, Mark Havercroft asked her, 'Miss Jones, are these really all your children?'

It was with a similar naivety that I said to Judy, the proprietor of the Applecross Inn, 'Isn't it amazing that you have all these locals turning up every night?'

Applecross, being in the middle of nowhere, doesn't really have locals. 'These aren't locals,' Judy smiled. 'Some of them are folk who come back once or twice a year. A few are workmen.'

And then it dawned on me. I wasn't the only one who'd been made to feel so welcome – it was everyone.

Earlier I'd arrived at the pub and checked my contingency fund. I had about £80. I had no clean clothes and all my batteries had been used up. 'How much for a bed?' I'd asked.

'I'll do it for £45,' Judy said, taking me upstairs. 'Would you like a bath?'

I tried not to sound desperate. 'Oh my God, yes please.'

Bathed, refreshed and wearing the least smelly of my smelly clothes, I'd wandered down to the bar. I craved lager shandy.

Judy and I got chatting. She's from Huddersfield and she came to Scotland 23 years ago. She hasn't looked back. She is great at what she does – running a remote pub with local atmosphere and great food.

Cue Jim. Jim had chatted to me on my way in. He was really interested and moved by the Walk a Mile thing. He is ex-forces, and has been involved with Help for Heroes. He was a great listener. 'Would you like something to eat?' he asked.

I'd been planning on cooking up some Supernoodles with the kettle in the room. 'Yes. That would be great!'

He got me fish and chips – fantastic – and I went mad and had another shandy.

'We're going to have a whip-round for you, and a raffle,' Judy told me.

I was taking a day off walking the following day, to get the full benefit of the 27 baths I'd had. So it was agreed that the raffle for her donated bottle of Famous Grouse would be drawn the following night at 9.00pm. The kindness of strangers …

The following morning I felt great. My legs were still a bit creaky, but pretty good. At breakfast I met Jim, his wife Ali (excuse any spelling issues there) and their lovely four-year-old boy, Ollie. They were so enthusiastic and friendly. They vanished to prepare for their day of walking and fishing.

I asked about laundry. This was done by the in-house laundryman, George, with a two-hour turnaround from manky to clean and dry. I went down to pay. 'No charge,' Judy said simply.

This had been a significant amount of comfort and pampering – for no charge.

I would be camping nearby, so we agreed that I'd come back for the raffle at 9.00pm. I had a relaxed day and came back to the pub at 7.00pm – still feeling clean in my recently washed clothes. I had money to buy tea, so I indulged in a Thai chicken curry.

I chatted to folk as they came in. The atmosphere was delightful as Judy did the hard(ish) friendly sell of the raffle tickets. £157 is what she raised – £157! The contingency fund was looking pretty healthy, to say the least!

But Judy wasn't done yet. I told her that I was going over the 'Big Hill' to Loch Carron the next day. Judy arranged for Hubert, my trailer, to be given a lift to her friend Viv at the Kishorn Fish Bar so I didn't need to pull him up the highest road in the UK, or get run over by him on the way down.

I got chatting to a couple of guys called Craig and Jamie. They'd grown up together and met up a couple of times a year to go on scary walks along ridges and the like – oh, and to get pissed. Far be it for me to say, 'A big boy made me do it,' but suffice it to say, Craig ensured we had several drinks, including a whisky, for the road …

I giggled as I slalomed up to my tent. What a great night, what a great place, what great people.

I awoke with a start realising that me, Darth II and Hubert had to be somewhere. We got to the inn, where I saw Judy and her sister. I had no idea how to begin to thank them, so in time-honoured tradition I threw my arms around them.

As I walked away, I thought to myself that it's little wonder that the Applecross Inn has won the Best Pub in Scotland award for 2012.

The road over this particular Big Hill is crazy – it's a single-track road which zigs and zags from one false summit to the next. Many folk on the road asked if I wanted a lift, but small, slow steps were the order of the day as I walked up through the clouds.

It was a little sad that, at the top, there was little to see. It was misty and there was some snow, but not much else. I smiled as I remembered speaking to the barman – who also drives the snow plough – the previous night. He'd said that the ice had been so thick and slippery that he'd had to use the blade of his snow plough as a brake to stop him from falling.

I went over the summit and was presented with a road that could be best described as hilarious. It's like a cross between the Cresta Run and the Italian Job as it veers and swerves its way down the mountain. I'll admit the descent was sore on the feet – but so worth it.

I got to the bottom to rejoin the main road I'd left at Shieldaig. By keeping it coastal I'd walked 40 miles instead of eight, but ... wow.

I got to the Kishorn Seafood bar and was met with the friendly face of Viv as she confirmed that she did, in fact, have Hubert. I got chatting to Eileen and Brain, a couple who live in Wemyss Bay, south west of Glasgow.

'You must come and stay with us,' they jointly smiled. So addresses and phone numbers were exchanged. What a hoot!

They left and I tried to pay. Viv explained that I wouldn't be paying, and that that was her donation. She told me that she'd had a brush with depression in the past and that it had been well managed with medication.

I asked her if she knew of any good camping spots, which is where I am now. I'm on the banks of Loch Kishorn, listening to wind, rain, the call of buzzards, the chatter of sparrows and the distant bleat of recalcitrant sheep.

What a few days. Walk a mile max.

Taken for a ride

There's one thing that the west of Scotland does well at this time of year – and that's provide water from the sky.

I walked round the southern shore of Loch Carron and, on seeing the Strathcarron hotel, I thought I fancied a shandy.

'It's a great provider of simple carbs and hydration,' I smiled at Ian, who'd bought me a couple of the said refreshments I was appraising. He's a builder up in these parts. Impressed with the sacred ramble, he saw fit to furnish me with a few drinks and, just as importantly, his time. Among other things he told me that his mum had been diagnosed with Alzheimer's disease – a condition that's often as challenging on the carers as the sufferers.

Like with so many illnesses, dementia sufferers and their carers can feel isolated in their plight – and yet there are currently 800,000 people in the UK with some form of the disease. Carers who are family members of sufferers save the UK over £8 billion each year.

Ian didn't dwell on this. We chatted about a whole variety of stuff before it was time for me to get on my way. Time to get on my way? Oh yes, let me explain …

The A890 has suffered a major landslide and, as such, is only open at certain times. I had hoped to nip across on the Strome Ferry that had reopened for a couple of months to help with the movement of Scotland's highland community. However, that was not to be – it closed again last month I think. I'd heard that a convoy system was in operation, leading cars along the railway line for a stretch before returning them to the real road. Maybe they'd let me walk along…

Er, maybe not.

My sense of all that is right means that, at the end of my journey, I'll have to return to this half mile stretch – because I was taken for a ride instead. No matter, it allowed me a bit of time out of the rain while I chatted with the driver. He'd had his own mental health problems and felt that his life had been made better by having folk who love him, good talking therapy and some medication. He was so open, so friendly and enthusiastic about Walk a Mile.

I reached my destination for the day, a small place called Achmore which, I'm reliably informed, means 'big field'.

As I was putting up my tent a girl, maybe 11 or 12 years old, walked up and asked what I was up to. I told her about my journey – then she trumped me by telling me about the two-year journey her mum and dad had taken her on: a cycle ride the full length of the American continent, from Alaska to the southern tip of Chile.

While I was remarking on what marvellous parents she had, her mum, Ingrid, appeared. We chatted briefly and she told me, during my wrestling match with my tent, that she was having a bunch of friends around for the evening and that I should come round to enjoy a roast dinner and a bath.

There it was again – the folk of the UK working their magic.

I finished putting my tent up and wandered over to their house, feeling a little guilty at being empty handed. I was welcomed in like a long-lost friend. Dad Sean and daughter Kate easily matched Mum's hospitality as their planned visitors arrived. I spent the whole evening with that fixed grin that only jamming a coat hanger in your mouth would normally provide.

They were so keen to tell me about their American adventure, how they'd done no cycle training before they left and that Sean built the bikes at the airport, hoping that all the bits were there. They rowed kayaks in between icebergs just off Alaska, with whales breaching nearby. They told me about the fantastic hospitality they received in Canada, the States, and central American and South American countries – with photos to match.

In among this Kate, wonderfully chatty and friendly, gave me her sheepy Easter cake and one of her Easter eggs.

Ingrid and I briefly chatted about the loss of our parents – by a strange coincidence she and I had both been rendered parentless, thanks to cancer, by the age of 25. We talked about how we never really got to know our parents as proper people, and not just acting in the roles of Mum or Dad.

But then we were straight back on the magic carpet ride. They told me about their tree planting, their other travels, Sean's sculptures of climbers, Ingrid's photography and their appetite for life and people.

Giving me hospitality came as naturally as breathing to them. There was a kind of travelling cowboy mentality – if you provide for others, others will provide for you. What comes around goes around. Karma, or whatever you want to call it.

As I was readying to head forth into the rain again this morning, one of their neighbours came round with a cup of coffee. It had all been so lovely, fantastic and delicious that I had to laugh out loud at the offer of even more kindness.

Skye and the 120 miles per hour mini-break

'But Dad, I want to see a golden eagle.'

'Shut up, you can see them on the internet.'

'George, what is the rule when you see someone walking towards you on your side of the road, pulling a trailer?'

'He'll get out of the way, Julia, just you watch.'

'But he doesn't appear to have anywhere to go.'

'Don't worry, *Julia*, the law is on my side.'

'Dad, can we keep the funny bald man on the bonnet of the car?'

'I really think you should stop now, George.'

'Julia, children, we have a schedule! It's people like him – look at him, bloody anarchist with his trailer – that cause chaos up and down the country.'

'Dad, I need a wee.'

'Sorry, the next scheduled stop is in Bristol.'

Ladies and gentlemen, welcome to the A87, the road into Skye. Good Lordy, they drive fast at you. I'm not going to stay on the road as a point of principle.

What does a break to the beautiful isle of Skye conjure up for you? A gentle drive through stunning scenery? Taking time to enjoy the symbiotic nature of human and land – the animals and plants upon it? Funny, really.

I am sure that somewhere in the highway code it says, 'Don't kill the funny bald man walking towards you with a trailer.' It may not be explicit – but I'm sure it's there somewhere in spirit.

I was astonished at the number of drivers who drove straight at me at speed in the belief that I'd vanish. I appreciate that people's time is valuable, but please, turning slightly or slowing down to negotiate the walking speed bump would be nice.

Skye is beautiful. Once I was off that particular main road I could take a look.

I walked past a family of cyclists – the youngest of whom was probably ten – all pedaling on in stoic terror. I wonder what it's like when it gets really busy.

Off the main road, I meet a lovely couple from Nottinghamshire, who tell me they are on a once-in-a-lifetime, two-year journey to go to all the places around the UK and Europe that they hadn't seen. They'd tried cycling on the road of terror and concluded they wouldn't require All-Bran for a week or two.

They've been all around the world and were pleasantly astonished at the beauty of this fair country and the kindness and warmth of the people in it (when they weren't trying to run you over).

I met a chap, Jeremy, who'd worked for Rethink – a charity that encourages folk to look at the situation of those with mental health problems. Google it – see what they're up to.

I'm afraid my listening skills weren't quite as they might be, since he'd stopped in the middle of the road and I was jumping in and out of traffic to keep it going. He told me of some places where I might be able to stick my tent up. This was more difficult than it sounds, since there were miles and miles of heather-covered moorland – no grass of note anywhere.

So on I trundled into the early evening. As I walked, I saw a guy on a three-wheeled chopper / motor bike thingy. He wasn't travelling at speed; he was just happily cruising up and down the same bit of road as me. He'd gone past me a number of times when he finally pulled over, and with a huge grin said 'Are you as mad as me?'

I reached out to shake his hand and said, 'Very probably.'

We chatted like mates who hadn't seen each other in a while. He talked about his beautiful chopper (just don't – I can't believe you have to cheapen everything) and how working on it, riding it and talking about it kept his own mental health in line.

He gave me his non-business card – and I gave him mine. He gave me some directions to some nearby flat grass. I walked off thinking we do mad things to keep us sane.

So, as directed, I walked up the dark and lonely forest track, following it deeper and deeper into the trees and only occasionally breaking my step to say, 'Lions and tigers and bears, oh my!'

I finally got to the clearing to find two firemen from Birmingham putting their tents up. They'd been given directions from a local hotel. I felt my directions had far greater kudos, having been given to me by a guy calling himself Mad Rob.

We talked briefly. We managed to cover the fact that they had to work longer for, and pay more into, their reduced pensions. Cycling around Scotland just gave them a break from all that. I told them to be careful – most of the conversations I'd had with English folk now living up here had started with, 'We only came up for a holiday...'

I went off and put my tent up far away enough from them so they'd be outside the blast radius of my snoring.

Tomorrow I'm definitely having a rest day.

And then, and then, and then ...

The day didn't start terribly well. I'd put a Compede plaster on the blister on my right heal. It was coming off slightly so I thought I'd remove it and replace it with a new one. Using my mum's tried and tested 'pull it off fast and you'll hardly notice it' technique, I pulled it off fast, removing a chunk of healthy skin.

We had a gusher. Suddenly my rolly-down mat thing looked like an operating table in the Crimean war. Finally, some of the bits and pieces in my first aid kit came in handy – the scissors to cut off the remainder of the healthy skin and plaster combo, the antiseptic wipey things to make sure I don't die of trenchfoot, and the moppy-uppy swabby things to er ... well, you know.

I stuck a blister plaster in the middle of the mess, pulled my sock on and seized the day.

Matt

Matt was a cyclist zipping around these here parts enjoying the incredible heat. He lives in Manchester and is in the process of starting up his own electronic publishing business, having spent too much of his life commuting three hours in and out of London every day.

No eye contact and no conversation.

Not Matt. I meant commuting in London. Do try to keep up.

We compared notes and off he went on his very happy and enthusiastic way. I felt that, just by talking to him, some of my batteries had been recharged.

John

Is a guy who works for Turning Point – a mental health charity. I had sought shelter under a tree from the beating sun in Arisaig.

He generously enthused about my little adventure and raced off to catch a train.

Andy

Wandered over from the hotel opposite and remarked that I hadn't done much walking from what he could see. He sported the best Amish beard I've seen outside of ... er ... you know, Amish land ...

He's an agricultural engineer and has enjoyed working much of his life in Tanzania. He was going back there soon. We chatted about Walk a Mile and he told me that his wife had bipolar and that this was controlled – more or less – with lithium. She had also experienced electro-convulsive therapy a number of years ago, which he feels only served to pickle her head further.

He thinks that having a stable environment and a steady routine has helped her with her condition. That and the fact that he monitors her when she decides that she doesn't need to take the same dose / any dose at times. I can't imagine ever playing around with my pills.

Andy Dempster, the writer of 100 Classic Coastal Walks in Scotland.

Look him up – I met him in a lay-by, so I didn't have to. We chatted about the hills he'd climbed and the hills he'd yet to climb, the beauty of Scotland and the ludicrously hot weather (to be fair this was an ongoing theme throughout the day) and how he felt that the originality of my story made it publishable.

He might have said some other stuff, but I'd floated off into a fantasy world of book signings and brightly coloured cravats.

The three generous walkers

This trio of men in their latter years had got together to ramble around some Scottish hills. They live in different parts of the UK, occasionally meeting up for little adventures. I told them my story; they gave me £30 and some firm, encouraging handshakes.

The cyclist whose name I have forgotten

About a mile up the road from the generous fellows I found some much needed shade. I'm sure it's detrimental to the cardiovascular system if you let the blood boil.

The nameless cyclist pulled up and joined me. He'd been pushing it a bit too hard. At first I was concerned; I thought he might be overly dehydrated or suffering the effects of heat stroke or something. But he was fine. I'm pretty sure my concern was some sort of projection.

We enjoyed a bit of light banter. He told me the guy who was going to accompany him on his Scotland journey had suffered a hernia. Cycling was probably not the best idea then.

He listened to my tale of derring-do and told me he wanted to help. He said he didn't have much but he was right in his assumption that every little helps. He pressed a £1 coin into my hand. It's hard to express the delight I felt at this gesture, at this guy who had little but wanted to share it.

Jean the French cyclist and Carla the German guide

Have I mentioned it was hot? I was sheltering in the shade of yet another small monument erected in the name of bonnie Prince Charlie. The batteries that I carry for my phone warn me not to expose them to anything more than 60 degrees centigrade. The one I'd kept in the top part of Darth II had gone a little wonky. No matter, it served as a good hand warmer.

Jean turned up on his bike with the biggest smile and the whitest teeth I've seen outside a Colgate advert. His English was monumentally better than my French (une banan – go on, guess what that might be). He was reliving his childhood by cycling around some of his favourite holiday spots in Scotland, Ireland and Norway. He'd been saving for years for this journey, and his smile reflected his infectious joy at just being out on his bike.

Carla turned up in her car. Jean commented that we were all travelling alone. I suggested we had no mates. He countered that by saying we were alone together.

Carla was doing some preparation for taking German tourists around the area. She wanted something a little different. I babbled extensively about my time on Eigg and Knoydart.

We took some photos and promised to meet up in that exact spot in twenty years. We were best friends forever.

Actually, in reality they took my cards and promised to look me up whenme.

JR the West Brom supporter

I am a Baggie. A West Bromwich Albion supporter. However, all my enthusiasm for my team pales into insignificance when compared to this man.

He was there in 1954 when we won the FA cup. Yes, yes, I'm sure you're all amazed and astonished. He started talking about players I'd never even heard of. He remembered specific goals; he could recount them as vividly as if he had just seen the game.

John, for that is his name, travels the west of Scotland in his motorhome. He has been fortunate enough to see otters and pine martins and all the other cute critters on offer up here.

After a quick calculation, I worked out that JR is 68. He lost his wife recently and is more than aware of his own mortality, having had two melanomas lopped off his neck. He warned me about heat stroke as he remembered that hot summer of '76 when it happened to him. It's not likely to happen to me, I told him. I shuffle from shade to shade drinking my own bodyweight in water as I go.

He's from Tamworth originally, and told me that he hates big cities because of the anonymity and the lack of a friendly smile.

All too soon, I was back on the road. I wanted to give this man more of me, but I had to find somewhere to pitch before sundown.

Roy the ex-soldier

I find Roy looking out at Eigg across the Sound of Arisaig. The sun was beginning to set and he was swigging from a can of lager. He gave me a big smile and offered me a can. Well, it would have been rude not to.

He told me about his time in the army. I admired his beautiful motorbike as he told me about the beatings he endured from his ... superiors (?) when he expressed opinions about the jobs he was on. For example, he received a smack in the mouth at Greenham Common for suggesting that the women there had a valid viewpoint.

He had a Bristol accent and he wanted to come and live in Scotland. His dad was Scottish so he felt he had some affinity with the place.

I told him that he and I both have Scottish accents, it's just that they haven't been universally recognised by the rest of the Scots.

He liked this. We talked about the pipes – I like *Amazing Grace* by the Royal Scots Dragoon Guards. His cousin and his family whizzed up – contemporary pipe music blaring from the car.

I had a brief chat with him. He told me how he had what he describes as a nervous breakdown a number of years ago, and resided in the Inverness loony bin (his words) for a month.

He feels he emerged from his madness with little memory of it. I asked him if he felt it had completely left him for good. When the nights get long up here, he develops a sense of dread and feels the world closing in on him. At times like that he drives back to his mum's in Glasgow – only to touch base, turn around and come back.

It works for him.

All these people – and more – in just a couple of days: this is what Walk a Mile is like. Join me, go on, you know you want to ...

Chris Young – media whore

After nearly two years of Walk a Mile, I had finally invaded England. It was a crisp, sunny day as I waved at passing traffic on the B road that runs parallel to the mighty M6 and its huge volume of assorted motorists.

I had a bit of time on my hands (when don't I? It still makes me laugh when Ella phones asking, 'Are you busy?') so I decided to phone the local paper and radio station.

Emily from the News and Star was very enthusiastic – just the thing to put a spring in the step. She would interview me and send out a photographer in due course.

Now for BBC Radio Cumbria. I was a little reticent phoning the BBC given the responses I'd received in Scotland. They didn't think my story is really news. But hey, I thought I'd give it a punt.

Imagine my pleasant surprise when I heard Sara from the mighty Beeb exclaiming, 'Wow, that's amazing! We'll try to fit you into a slot today.'

'I, er ... cool!' I declared. I'd had my own radio show back in the day on Radio West Fife, a hospital radio station attached to the local Dunfermline hospitals. My greatest achievement had been 'Let the blood run free', the hospital soap. That, and the fact that we'd received complaints for talking about the Karma Sutra on the late evening show.

Complaints meant folk were listening!

As I walked into Carlisle, a man and his dog drew level with me. He asked if I was going far. I told him about the walk and he shared a bit of himself. His name is Jerry and he heads up a clinical team who work in operating theatres in the local hospital.

I somehow managed to stifle my Tourette's-like urge to talk about Jerryatricks and / or Jerry and the Pacemakers. He told me how, in the light of the reports about Stafford hospital, staff at all levels and of all professions were feeling the squeeze of stress in their jobs.

I asked if there were systems in place should the stress of the job begin to get on top of folk. He told me about the human side of the job – about the shock experienced by himself and others when they come across friends and family in A&E. They are offered counselling, but, as a rule, most staff are reluctant to accept it. Because it's a sign of weakness? Denial? Who knows? Some folk use their line managers at these times. But what happens if it's your boss who's causing you stress?

I got a call from Sara at Radio Cumbria. I was going to be on Caroline Robertson's show at 3.40pm. How exciting!

I decided to go to a local café, The Chimes, opposite the cathedral, and have chips and cheese. A heart attack on a plate. I clattered in, knocking a chair over and receiving a Paddington Bear hard stare from the proprietor. I told her about what I was up to and lo, I was indulged to free hospitality.

Radio Cumbria wasn't exactly like Radio West Fife; they had all kinds of shiny things and more than one microphone that worked. I really enjoyed myself. The presenter, Caroline Robertson, was right dead friendly and I was put at my ease instantly. I could see my celebrity life rolling out before me ... the One Show, Clare Balding's rambling radio show ... book signings ... (best write it first) and so on ...

My media ego was further massaged the next day when Louise, the photographer from the newspaper, caught up with me and I did exactly as I was told. Well, there's a first time for everything.

So that was all good fun, and I'm getting the story across too. What more could I want?

The three-pronged approach to dealing with mental health problems? Honesty, honesty and honesty ...

Today I met a man of about 60, mending a wall while his dog bounced about just for fun. I briefly told him about what I was up to and he told me his tale.

About 30 years ago he'd been working flat out, feeling the stress of it all but getting on with it. Like so many others, I guess.

But then a few simple things contrived to push him over the edge. Nothing terribly profound or life threatening, but just a gentle nudge to send him too far. First of all, he had to get his car fixed. The weather was bad– snowy – and the guy with the part he required wouldn't deliver it. His car was still functioning, so he drove off into the snowy night to get it. The experience caused him a great deal of stress.

He then started struggling to sleep. He was worrying about something and nothing (his description). He also found the prospect of completing the (usually simple) paperwork for his livestock almost impossible. He asked a friend round to help with it. After a bit his friend said, 'Where are the debts?' But there weren't any debts – he wasn't worried about money. He was just unable to function properly.

He believes if his GP had acted swiftly by giving him antidepressants he'd have been fine. As it was, he fell into a ten-year spell of a depressive illness, his mind slow and sluggish, thoughts of suicide haunting him.

With the help of a light box and the right medication, he feels more in charge of his mental health than ever before. He relapses from time to time, experiencing what he describes as breakdowns, but he gradually bounces back to a more functioning person, given a little time. He understands that depression is something that is common in his family, but that this is a truth that has taken a long time to come out.

People in his family say they have a virus and recurring headaches – all, he believes, smokescreens for their mental health problems. He had an uncle who he suspects took his own life after long periods of viruses and headaches. He walked onto a busy road and was killed by the traffic.

He described other folk in his family who, he feels, hid the shame of their mental health problems, with the result that they suffered more in isolation. They believed they should just pull themselves together.

He was angry when he told me that you don't get that reaction with physical illnesses. That's why folk in his family talk of headaches and viruses – hiding the problem, but not moving on. He has prostate cancer, with all the symptoms that go with it. But he says this physical illness doesn't affect him one tenth as much as his breakdowns.

And so he told me what he believes is the best way to deal with mental health problems: honesty, honesty and honesty.

'Say it back to me,' he said.

'Honesty, honesty and honesty,' I said.

'Good, I was just making sure you got it in the right order,' he said.

Dumfries

They call them ear worms, those tunes that play over and over in your mind, unwelcomed – and, in this case, unexpected.

Every time I thought of my destination – Dumfries – the theme tune to *Magic Adventures of Mumfie* started to play in my head. The problem was that it wasn't a very good recording …

'Mumfie is an elephant, a something little elephant, who always something something every day …'

I was striding out confidently in the knowledge that I had, possibly, the choice of four places to stay in Dumfries … is an elephant, a … something little elephant…

It was a crisp, sunny day, but I had awoken earlier to a weather report saying it was -5 degrees where I was. *Ridonculous*, I'd thought. I was positively toasty in bed. So I'd gone out – and found Narnia.

One of Hubert's (metal) handles had ventured outside so, without a thought for my own safety, I had grabbed it, only to feel my hand gently weld to it. And that's why, officer, I had a two feet-long metal handle in my sleeping bag with me.

I've digressed. Gradually all four of the possible hospitalities evaporated throughout the day, leaving me talking to a guy from

Lancaster who was leaning on a wall. He presented me with a bottle of Vimto and some directions as to where I might pitch. In among all this I cried out to Facebook and the Twitterati, such was my disappointment at having lost all my places to stay. There was a flurry of activity as I found a perfect field and whacked the tent up.

I decided today would be perfect for a rest, and so I have lounged like a loungy thing all day. Until, that is, I heard from a chap who'd read my *Sun* article. He wanted to meet up. Who was I to refuse?

There came a 'Chris, are you there?' from outside the tent. Since I knew I was having visitors, I washed (wet wipes) and put on some clean clothes. I smelled like a nursery.

The chap, who will remain anonymous for reasons that will come clear later, thankfully chose not to comment. He whisked me away to McDonald's for my tea, furnishing me with a Big Mac meal and a chocolate muffin. We talked about a whole bunch of stuff, including what made him want to help. He said he was soft hearted.

He told me he occasionally saw things or people he wanted to support. 'After all, you can't help everybody,' he said.

I asked if he'd had any experience of mental ill health in his life. He said no, but he has a granddaughter who has dyspraxia, minor learning disabilities, and some difficulty with coordination and emotions. But she was happy, he was very keen to stress. You play with the hand you're dealt.

We chatted more about something and nothing. I asked him how many children he'd had. He said three, but there were only two now. In the middle of a busy McDonald's I said, 'What happened?'

He told me that when she was 17, his daughter had entered a suicide pact with her boyfriend. They'd taken their own lives.

He still thinks of her. He comes across as a proud man – god, that sounds nebulous. He's a man who plays his cards close to his chest. He'd first said he'd had little to do with mental health issues, and now this.

He held my gaze. Again he said something along the lines of 'You just get on with your life. I've got my grandchildren.'

We talked a little more about what I was doing and the impact of mental health. He smiled as he said I 'didn't look like one.' He also drove me around a bit to ensure I knew which way to go in the morning. As I got up to get out of his car, he put £10 in my hand, apologising because it wasn't much.

I thanked him, saying goodbye as if this was the last time we'd meet. He smiled with a little twinkle in his eye and said he'd meet with me again if I told him where I was – after all, he has a car.

It's hard to say how touched I was by this gently spoken and unassuming man. I really hope we meet again.

Ripples

A thousand years ago, when I started this ramble, I stressed the point that love, kindness, generosity and trust were every bit as contagious as hate and prejudice.

Very early on in my journey I met a man who galvanised my faith in my fellow folk.

The other day I received this sad email from his son ...

Hi Chris. Thank you for your kind words about your encounter with my dad. I'm sad to say that Dad died earlier this week after struggling with cancer over the past year. While digging into Dad's background, the undertaker stumbled across your blog. You summed up my dad to a tee, so much so that we asked the minister read out your blog as part of the eulogy. Dad would have been pleasantly surprised to find himself on the interweb.

Thank you,

The young Donald Sutherland.

I'm not afraid to say I shed a tear.

It was obvious that I wasn't the only person who'd experienced the kindness of this lovely man.

Normal

If only …

Last night Ella and I had what I'd call a grown-up conversation. For the purposes of this it doesn't matter what the guts of it was, but it's the kind of normal conversation that that couples have up and down the country.

But just at the point where normal folk would be entering into an intense exchange, possibly even a heated debate, I mentally slip a gear. And then … well, nothing. I'm lost in a world of the fizzing brain. Thoughts come and go so quickly it's impossible to fixate on anything. This time even watching endless American cop shows didn't help. I was unable to concentrate on even the most simple of plots.

The urge to self-harm was massive. The urge to take my own life so tempting. Thoughts of graphic violence to myself paraded through my mind. Invasive thoughts came, unbidden, in wave after wave of shock and awe. Intolerable.

Almost intolerable.

Ella asked if she could hold my hand. Ordinarily a loving, cuddly kind of guy, it's all I can do to touch her for a minute or two. I take pills – Quetiapine and anti-psychotics. In retrospect I should have played the oh-so-rare diazepam card.

My inner mantra was barely audible in among all the noise. *This will pass*.

My eyelids twitched. Stress mounted. *It will pass*.

Medication gradually did its job. My mind fought like a recalcitrant child, refusing to go to sleep.

I got up to go to bed. Ella said goodnight. I couldn't even look at her. She said she'd be up soon, but I was off in some dream – playing football ... racing down the wing ... acting as part of the team ... enjoying the joint ebb and flow ...

And then I awoke into this ... this *state* that professionals – that *I* – call dissociation. A fugue state where there appears to be a satellite delay on my perception of the world. Everything is distant. Everything is a dazed misrepresentation of yesterday. I can't focus on reality. Everything is too much.

Unlike last night though, there is no intensity of feeling.

Nothing is real. Nothing. I'm not real. Nothing outside my head is real. I've described this as having my head under the water at a swimming pool, in that my focus on the world is weirdly displaced. I'm numb. I've no sense of caring. I feel no emotion. None.

In trying to explain it to folk in the past, I've described it as feeling like being in shock. It feels like this has been happening more frequently this year. And there's nothing I can do. I chant the inner mantra *it will pass*. So I guess that's not nothing. And look, I'm writing a blog while I'm in it.

In the past it has lasted anything between an hour and three weeks. In recent times it appears to have settled into three or four days. At its most particularly intense I have believed I was a young child, perhaps reverting to a time when I felt most safe.

Other times I feel like an omnipotent being, a Christ-like individual. Surely if my mind is the only thing that truly exists, that must be the only answer. The irony of the fact that I'm an atheist isn't lost on me.

At times in the past, I have self-harmed with great gusto, just so that I could feel something. Anything.

Today I have pills. I have my mantra, and the gentle pulse of the cop show in the background.

Just another Walk a Mile kind of a day

We arrived in sun-drenched Grange yesterday evening and were immediately whisked away by the folk at the B&B. We went to see lovely outdoor production of *Alice in Wonderland*, featuring Lucia, the daughter of the household.

We had a leisurely start to the day, ambling around Grange and taking some pictures for the August edition of *Corby Spirit*, a local magazine serving the town of the same name. We also scoffed a delicious brunch of a bacon roll and the creamy delight that is the 'Bee Sting' – a custardy, rolly thing, a perfect mixture of carbs, sugar, protein and fat to launch me on my way.

The sacrifices I make for this walk....

I just knew things were going well today. Ella and I had said our goodbyes. I was striding out manfully, seizing the day, when I heard 'Christopher! Christopher!'

Someone had thrust £5 into Ella's hand for the purposes of contributing to the ramble. Splendid.

I walked off into the coastal countryside, the sun high in the sky and the pungent aroma of wild garlic gently coaxing me on my way. I met a couple from Liverpool who have recently moved up to sunny Cumbria. I told them what I was about and before I knew it, I was in the middle of a typical Walk a Mile kind of a chat.

Here was a couple who'd been slapped in the face with mental ill health. The cheery woman, enjoying this sun-drenched day, told me about her sister's suicide in the seventies. She'd been a business woman with a family, keen to project an image to the world of someone who was capable and successful. A woman, according to her sister, who never spoke of emotional stuff – who played her cards very close to her chest. It was interesting to hear men don't have the monopoly on this. It was sad to hear about the son's anger, how he felt abandoned, deserted.

As she pressed money into my hand, the woman told me what a great thing I was doing. It's funny, after an experience like meeting these lovely, open people, it doesn't feel like I'm doing a great thing. It feels like I'm doing the *right* thing.

I walked on in true British style, looking for shade out of the sun, all the time thinking that talking about this must be the right thing to do. I was manfully sitting in the shade when four walkers wandered up. They asked my about the ramble. And then, as so often happens, off they went.

I was just gathering my things together when I heard running and a voice behind me. 'Have you got a pen?'

'Er, yes,' I said, rummaging in my sporran.

This was one of the women from the group. She wrote down her phone number and told me there would be hospitality on offer when I got to Heversham tomorrow night. Excellent (in true *Bill and Ted* style).

I wandered on for a while, stopping regularly. The heat was most impressive. I happened across a couple of cyclists. Mr Male Cyclist told me about his meanderings. He loved to stay outdoors. In his younger years he'd taken to the roads with little more than a hammock and a belief that somewhere there'd be two trees the correct distance apart.

Another couple of cyclists turned up and the story exchanging began again. With a chipper, 'We're off, you're beginning to repeat yourself', the first couple rode off.

The very enthusiastic male in the new couple fired off lots of questions, and answered a few himself. He told me they'd just come back from the Outer Hebrides where they'd met a man on a similar mission to me.

Only he was doing it on an electric scootery thing – the very sort sold at disability centres and the like. Cool. He was towing a small caravan with his two cats on board. Wild. He complained that his buggy wasn't quite making the distances promised to him by the manufacturer. Not really that surprising.

There's always someone doing something just a bit more ...

After this most entertaining exchange, the cheery bearded man and his partner made off after thrusting £10 into my hand and telling me that not only do Jain monks walk naked – with a person sweeping gently in front of them so as to cause minimal damage to the world's fauna – they also have, on occasion, gauze over their mouths to prevent the digestion of errant insects.

What a day. Somehow my whole journey was jammed into six hours.

Small steps

Today I'm sitting in Ella's front room, setting myself small goals which may or may not come to fruition.

Opening the blinds was a big step. The world feels cacophonous, but I've done it. That said, I feel a little stripped bare.

Tomorrow I'd like to take a walk outside. Ilmington isn't a terribly threatening place. It's a picturesque village in middle England with delicious yellow Cotswold stone houses. The weather is pretty mild. On Wednesday, I'm hoping to go to my favourite Chinese restaurant for lunch.

These are all starters to the main course – a short holiday to a little seaside resort in southern Spain. Something that normal people do all the time. It sounds like the right thing to do. Surely it will have therapeutic benefits. Surely these are all little steps in the right direction.

I'm going to bring you along on this part of my journey. Today, outside feels a little optimistic. It's bright, it's loud, it's brash. Here in the front room the LOUD TV offers me some escapist solace. When I look elsewhere I feel dazed. My lips are pursed. I'm following the plot on TV, having mislaid it in real life. In good coaching / counselling / cognitive behavioural therapy style, I'm visualising what the outside might look like / feel like / sound like / smell like.

I've got a small route round the block planned. I won't rush. If I see someone I know I'll briefly pass the time of day calmly. The walk will take about 5–10 minutes. It'll be no problem.

So … welcome to Tuesday. It's a cool day – there are a few more clouds than you'd find in the *Simpsons* sky. I've had some Shreddies. I'm charging my phone up so I can call Ella, should things go belly up. This is kind of unrealistic as there's almost no phone reception anywhere in town, and Ella's not around this morning.

So it's probably a good thing I'm on my own. I'll take my computer scrabble shots. I'll get dressed. I'll watch a bit more TV.

How do I feel? Well, I'm trying not to. I'm trying not to attend to it … I'm focusing on the task in hand. But there's a bit of a quandary: I'm scared to feel and I'm scared not to feel – what kind of strange limbo is that?

Okay. I walked out of the house – pausing, where I could, to take snippets of film. Johanna would be proud.

I saw a guy I knew. Stomach lurch – impulse to flee. 'Morning,' I smiled amiably.

I walked around the edge of a local pond, taking in the sounds and sights of a pre-autumn day. A vibrant blue dragonfly buzzes by, and the wind mumbles through the leaves of the oak and horse chestnut trees that hug the route. I feel that distant connection to *the* walk. The sky, the clouds, the smells, the puzzled.

Just as I near Ella's house again I see the post lady and the red post van. I have to stop. I listen as she walks up Ella's path and returns to her red box on wheels. What was I afraid of? A conversation that transcends 'Good morning'?

Then, suddenly, I'm caught in an alleyway frequented by dog walkers. Here comes one now. With nowhere to run and my heart pounding, I say 'Good morning,' with a big (exaggerated?) smile. Then I go back to Ella's without further chicanery.

I did it though. And I think I can do it again. Not right this second. But soon.

Tomorrow involves Chinese food. And a lot more people.

Let's wait and see ...

Small steps 2

No whizzes – no bangs. Yesterday went well, I think.

I walked around Ilmington for about ten minutes. The world felt astonishingly loud, huge and bright. The air in my lungs felt different. Cleaner. Fresher. But I did it. I even did a bit of filming. I spoke to a couple of folk. I got back and I felt, okay.

Today is the next step. A trip into Stratford upon Avon and a Chinese meal. I can't drive. My depth perception has gone to pot. Ella is positive, kind and supportive.

I imagined lots of people just walking, going about their business, shopping, maybe going to work, perhaps doing that holiday thing. I'd imagined going into the restaurant. It's familiar, the folk are friendly and the food is fabulous.

In reality we parked in a quiet car park, took the two-minute jaunt round the corner and were met with smiling faces (my heart was pounding at this point). We knew exactly what we wanted: ribs to start, Thai green chicken curry for me chicken udon for Ella. The place was pretty empty – there was just us there. I calmed down pretty quickly.

As ever, the ribs were magnificent and the curry was just a bit too much. We got back in the car, and went home. I was okay. I'd done it. Well, more to the point, *we'd* done it. I was a little dazed. There was an option of going out in the evening to celebrate a friend's birthday. It was tempting, but a little voice in my head said 'small steps'.

There's a whole mixture of stuff going on just now. I'm trying to just be in the moment, but I also think about the holiday, the drive to the airport, the people, getting onto a plane and all that frippery. The promise of empty beaches. The thought of returning to the walk. Doing it quietly. But there are a bunch of people around the Wirral who've offered to walk with me, who've offered hospitality and a friendly word.

But, one thing at a time. Small steps. We'll get there.

I have to do a talk at the Barrow in Furness Mind event. Now that's just bread and butter to me, isn't it? I need to be contacting universities to look at the possibility of lectures and whatnot.

Whoa there. Small steps.

I need new boots. What will it be like to walk again? I've lost some fitness. But I don't need to rush. I can see some friends then break myself into it gently. It'll be fine.

Weirdly, I'm missing the familiarity of dissociation. The world's more real now. I'm in danger of feeling fine, borderline dandy. What happens if ...?

Shush now, small steps.

What's the worst that could happen?

It had been an easy ramble along the Wirral way on the south side of said peninsula. It was rainy, but hey, I've experienced vastly worse. As I walked, I kept my eyes peeled for a suitable point to put Marvin (my tent) up. I noticed there was a country park with lots of space to pitch up on my route.

Since there is no right to roam law in England, I wandered up to the visitor centre and asked if I could camp on their grounds after telling the front of house man what I was up to.

He told me he couldn't allow it. It's a council area and he couldn't authorise it. I asked if he would do anything if I camped out of site … er, sight. He restated his point. He wasn't for shifting.

I chatted a bit more about what I was doing. He told me that folk with mental health problems were supported in doing work around the park. I told him that I rarely found myself in this sort of pickle (at the same time thinking 'what's the worst thing that could happen if he, as a fellow citizen, told me that he would turn a blind eye?')

He phoned a nearby static caravan park. 'They might be able to be more flexible,' he told me. I just need to go round and have a chat. Then he said, 'In 20 minutes, we'll all have gone home. There will be no rangers here after that.'

I felt he was giving me the nod, so to speak. That said, he had spoken to the chap in the nearby caravan site, so I thought it would be rude not to take a wander across. The chap met me with a very warm handshake – smiling and listening to my tales of derring-do. He was happy to allow me to camp, but since he was the member of a committee, he had to phone a couple of others to get the absolute okay. He described what I was doing pretty well, and then said something like, 'No, he's raising awareness. He's not mental, he's a good guy.'

What to do? I felt that this man in front of me was also a good guy – although I felt the need to shoehorn in the fact that I was both mental (at times) and a good guy.

The committee agreed I could stay – in no small part due to the enthusiasm of the chap standing in front of me. 'So, what was your motivation to do this?' he asked. An in! And so I was able to tell him that I had a mental malady, even though he'd given me the all clear. We stumbled around the subject a bit, but we did okay.

I went to put Marvin up and was obviously delighted to hear and feel one of the tent poles break in three places and tear through the fabric. After all that negotiation, I was tentless.

I fought with poles and tent for a while. All I needed was to make sure Marvin would stay up for one last night. With much jamming, coercing, and oh-dearing, I managed to make him look almost tent-like. Almost – he still looked like something that might have had a chance of winning the Turner prize.

The friendly chap had invited me to pop in for coffee at the campsite bar later. The combination of an early morning tomorrow, psychological fatigue and a buggered tent made me politely decline.

Lying in the sleeping bag, listening to the rain, I was delighted at the cascade of offers of support coming through the interweb. I told these generous folk I was fine for the night. But the world wasn't done with me yet.

'Is he awake?' a young voice said.

'I don't think so.' Possibly her mum.

'Hello?' That was definitely me.

Before I knew what I was doing I'd been welcomed into the pub and furnished with a lager shandy. I sat chatting with Leah (Mum), her 11-year-old daughter Karen and her husband Phil. In that friendly atmosphere we talked about all things Walk a Mile and mental healthy. It took no time for folk to become open and honest.

Leah went out with her daughter momentarily. When they came back her daughter spoke very quietly to me. 'What do you like?'

I looked at her mum for a bit of guidance. When there was none, I said 'I'm not sure what you mean.'

This smiling young person came back with, 'Do you like salt and vinegar, ready salted or cheese and onion? Do you like lemonade, coke, or shandy bass?'

'Ready salted and shandy bass, I think,' I said. And off she went.

Leah told me her daughter had described me as 'a nice man' and wanted to help. She had some money from helping with the bingo. With a smile, Leah gave me £10 to help me on my way. Her daughter then came back with crisps and the shandy bass.

'Thank you.' I was blown away by this.

'I've got 30 pence left,' she said, giving that to me as well. I looked at her mum and she nodded vigorously.

I goodnighted into the night and lay awake for a while thinking, well, 'Lordy!'

Ella is coming up tomorrow to help me get a replacement for Marvin. I'm not afraid to say it'll be lovely to see her.

Folk, who may not completely understand, reach out to help in their own way. People who do understand need to be held back to stop them charging to the rescue. If that's the worst that can happen ...

Think Again

There really is no way to dress this up. This is a hard story to tell, read, or live through. It's a story that opened my eyes and humbled me all at the same time. But it's a story I'd like to pass on. I've kept folk anonymous, given the circumstances.

I was staying in a campsite and word had got round that I was doing what I'm doing. A group of kids who'd been merrily marauding about the place had finally decided it was time to corner me and drag the story out of me. I like an audience, and they were great fun, firing all kinds of youthful questions at me. I'd been drawn to a young guy of 11 or 12. He had a shock of blonde, curly hair and two hearing aids. He was full of questions and listening keenly. I had to be actively mindful of the others in the gang – I could have chatted to him all day.

Later, his dad wandered over, to hear about what I was up to and also to share their story.

When his son was about six months old, he contracted meningitis and septicaemia. They thought they'd lost him but he rallied and pulled through. Unfortunately his hearing had been profoundly affected – which meant he'd had to wear his hearing aids since then. When the kid was about eight years old, Dad wandered in on him in the kitchen to find him holding a sharp knife against his wrist.

All kinds of thoughts hit him like a tsunami. *What's wrong? What have we done wrong? Is this attention seeking? Is this something to do with his hearing?*

They took him to his GP. The GP referred him quickly onto the Children's and Adolescent Mental Health Service – CAMHS. Dad felt that in no time at all they were talking to a child psychiatrist. His eight-year-old son – his beautiful boy – told the doctor that he wanted to die.

The question that stood out for him was this: 'What stopped you from doing it?'

'Nothing,' was the bland reply. His dad told me how shocked he'd felt at this young boy's deadpan expression. In later discussions with CAMHS, he was told they nearly took his son into hospital there and then for treatment.

Over the past few years, he and his wife have been delighted at their son's improvement – a combination of medication and therapy has helped them all move forward. Dad tells me how this has been a sharp learning curve for him. It's a world they'd never expected to find themselves in. He's read as much as he can around the subject of childhood mental health.

There appears to be a bit of a blur between self-harming and suicidal behaviour with his son. He was prone to both. They approached the school to discuss the issues in an attempt to ensure their boy's safety. They asked that he was monitored more around sharp instruments. Dad felt he was met with disbelief and ambivalence from the teaching staff, who felt his son was attention seeking. They had to visit school a number of times to reiterate there was no risk of him coming home with drawing pins in his pockets.

But that, he says, was then. The relationship with the school has improved, although he doesn't feel they fully understood. Now he can give his son a row for being naughty without fear of causing him to go into a psychological decline. He seems to appreciate that he's loved even when he's sitting on the naughty step. Stuff that so many parents take for granted ...

Given all the reports on social media on the internet, they've been reluctant to give him access to it until he's at least 40. That said, he uses Instagram.

One night, Dad told him that was enough for the evening, and that it was time for bed. His boy was unusually determined to keep using his little bit of social media. Instead of wading in, he had a chat with his wife and a friend – both had been monitoring recent developments on Instagram. Their son had told his social media world that he hated his hearing aids.

Instead of the bullying that we've been told to expect from the world of the interweb, their son was met love and kindness. Friends told him he was fabulous, great, wonderful, that he looked great and that they could hardly notice his hearing aids.

It's hard to get this across – but the way the Dad told me about his son's virtual (all real) friends – well, it put the hairs up on the back of my neck and brought tears to both our eyes.

They know they're not out of the woods yet. His son still sees a psychiatrist; when he feels low he's still inclined to isolate himself and, because of his hearing, he often feels paranoid in groups, especially if people are laughing at something he hasn't heard. They all feel they have learned a lot, though, and are managing the situation with support.

It's always been a bit of a quandary to me as to what age folk should be before we start talking to them about mental health. So I asked this dad, who'd clearly become a bit of an expert in this thankfully small field.

He thinks eight years old would be a pretty good starting point. How we do that? I'm not terribly sure. It was so hard to feel the pain of this particular journey, but to hear and see Dad's relief as the story unfolded was an absolute pleasure.

I so wanted to hug him – but we did that manly handshake thing instead. He thanked me for what I was doing. I was really taken off guard with this – especially after all they'd been through and all they'd done. Without missing a beat, he thrust £20 into my hand to help me on my way.

I'm not sure if there's much more I can say.

As seen in Criminal Minds, or Whoops, I did it again.

It was hot. I was sweating like a hot thing in a hot place.

John the farmer spotted my discomfort. 'Hi there.'

This was the same 'Hi there' given to me by Donny Sutherland and many other folk who've fixed me with their friendly auras. This 'Hi there,' meant 'You're coming into my home and you're going to tell me what you're doing and I'm going to look after you for a bit.'

'D'you want a cup of tea?'

I remember reading somewhere that cold drinks cause your body to close its pores because it's reacting to the cold, and as such, has the opposite of the desired effect. Hot drinks, on the other hand …

Listen – *you try* being inside my head for a while. If I have to listen to it, so do you.

I happily accepted the tea while explaining a little about what I was up to and hearing a bit about the lot of a farmer. John told me that subsidies from government and Europe were mysterious entities. Mysterious in that the powers that be were constantly shifting the goalposts. They'd award them for cattle, then only breeding cattle, then dairy herds, then land.

My head was spinning. It made me think of the Monty Python sketch about where first years should hang up their coats.

We had the 'where are you planning to stop for the day' conversation. I said soon, given that I might evaporate. I said I might revert to my 'walking at dawn to avoid the heat' policy to ensure I could knock some miles off. John said I could stay in his static caravan to set me up for my transition to stupidly early mornings. Yes, yes, yes! I tried not to sound over keen, but YES!

He told me that he, his sons and daughter have something to eat at about 6.30pm and that I was welcome to join them. I had the best shower of my entire life and caught up with a few blogs. I might have fallen asleep too.

John came round at about 6.30pm. He said supper would be in about 20 minutes, and then vanished. I never saw him again. One of his son's girlfriends … er, the girlfriend of one of his sons, Helen, came over with a great big plate of carbohydrates and a bunch of questions. I talked about my crispy sunburnt arms and she told me how she'd had her back to the sun while working, causing similar crunchiness.

She asked me about my mental malady. I said I had borderline personality disorder. She'd never heard of it. No worries, not many people have. 'Have you ever seen *Criminal Minds*?' I asked.

'Yes, I love *Criminal Minds*,' she smiled.

'It's usually me whodunnit,' I grinned. There, I'd done it again. Making light of it? Scaring people with it? Using irony?

Being a bit of an arse with it is what I was doing. I think I redeemed the situation by describing some of the emotional effect it has, explaining that as a condition it's hugely over-represented in male prisoners, and that my particular pain in the arse was dissociation. First impressions last, Christopher – save the dodgy gags until later. If ever.

Being the star in every episode of *Criminal Minds* is not a unique selling point. I'm writing it out in my best handwriting 1000 times.

Also, wonderfully entertaining as *Criminal Minds* may be, it isn't a good reference point for learning about people with mental maladies. But I don't think I was too scary, as Helen's joined up to the Facebook group.

Probably just to make sure I leave the area.

Where do you want Walk A Mile to go?

This may come as a massive shock, but I'm going to let you into a secret. Walk a Mile in My Shoes wasn't terribly well planned.

The idea was fed by a number of things: I'd used my excellent group psychotherapy to retrace my steps. I'd had to go back quite some way to find the pre-social work me in my own mind. At the age of 12, I made a pact with myself that I was going to be there for others who found themselves in crazy, out-of-control situations that the young me now found himself in. Prior to that, my world was fabulous – so why not take a look there?

I'd also come to realise that, although my mental health malady wasn't curable, it was potentially manageable. And not just by me, but through the support of others – primarily Ella – who'd come into my world and taught me that anything was possible.

Through the media and speaking to folk around me, it was clear that mental health stigma was still rife in the UK. Not through any kind of malice, but through ignorance – an ignorance that was fed by the steady sensationalist drip from the media.

I loved to write. I loved talking to folk. I loved people; I found them thrilling, nourishing. I loved sport and being outside. I remembered walking holidays with my school where we went to Edale in Derbyshire – the start of the Pennine Way – and just how beautiful that world had been.

So, as you can see – the vast majority of the work was done in my head. Throw in a healthy slice of Satish Kumar, and I was off. The physical practicalities meant gathering clothes, an iPhone and camping gear for all eventualities. And that was all I needed.

Oh, and faith. Lots of faith. Not in any bearded deity in the sky – but in people. I'd convinced myself, and I knew that I could convince others, that people are fabulous. And that people could be – would be – generous and hospitable given the slightest opportunity.

Having Johanna Wagner, film maker extraordinaire, certainly helped.

Walk a Mile in My Shoes isn't just about me though. I don't think it'd be terribly interesting if it was. I think there are enough so-called inspirational tales of derring-do to keep the world sated forever.

It's about you lot. So, what next?

I'm getting physically fitter and lighter as I walk around listening to mental health stories and undergraduate psychology lectures. But what else can Walk a Mile be? What can it become?

Yesterday, I met up with my lovely friend Donna in the town of my birth, Corby, to further my thoughts about what next. Donna will soon be the proud owner of a large community building in the town, with a hall, stage, kitchen, parking, and bags of potential.

We chatted about it. We went to look around the outside of it while she described her hopes and dreams for the space, while ideas for Walk a Mile Rebooted grew in my mind. What if we gathered some like-minded people around to plan for the future of the campaign?

What if we gathered others too? People who we wouldn't immediately imagine would fit the Walk a Mile stereotype (if there is such a thing) – but whose thoughts and opinions could be just as valuable?

What if we could gather folk from different walks of life? People with a whole cross section of views and opinions on this – whatever it is? People from different races, cultures, political parties, different backgrounds. People with different beliefs and opinions – people who've used mental health services, people who haven't, carers, friends, people who've never dipped a toe in that world? People who work, people who don't? Professionals? Those working in mental health? People who work in / for the benefits system? What about local politicians – councillors and MPs?

A gathering of lots of folk with a simple starting question: 'What's it like to be you?'

From there? Well, who knows?

I'm aware that there have been times when I've been winging it a bit – especially in the tail end of last year. It became obvious that there wasn't an infrastructure upon which Ella and I could rely.

I wonder if we could make it all a bit more solid?

CHAPTER 16

SEE ME SCOTLAND

By now I'd walked thousands of miles (mostly in Scotland, but in parts of England, too) and talked to probably thousands of people. It had been hard, joyous, miserable, and amazing – all in equal measure.

But it was time to ramp things up a bit. I'd already been making noise about mental health. It's just that now I wanted to be even louder.

Essentially, I'd noticed that although people with mental health problems and mental health professionals all have a large presence on social media, there didn't appear to be much crossover between the groups. Professionals and people with mental health problems tend to meet under stressful circumstances – for example when a person visits their GP hoping for services when there are none, or when a person becomes so ill that sectioning is seen as the only option.

As a result, stigma and discrimination exists between the two groups. My feeling is that where there is a lack of social experience – virtual or otherwise – there is scope for the insidious tendrils of ignorance, prejudice and stigma to encroach ... yes, on, and from both sides.

Our brains are fabulous. Where we lack knowledge / perceptual information they perform a pretty groovy trick called 'completion'. For example, if we are briefly shown a familiar shape but with part of it removed, – we will perceive a complete shape. Our brains fill it in. Pretty funky, eh?

We do the same with all our experiences of the world – which serves us pretty well.

However, at times, and with very little evidence, our wonderful minds will come with a pile of old ballcocks. Ballcocks that we'll reinforce with any 'evidence' we find about the place, including the interweb.

Walking around and talking about mental health would only provide a starting point for change.

It was with this in mind that I began talking with See Me: Scotland's programme to tackle mental health stigma and discrimination. They're funded by the Scottish government and Comic Relief, and are managed by SAMH and the Mental Health Foundation.

After a series of exciting discussions, our two initiatives decided to get together and run a series of events to bring mental health professionals and people with mental health problems together. Other interested parties – carers, family members, volunteers – were invited too, to literally walk a mile in each other's shoes. At these events there would be barriers; people would meet on a level playing field. We would divide people into pairs using T-shirts with either a red or green logo on them.

Our first planned Walk a Mile event was to take place in September in Edinburgh. We were to walk the Royal Mile, which goes from Edinburgh Castle down to the Scottish Parliament. (The one that – shock, horror – isn't actually a mile. It's actually 0.89 miles. But 'Walk 0.89 Miles' sounded significantly less catchy.)

We were looking for people to walk with me and others to talk and share their stories. We also started to look for artistic types to come up with ideas for a Walk a Mile Logo.

The aim was to get people to undertake this ramble with someone from another walk of life. We were particularly interested in pairing up a vast array of healthcare / social care professionals with the equally broad group of folk with lived experiences (who may or may not have used services).

The wonderful See Me team agreed to fund the event and pay for our shiny new logo and website, where people could share their experiences of this walk and others. I've got to say I was rather excited about all this.

CHAPTER 17

THE TIP OF A RATHER LOVELY ICEBERG

On 3rd September 2015, hundreds of people took to the streets to walk a mile in each other's shoes. There was no raging against the machine – just a bunch of folk walking and talking about mental health issues and what that meant from their perspective, in five different towns and cities.

This – we hoped – was going to be a distillation of what is fabulous about Walk a Mile and the people I'd met so far around the UK. It was a simple message really: that people are interested and interesting. That folk, when put in the same social space, are very quick to rejoice in their similarities and put their perceived differences to one side. This isn't rocket science.

At the end of the day, my face ached because I'd been smiling so much.

My role for the day had been made so incredibly simple by the wonderful, hardworking Eleanor from SeeMe and the rest of their dedicated team. My role? It was pretty much to ponce about, chatting, shaking hands and hugging folk. It's a hard job, but someone's gotta do it.

People I'd never met before came up to me with smiles that suggested we were long lost friends. They could have been any one of the following kinds of folk:

Walk a Mile Participants

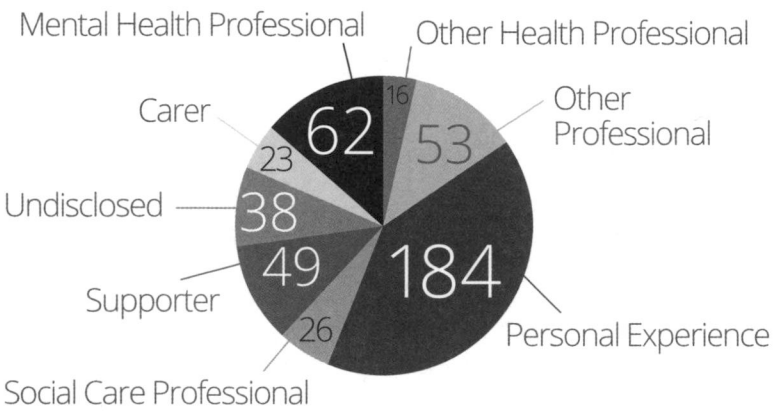

Figure 1: Walk a Mile Participants.

But their only difference on the day was whether they had a green smiley face on their shirt, or a red one.

We started with a simple question: 'What brings you here today?' And it all just bowled along from there.

As well as the lovely buzz of the event evolving around me, some of my highlights were seeing the lovely Teen and Stewart, along with a few other friends I'd made along the way. They'd all continued to support me in a variety of ways as I trundled around Scotland.

I chatted to a woman who saw her spell in prison as a positive experience, because that's where she'd first received her diagnosis of borderline personality disorder and, as a result, had started therapy to help manage it. She'd brought her social worker along for the ride.

This same social worker spoke to me about her own struggle with depression – much to the surprise of the woman who'd invited her. Clearly we have more similarities than differences – you just have to scratch the surface.

Earlier, I'd walked with Jamie Hepburn, the Scottish Minister for sport, health improvement, and mental health. It was a situation similar to those 'what would you do with three wishes?' scenarios. The one where your third wish is invariably, 'I'll have three more wishes, please.' We sorted that out very early on – Jamie agreed to meet with me at a later date to talk more about all things mental health.

I liked his trusting disposition – right from the start he agreed for our conversation to be broadcast to the world using the periscope app on my phone. That, for me, was a pretty good place to start.

I ended the day talking with a woman who wasn't wearing one of our t-shirts. It turned out she'd just popped out to buy some hummus. She's seen our merry band wandering down the Royal Mile, liked the cut of our collective jibs, and joined in.

That's the Walk a Mile way.

We appeared on BBC Radio Scotland, Scottish television, and in the Edinburgh News. We'd really managed to make a noise about mental health.

But this was just the tip of an increasingly growing, rather lovely iceberg. An iceberg that includes you lot.

CHAPTER 18

I'M NOT GOING TO GET ANY BETTER

There, I've said it. And fuck, that's a whole weight off my mind. Imagine the guilt, day in and day out, I feel when I find I haven't recovered.

I know I have a bunch of symptoms that, when clustered together, attract the label of borderline personality disorder. A label that, to the vast majority of the population, is completely meaningless.

It's a condition that's been with me all my adult life, with two major epicentres – one in my teens and one in my forties.

These days my symptoms are mainly dissociation – 'derealisation' where the world becomes unreal. I have hallucinations of ridiculous things: the last one was of an astronaut silently climbing through the ceiling above our bed. They are surprising and occasionally shocking. I have invasive thoughts of extravagant and violent self-harm, with suicidal ideation mixed in at times. I have paranoia where … well, I'm sure you know what paranoia means.

Roughly translated, it means I effectively lose four months a year. I don't believe any flavours of further psychological wizardry will improve or change my symptoms in any way.

Well, that's not a very positive message! What about hope? What about recovery?

Well, there's the thing. I *have* recovered. This is what it looks like. This is *what my* recovery looks like. Don't let the word 'recovery' be hijacked by the powers that be. As soon as someone else defines your recovery, it stops being recovery.

We've learned how to manage my BPD. When it happens, it's still shit and I still need a lot of help. But we manage it very well. I use meds, darkened rooms, loud cop shows, and gentle inner mantra. *It will pass. It always does.*

The rest of the time, my life is great. I'm not the problem. Sure, I *have* a problem, but I'm not it. Today, as on most of my good days, I'm not thinking, 'Why can't I just fit in?' I'm not saying I have nothing to offer myself and society. I know, like millions of others, I want to contribute to the world in a way that has some meaning to me.

But we're not the problem. The problem is government policy, laws, regulations and rules that openly discriminate against me and a bazillion others like me.

I'm not the problem. And you're not the problem either.

Action is needed for any change. We need to take action. We need to work together to end this.

I'm not going to get any better. It's huge parts of the system that need to get better.

So where do we start?

CHAPTER 19

THE BEGINNING OF THE END, OR THE END OF THE BEGINNING?

My work here is done. Join me and the ticker tape parade as I high five my way down the Mall to receive my M/O/CBE from Buckingham Palace, saluting Walk a Mile for curing mental health stigma ...

I can almost hear that marching band. Better still, the Proclaimers singing, 'I would walk 500 miles, and I would walk 500 more' as the massed throngs celebrate our wonderful achievement ...

And we're back in the room.

Well, you can't blame me for a bit of complacent optimism. Since I wandered out of Edinburgh on the 6th of April 2011, with my backpack full of peanut M&M's and Super Noodles, I've spoken with thousands of folk around our lovely island about mental ill health. Together we've demonstrated time and time again that people are fabulous. They're kind, trusting and trustworthy, interested and interesting. They're wonderfully hospitable – you just have to give them the opportunity.

Thanks to Johanna Wagner, we have a feature length documentary that premiered at the Scottish Mental Health Arts and Film Festival – one day, it might actually be completed to her satisfaction ... until then though, we'll continue to know her as 'Just one more shot' Wagner.

With the support of See Me, we have now run around 25 events around Scotland. See Me picked up the Walk a Mile brand and we have a shiny new website. Off the back of this, we've developed the charity Walk a Mile in My Shoes, furnished with trustees with a great depth and breadth of expertise. Our aim is to bring the walk and the events to the rest of the UK.

On a personal level, I've made it as far as Porthmadog in North Wales so far. It's my aim to restart the walk from there, sometime in the Spring of 2018, and continue to make my way around the country.

Every day we raise awareness and share up-to-date information about the world of mental health, with the 40,000 or so folk who follow us on social media. We've had miles of column inches in local and national newspapers, and coverage on local and national radio and TV...

And look, thanks to the fine folk at Trigger Press, I've written a book!

Please excuse me as I put my feet up, don my Paisley Housecoat and fez, and light my pipe. I've enjoyed regaling you with tales of derring-do of my rambles around our lovely island ... Cognac? Don't mind if I do...

But in the words of Winston Churchill, 'Now this is not the end. It's not even the beginning of the end. But it is, perhaps, the end of the beginning.'

Now is certainly not a time for complacency. Sure, we seem to be talking more openly about mental health, but what has actually changed?

People may be fabulous, but the systems that we have in place to support folk with mental health problems are idiosyncratic, vulnerable to an area-to-area postcode lottery, often insufficient, and occasionally downright discriminatory and prejudicial against the very people they were set up to help.

I should say I'm talking specifically about the UK here, my own country. Things might be quite different in your own country, for better or for worse. But this is the state of things in the UK as it stands today.

We have a benefits system that actively discriminates against people with mental health problems, with application forms for disability benefits that all but ignore the mental health issues that many applicants experience. We have a housing benefit system where, because of regulations set down by many mortgage companies, private landlords are prohibited from renting their properties to people on benefits – many of whom have mental health problems.

We've had a draconian system of sanctioning people on benefits, where people with mental health problems are hugely over-represented. There was a 600% increase in the number of people with mental health problems being sanctioned between 2011 and 2015. This means that their benefits are stopped for anything between 3 days and 3 years, leaving many to the mercy of unscrupulous money lenders with interest rates in excess of 1000%.

We've watched, with feelings of impotent helplessness, as health and social care services have been pared back further and further, making a complete mockery of the phrase 'efficiency savings'. Services, staff and most importantly, people with mental health problems are buckling under pressure.

This has led to a siege mentality, where managers in health, social work and the third sectors battle jealously for their budgets and fiefdoms. There's a silo mentality as they batten down their hatches, often with scant regard as to how their services can dovetail with others, both within and outside their sectors. This leads to meaningless – and, at times, bizarre – competition as people with mental health problems cascade through the massive holes in the safety net.

This leads to service user experiences where folk are sent off to hospitals hundreds of miles away, where people with severe conditions are told they've 'just got a touch of schizophrenia', and where the 'least ill' people are shunted out of services in favour of people who have a greater immediate need.

As services have declined, the prison population has risen in England and Wales by 90% since 1990 to 85,500, in Scotland by 62% to just under 7,700 and Northern Ireland by 49% to 1,600. There's no coincidence that a massive 75% of inmates have mental health problems.

I know what you're thinking – you're thinking it's not all bad news. Didn't you read somewhere that a huge, life changing, £1.3 billion has been earmarked for mental health services over the next 4 years? Won't that be funding 21,000 new professionals who'll be providing 24-hour services, treating an extra million people by 2021?

Ignoring the fact that this boils down to £15,476 a year per professional – a princely sum that'll give you between a third to a half of a psychiatrist (or approximately 1/5 if they're a consultant) – let me draw your mind back to the great £800 million disappearance of 2016.

You may or may not remember that mental health services in England and Wales were promised this massive sum, with the promise that things were going to change. You, like me, might be a little disheartened when you discover that this £800 million – a sum that was never ringfenced for mental health services – was swallowed up as a 'contingency fund' to offset deficits elsewhere in the NHS.

So, what happens with the £1.3 billion we've just been promised remains to be seen.

What we do know is that when professionals and mental health punters encounter each other at the coalface of service provision, stress is never far away. Stress occurs where people with a lived experience of mental health problems are desperate for services. Stress happens because professionals, often the gatekeepers, know that these services are often scant and, at times, non-existent. Stress is caused when the situation deteriorates to the point where a person needs to be detained under mental health legislation.

But all that's just money and politics, isn't it? Well, no. Depending on which study you manage to Google – there are a number around – people with mental health problems are expected to die, from physical illness, between ten and 20 years earlier than the wider population.

Suicide remains the biggest killer of men under 45 and women between 14 and 21 in the UK, with over 6,000 people taking their own lives every year.

This isn't all down to deficits in health and social care though. People with mental health problems feel the bite of exclusion in almost every area of public life. For example, only 13.5% of people with a long term mental health problem find themselves in employment when around 80% want to work. This is often due to the preconceived beliefs of their potential employers – beliefs that are often based on little more than what they believe they've learned about mental health from the media. A media that is often sensationalist, portraying people with mental health problems as scary 'others' who mean them harm.

I could talk about more here, but ultimately, it would just feel like a shopping list of doom.

But it's not all bad news. There's hope. This is where you come in. You can make things change. Yes – YOU.

Neil Thompson, a man much wiser than me, tells us that prejudice and discrimination happens at three levels.

There's the personal level – for example when I bump into folk on my coastal ramble; a cultural level, where beliefs and prejudices are held by groups and / or communities (for example the groups and communities we bring together at our #LetsWalkAMile events), and a structural level, where prejudice is entrenched in the structure of a society at a government level. An example of this is austerity measures that target vulnerable groups, including people with mental health problems.

We're aiming for a 'trickle up' effect, where the attitudes of individuals have a positive influence on cultures and, ultimately, this will change the way people with mental health problems are perceived and treated by government agencies and society in general.

With Walk a Mile in My Shoes – the coastal walk and the events – we are using Intergroup Contact Theory. It's a tried and tested method that helped to challenge and change racial stereotypes in the United States in the 60's, by getting different groups to work together to achieve goals that are mutually beneficial.

With Walk a Mile there are no hierarchies or uniforms. We all meet on a level playing field, cooperating to achieve the common goal of walking a mile in each other's shoes, (or getting this particular wandering loon around the edge of the UK). Add to this the support we've had from See Me and the 40,000 folk on social media, and we've got all the ingredients to begin to break down mental health discrimination.

And what have we found? Time and time again we've made the wonderful discovery that people are fabulous. People from all walks of life are keen to talk and, more importantly, listen (my mum always said you've got two ears and one mouth for a reason).

I've been told by some that we won't change anything by 'being nice', that we need to meet discrimination and perceived prejudice head-on, stamping out the stigma whenever we encounter it. Many will challenge non-PC language whenever they come across it.

This is where my views and methods diverge from many of my fellow campaigners. I believe errors in language are not necessarily

Condition	Meaning	Example	Evidence
Equal Status	Members of the contact situation should not have an unequal, hierarchical relationship.	Members should not have an employer / employee, or instructor / student relationship.	Evidence has documented that equal status is important both *prior* to (Brewer & Kramer, 1985) and *during* (Cohen & Lotan, 1995) the contact situation.
Cooperation	Members should work together in a non-competitive environment.	Students working together in a group project.	Aronson's 'jigsaw technique' structures classrooms so that students strive cooperatively (Aronson & Patnoe, 1967), and this technique has led to positive results in a variety of countries.
Common Goals	Members must rely on each other to achieve their shared desired goal.	Members of a sports team.	hu and Griffey (1985) have shown the importance of common goals in interracial athletic teams who need to work together to achieve their goal.
Support by Social and Institutional Authorities	There should not be social or institutional authorities that explicitly or implicitly sanction contact, and there should be authorities that support positive contact.	There should not be official laws enforcing segregation.	Landis' (1984) work on the importance of institutional support in reducing prejudice in the military.

Figure 2: From www.in-mind.org/article/intergroup-contact-theory-past-present-and-future (Jim A. C. Everett, 2013).

indicative of poor attitudes towards people with mental health problems. If I met people head-on every time they used the words 'crazy' or 'mad' in my presence, not only would I have received little or no hospitality, but I'd have missed out on the opportunity to really hear what they thought about people with mental health problems – and, more importantly, how they wanted to help.

I believe that using 'wrong language' as a measure of prejudice and discrimination is neither valid nor reliable. I also believe that having zero tolerance for language you deem to be undesirable causes more harm than good.

When was the last time you won an argument or changed someone's mind by telling them to shut up?

Walk a Mile isn't about being nice – it's about engaging folk in a meaningful, respectful way, taking the time to see things from their perspective. It really isn't rocket science. Remember the words of Jo Cox: 'We have far more in common than that which divides us.'

Walk a Mile – as the name might suggest – isn't just about the talk though. Somewhere there's a walk. As a social worker, I found that often folk found it difficult to be open and honest in an interview scenario, whether it be in the stark surroundings of a local authority office, or even in their own homes. Introduce a setting that alleviates the perceived pressure of the situation – I've used anything from a game of football to a drive in the car in the past – and people are able to speak more openly. A walk around a local park often does the job nicely.

It would be easy here to equate a lovely ramble in the countryside with good mental health. Good physical health means good mental health ... E=MC2 or some such? But speaking from my own experience, I love walking along the coast (well, anywhere really, when I'm feeling well). *However*, when there are bats in my belfry, the very idea of leaving the safety of the house is almost intolerable. So, before you dive headlong into the phrase, 'You just need to get outside in the fresh air ...' have a think before you piss someone off.

I also hope that my story will be part of a wider, sensible conversation about what we mean by child abuse, and the long-term effects that this can have on an individual. As long as the media maintains the rhetoric of paedophile rings on the internet, with evil gangs of men scouring the streets to prey on vulnerable teenage girls, we are ignoring the uncomfortable fact that the vast majority of child sexual abuse – over 90% according to the NSPCC website – is perpetrated by people already known to the child.

Yes, these gangs exist. Yes, we need to take care of our younger folk when they use the web. But as long as we keep the myth going that that 'stranger danger' is where the majority of the risk lies, then, sadly, things won't change. We'll continue to look out for weird hybrid of the Child Catcher out of *Chitty Chitty Bang Bang* and a slimy, middle-aged man with a car full of puppies and sweeties. All the while, the real abusers – plausible, friendly, socially skilled people who look like you and me – will continue to slip under the radar.

Worse still, we'll continue to negotiate with victims of abuse when their abuser doesn't fit this sinister stereotype. Somehow, the perceived impact of that abuse is lessened when the abuser is seen as similar to us. If we keep this up, victims of abuse will continue to fail to report what has happened to them, through some sadly misconceived notion that their mistreatment doesn't somehow fit the mould. They'll continue internalising it, blaming themselves, keeping it secret ...

On top of this, we think we have a clear image of what a victim of childhood sexual abuse looks like: a child, usually clutching their head, curled in a corner in a black-and-white, or sepia world. You've all seen them. But my truth is so similar to many men who finally seek the help they need in their mid-forties. That's a lifetime of self-medicating, trying to deal with feelings of self-loathing, and denial – as any number of mental health problems develop a firm foothold, making them very difficult to shake.

It's essential we don't vilify people with mental health problems and complex needs. Often services are designed to fit the needs of the service and not their clients / patients / service users.

So, in short, this is not a time for complacency. Yes, we've done so much but we've still got a lot to do. If we work together, there really is no limit to what we can achieve.

CHAPTER 20

YES, I'M STILL NUTS

For me, life's pretty good. Yes, I'm still nuts. I still dissociate for roughly a third of the time. I still experience the raft of symptoms that come with borderline bastard personality disorder, including uninvited rage, fears that the people I love will leave me, urges to self-harm in wild and imaginative ways, and, of course, my old friend suicidal ideation. I don't see that changing anytime soon.

No, you're right, that doesn't sound pretty good. It feels a bit like I've just tried to sell you a car only to tell you it's falling to bits.

Things are great. We manage those imposters as they rear their ugly heads. We put them in a darkened room with loud American cop shows – distracting them until they give up the ghost and wander off until the next time.

And ...

I got married to the lovely Ella at the end of September 2017, galvanising the fact that I'm part of her wonderful world. She sees things in me that I often fail to see in myself, and after years of trial and error, we've learned to manage me. I've learned to accept that even though my condition can curtail what I do, it doesn't define me ... and that applies to every person I know with a mental health problem.

Walk a Mile is continuing to develop in all kinds of ways, growing wonderful arms and legs that I'd never imagined ... but that, dear reader, is another story ...

I was once told that you don't write a book to make millions. You write a book to start a conversation.

I'm all ears.

Walk a Mile,

Chris

ACKNOWLEDGEMENTS

Thank you to Ella, for all her long distance feedback when I started writing again. I'd also like to thank Trigger Press and my editor Stephanie Cox for all of their hard work and patience.

the *Shaw* mind

FOUNDATION

Supporting children, adults and families
for better mental health. **#lets**do**stuff**

Sign up to our charity, The Shaw Mind Foundation
www.shawmindfoundation.org
and keep in touch with us; we would love to hear from you.

*We aim to bring to an end the suffering and despair caused
by mental health issues. Our goal is to make help and support
available for every single person in society, from all walks of life.
We will never stop offering hope. These are our promises.*